Nine Lives

Nine Lives

Goldie
with Paul Gorman

SCEPTRE

Some of the quotes in this book are reproduced with the
kind permission of Smoking Dogs Films
from the documentary *Goldie: When Saturn Returnz*.

Some names and identities have been changed in order to protect the integrity
and/or anonymity of the various individuals involved.

First published in Great Britain in 2002 by Hodder and Stoughton
First Published in paperpback in 2003 by Hodder and Stoughton
A division of Hodder Headline

A Sceptre paperback

1 3 5 7 9 10 8 6 4 2

A CIP catalogue record for this title is available from the British Library

ISBN 0 340 82479 4

Typeset in Sabon by Palimpsest Book Production Limited
Printed and bound in Great Britain by
Clays Ltd, St Ives plc

Hodder and Stoughton
A division of Hodder Headline
338 Euston Road
London NW1 3BH

To Chance, the light of my life.

Contents

Preface

When I first thought about writing a book about my life, it wasn't the right time. Well, I guess it's never the right time, because life unfolds on us every day. And when you approach the top of your climb, a new horizon appears, and more 'life' reveals itself, making another beautiful page to learn from . . .

This is about my life. It's about the window of my spirit and all those beautiful people that shine light through my soul, creating prisms of ideas, views, passions, fears, loves and dreams that we sometimes take for granted. It's also about the strength of faith that we all have hidden inside us somewhere. I'm just so glad that I've witnessed life through the sight the Maker blessed me with.

This is the story of a boy who, given belief, followed a dream. The belief was left by the strangers of the future, the ghosts in our lives both past and present. The taboos, the déjà vu, the things we never knew . . .

Now is the time when I want to share this with you, the slow photograph of life and how it was taken. I believe strongly in faith and I have felt the wrath of fate. Only now do I realise that through faith and knowledge, we become conscious of our place in the universe around us. It is down to us to find the many ways and keys which do exist to transcend the 'shell' in which we live in. To open them is to turn another page . . .

I've arrived, having survived my time in care, as a B-Boy, as a trainee dread, wannabe gang-banger, graffiti artist, Miami Funki Dredd, producer, superstar DJ, actor and celebrity.

I'm none of those people; I'm the sum of them.

I'm Goldie, a chameleon, a complicated character, shape-shifting all the time.

I'm Goldie, the cat with nine lives.

Goldie
Hertfordshire
October 2002

Introduction
by Paul Gorman

I first heard about Goldie in the eighties when he was one of the prime movers on the hip-hop art scene. He had introduced a distinctly British take on this essentially American style and finessed it into an art, and was duly recognised for this, exhibiting around Britain and in his mecca, New York, where he met and surpassed his heroes. At the time Goldie was compared to Basquiat: untutored, raw, complex and definitely the real deal.

Goldie has a ferociously restless nature, and it was no surprise that in the nineties he'd transmogrified into a leading figure in dance music by the time I first encountered him, in the haze of a club in Cologne, where he and his crew had just stamped the identity of hardcore drum'n'bass upon a dull music biz convention. The unforgettable 'face' of this underground British sound swiftly became an international star, collaborating along the way with major pop icons and fusing drum'n'bass with such contemporary classical influences as Górecki in a startling series of releases.

Having conquered the spheres of art and music, and become a celebrity in the process, Goldie moved outward on all fronts, owning a successful club and record label and expanding into fashion, TV and, of course, acting.

But the tabloid front covers and *OK!* spreads belie not only his creative achievements, which would be worth writing about in themselves, but also his life, which is as hair-raising, tragic and hilarious as sitting alongside him as he guns his Ferrari F1 to 170 mph. Trust me, I've been there.

It was obvious to me from the get-go that this book would

not be an empty exercise in name-dropping, like so many other celeb bios. Goldie likes to test the limits of anything he enters into, and it was clear that he wanted the book to be a reflection of himself and his work: honest, raw, funny and envelope-pushing. I've interviewed thousands of people, many of them celebs and pop stars, but have never encountered such a brutally open person as the man they once called Clifford Price.

To spend time around Goldie is to lose time as he weaves his tales of urban blight and spiritual faith. We spent days together, at his house, with me nervously eyeing the dog and the snake, on the road, at photo shoots and even once in the sweat room of the Sanderson Hotel. There, in typical Goldie style, as I melted in the infernal heat, he got down on the floor and started doing press-ups. I slunk away.

'For real' is a phrase bandied about too readily in popular culture, but I hope *Nine Lives* demonstrates that Goldie is just that: there is substance and depth to his life and work. And his story is unique: this is the tale of how a neglected and abused child fought off his considerable shortcomings and backed up his loud mouth with serious talent.

Paul Gorman
London
October 2002

1: Mother

Clifford Joseph Price is born to Margaret Kierney McVeigh and Clement Price in Walsall, West Midlands, on 19 September 1965. At the age of three he is put into the care of the social services and is not reunited with his mother for fifteen years. The complexities of their relationship are expressed on the epic track 'Mother'.

"ENTRAPMENT"

I SEE THE WHITE GHOST.. AS SILENCE IS CRACKED
BY DAWN.. I FEAR OF THE MOST.. WHEN MY
BODY IS TORN.. "IT MOURNS"..

FRAGILE IN THE PASSAGE WHERE I HAVE BEEN
SO MANY TIMES BEFORE.. "FINDING WHITE NOISE
IN THE ROOMS WHERE I WALK.. WHAT I'M
I TRYING TO FIND.. "SEARCH FOR DIVINE
.. IN A BLIND.. "DRAWN IN BY A FORCE..
.. THAT SETS ITS COARSE".. "AND I AM STILL
.. A DAWN.. "A FREEZE FRAME.."..A LIFE FORCE
.. PAIN RUNS THROUGH THE REMAINS..
AND I CANNOT STOP THE PULSE.. THE RED
IS BLUE.. IN SEARCH FOR TRUE".. MY
WITS MAY BRING ME BACK.." DOES MY
.. "SOUL BESTOW THE EDGE. DID MY FATE..
.. UPHOLD A PROMISE.. "A DEAL ALREADY
DONE.. "BUT MY BODY".. DID THE RUIN..
"TIRED IN I.. MY VEINS' RUN DRY AND..
HOPE OF FAITH.. TO GET ME THROUGH..
THIS SIGNS MIGHT ONCE MORE.. AS SILENCE
KNOCKS MY MIND'S DOOR DOOR.." IT LETS
ME KNOW "I'VE BEEN HERE BEFORE..—

"IN HONOUR TO YOU FATHER"
"TROJAN".. R: EVANS.

Way back in the mid-sixties my mother fell in love with a black man when they met in a pub in Leeds, where my mum was singing show tunes and ballads, that kind of thing. That was how she survived – she had made it out of the tenements in the Gorbals in Glasgow, at that time the roughest place in Britain, well tough.

That night in the audience, when she was singing 'Danny Boy' or whatever, was this very proud Jamaican guy, tall, good-looking and about ten years older than her. She loved him to death, apparently, just fell for him right there and then. The story goes that she got caught the first time they slept together and there I was: BAM! Supersperm!

Margaret Pusey: I come from this big Glaswegian family – there were twelve of us – and by the time I was twenty-two I was singing Scottish and Irish songs in this pub. I was a real innocent. One night in the audience was this guy, and he just charmed me off my feet, as they do.

When she became pregnant my mum moved down to the Midlands to be close to my dad, who had a job at one of the car factories in Wolverhampton, and I was born in Walsall Manor Hospital on 19 September 1965. That's 19/9/1965.

Lot of nines in that date, you'll notice. Nine is my number, and a very special one across all cultures. In Chinese numerology nine is associated with eternity and power, and in astrology – which I believe in, I don't care what anybody says – the Number Nine Life Path is all about understanding, which is what I'm trying to do with this book; get some understanding out of the chaos and creativity which have been my life so far.

Nine represents balance for me, and I'll always go for that number rather than, say, fourteen, which just doesn't work for me. I'm very superstitious, and if I get on a plane and I'm sitting in a seat with the wrong number – say, fourteen – then I'll change it. I'll be the one checking every number on the ticket, adding, subtracting, dividing just to make sure the ultimate number is right. So, as I say, nine's been very significant for me. Watch out for it as it recurs throughout this story.

Wendy Mandy: I'm Goldie's therapist and spiritual guide. We're pretty close – in fact he calls me his 'spiritual mother'. I can be very specific about past lives, but it's a subject which can sound ludicrous, so I'm reluctant to go into it. But this is important: I truly believe there is a past life which has dogged Goldie and which he is trying to enact now. If it sounds naff, it's because it's the one which everybody claims to have. But in his case I really believe he was an Egyptian, a pharaoh who let his people down by abusing the power he had. And now he's paying for it, by painfully learning how to use that power properly, by coming through at the bottom of the pile; an unwanted child in a pretty desolate area where there was very little culture, very little anything. And his task wasn't to learn how to be great again, but to learn humility through achieving recognition properly. Does that make sense?

I've always had this feeling that I've been here before and that I've lived other lives. It's not only Wendy, but several people – spiritualists, numerologists, white witches, you name it – they have all told me I have an old soul. And I sometimes think I couldn't have picked a more complicated body to come back in.

Anyway, back in September 1965 there I was. Me. Clifford Joseph Price. It would be a long time before I became Goldie.

My earliest memory of this life is of being in a small room on a hill in the flat my mum had in Wednesbury Road, Walsall, where I was born. Sometimes I can catch the smell, a combination of musty wallpaper and the gas heater that stood in the middle of the room. I remember it so well because it fell on me once; I've still got the scar on my leg. I was cooped up in this little place and two years later along came my brother Melvin and then things started to get crowded. But I was very close to my mum. We all shared the bed and I can remember her holding me by her side; like any kid, I loved her deeply and thought she loved me back.

Margaret Pusey: My family just didn't want to know, because it was such a scandal to be with a black man at the time. But I wasn't with him because he was black, it was because we fell in love. I got a lot of grief because I was with him, and nobody really wanted to know. It was tough.

And my dad was rarely around. He didn't really love my mum. When he was there, he used to mistreat her and life just got too much. To me he was just a presence, the dark figure, and at that age I couldn't really tell if my actual dad was him or this other guy who was on the scene and would soon become my stepfather, Pusey. I never knew his first name – he was always just Pusey to everybody. My mum was caught between two black men who were doing what they do. In black culture, it seems to me the sole job for men is to reproduce, and it goes against the whole concept of the nuclear family in Western society. This is what a lot of black men did then and do now: they complicate the normal situation by leaving kids in their wake.

Margaret Pusey: His daddy was one of those men who would go to a town for a year and then would up and leave and go to another town. He just wanted to do what he wanted to do. So after he left I married Freddie Pusey.

Like my mum says, she couldn't hold my dad down, so she grew to love Pusey, who was much more around, but she also grew to fear him. He was a very dark character, a proper black man. He would sit on the edge of his chair waiting for something to happen.

Many years later, when Pusey died, it was said that he was killed by his ex-wife using *obeah*, the black magic art from Africa. He always used to wear different-coloured handkerchiefs to ward off different types of evil and, as he lay dying of cancer – which spread so fast that the doctors couldn't do anything about it – he asked me to get him a suit to bury him in. But he said: 'Make sure you cut the pockets out of it,' an *obeah* thing to make sure the spirits don't rise from the dead and throw stones at the living.

Even when I was two or three I sensed Pusey was a very dark geezer, and we never really got on. Sometimes my dad would stop by and take me away; I remember him driving me down to stay at some place in London and watching in wonder as he took his hands off the steering wheel while he was driving and clapped them together to entertain me. I stayed at this big white house in south London with these people for a while, maybe because my dad planned to take me to Jamaica.

The way my dad tells it, Pusey never liked me and forced my mum to put me into care, because I saw him in bed with her before they were married, and I told my father. That's what my father told me when I eventually tracked him down years later. I can't really remember because I've buried so much of this stuff.

Margaret Pusey: When Clifford was about three or four, his father, Clement, came and took him away to London where he lived for a couple of years. I couldn't stop it happening. I found out that Clement was thinking about taking him out of the country and went down to London, and the social services got involved.

I was put into the care of social services. This is how I came to leave the family: one day I was sitting in that little room with the musty wallpaper and out of the blue I was told: 'This woman's come for you, to take you away.' The woman was Miss O'Connor, who had been appointed as my social worker, and that day she put me in this makeshift residential home, before I was fostered out for the first time. I've always had a bad time about that because, while I assume it was my mum and Pusey, I still don't know who signed the papers and actually gave me away. As I grew up one of the things that always got to me was: Why was I the only one to go? Why not Melvin as well? He was only a couple of years younger, so if she couldn't cope with me, how about him?

Margaret Pusey: With the life I was having, I couldn't have coped. He must have thought to himself: 'Why doesn't my mummy want to take me?' But it wouldn't have been a life for him. Not watching me getting battered and hungry and running [sobs] and running . . .

My mum just couldn't take it, but I wasn't away for just a few months; I was in the care of social services for a very long time, and I can hardly remember my mother's visits. She maybe came once or twice, but that was it. Because I was told my mother couldn't cope with me I always felt a complete failure in life, right up until the fame started to happen, I guess. And even now there's still that big failure button which I press if anything goes wrong.

Gus Coral (friend/film-maker): I've met her a few times and I gained the impression that Goldie owes his mother a lot as far as mental toughness is concerned, and it seems to me that she also gave him a direct attachment to real life.

That could be true, but that was only later on – for fifteen years she was absent and I had to learn to live by myself. It's in everybody, a human instinct, to want to be mothered, to be loved, isn't it? I think the main reason I have done what I have done – graffiti, art, DJing, music, acting – was because I wanted to be loved by everyone. Because I never had it from her.

Towards the end of my time in care, from when I was in my mid-teens, I was shifted to this place called the Lew Joseph Children's Home, which I write about later. When I was there Melvin used to come and see me, and I realised that he lived with my mum really close by. I started to think about all the things he told me about family life, and then when I was about seventeen I decided that I had to go home. It took me a while to pluck up the courage – maybe six months – but eventually I ran away to the estate where Melvin said they lived, Heath Town, which was like Metropolis to me, all these walkways and balconies which meant you never had to walk at ground level. It's quite a big place and I asked around for hours for Margaret Pusey, and then this neighbour pointed to a flat on the fifth floor of Chervil Rise and said: 'Well, there's a little Scottish woman that lives there.' The door was open, number fifty-one, a green door, and this little woman came out. She said: 'Come in, son. Have a cup of tea.'

Margaret Pusey: I was in there with the door open, because I loved to leave the door open. And I heard this voice going: 'Do you know a wee Scotch woman that lives around here?' And I thought, I know that voice. It was Clifford with two big bags. He just moved in and said: 'That's it. I ain't going back to that home.'

She wasn't working. My mum never worked, not that I've ever seen anyway. She was living in Chervil Rise with Melvin and my stepbrothers Stuart and Jo-Jo, who was no more than a baby then. Also living there was my mum's new geezer Slim and his daughters Marie and Annette, who was Melvin's girl. Complicated isn't it? But that was what life was like in them days and it's still like that now.

I really felt I was home in Chervil Rise and I stayed there for six weeks until two CID officers caught up with me and took me back to Lew Joseph. They found me skating at my favourite haunt, Whispering Wheels – which you'll hear all about later – and literally dragged me off the rink and carried me to the cop car still with my skates on. Back at the home there was hell to pay. I was deprived of all my privileges for two months and then my case was reviewed, to decide whether I should go back to my mum. She did have a turbulent life, and the men in her life had contributed to that.

But they decided I could start to go back home to her for weekend visits. Sometimes I'd go home and there was nothing *at* home. She'd do this all the time – take all her gear with her and go off back to Pusey, who she started seeing again after things didn't work out with Slim, and try to make a go of it again. So I'd go back to Lew Joseph on Monday saying: 'Yeah, I had a great weekend,' when really it was just me and Melvin. Finally the people at the home said I could stay with her permanently and I moved in. And I soon got used to the fact that sometimes my mum would fuck off, but she would always come back because Pusey would end up beating her badly.

So you can see how life was for my mum. But our relationship was really good at that stage. I enjoyed living at Chervil Rise, and when she was gone it would only be for about three, four weeks. She managed, that was the main thing.

I never rowed with my mum while I was living with her. I didn't really have the anger that I feel now over being deserted for fifteen years. I never questioned her, until recently. And now I keep on asking myself the same question: Why?

I get on better with her now than I ever have but we've still got a long way to go. When I see my mum she sometimes cries, because she has also had a very difficult time dealing with the fact that we've never had a truly close relationship.

Wendy Mandy: In cases like this, you need to understand where you came from and what happened, so you can put the last part of the jigsaw in. Goldie does understand what happened but there is still guilt about Mum. He has taken up her guilt and shame. Intellectually, as an adult, he knows that she didn't mean to desert him, but the infantile part of him is never going to mend unless he mends it himself. Any amount of apology from an adult does not help the stuck child within.

All of my feelings about my mum, and what's happened between us, are poured into 'Mother', which took up an entire CD of my album *Saturnz Return*, and has a thirty-piece orchestral backing, moving from conception through the anger and rage and sadness to fulfilling my destiny with her. You have to listen to that with headphones on, in one sitting. It's intense and harrowing but it tells the truth. My mum knows that. It's really crazy because I could never ever speak to her, have a real conversation about life. So I gave it to her and said: 'Put it on and listen to it alone. Just give me one hour of your life and listen in perfect solitude.' The first time she heard it she wept.

Margaret Pusey: I sat in a room all on my own and listened to it and cried like a baby. I really broke down, because I felt all his feelings that had haunted him when I played it. Then I phoned him and told him it was the best thing he had ever done. But listening to it was heartbreaking.

'Mother' is sixty minutes long. Do you think I can sum up everything that me and my mum went through in five minutes? I can't do that. All I can do is start and finish – however long it takes. I still love my mum and I hope she loves me. I go through all the pain of my relationship with her in that one song, and it takes that long to get it off my chest. It killed me, that track. Afterwards I just fell to pieces, I was crying for two days. It tapped into things I never thought I was capable of. The outcome of 'Mother' was: 'Do you get it, Mum? Do you understand what we went through?' And I wanted to hear her say: 'Yes, I do get it. And I'm sorry, son.' But I never got that. A few years back there was a documentary made about my life, called *When Saturn Returnz*, when my mum and me talked about 'Mother'. She broke down and we comforted each other during the filming of the documentary, but I still felt robbed of the moment. Although I wanted to show people that we could hug and say it was OK, in reality it wasn't enough. I wanted her to say: 'Look, son, come in this room for a second, away from the camera, because I want to tell you I'm deeply sorry.' I think maybe if my father had shown more love to her then things would have been different.

Margaret Pusey: If anything happens to me, I'd love him to play it at my funeral. That would keep me going.

With my mum I wanted to love her so much more than I was allowed to. A few years ago I was told that Eskimos have not one word for snow but more than a hundred: thick, thin, snow that melts quickly, stays frozen, this way, that way. I realised that the word 'love' doesn't stand for anything, because there are so many different varieties, and I've had to work out exactly what my love for my mother is. I've always avoided the question, up until now.

I do love my mum, and now I have come to a stage in my life when I have been able to deal with our situation on a primal level. The time has come for me to let go and put it behind me.

Sonik Terrorism "
CHAPTER 1 —
" HERE COME THE DRUNK —
..." THE " ROOTS OF OM" ~
WAY BACK ~ BEFORE ~ THE
VOICE OF SONG —
THE SORROW TALES OF WAR ~
AND WAILS ~ THE BARBARIANS
FROM WITHIN . "AGE RISING —
' TO FIGHT'. EMANCIPATION —
AND .TRIBE . THE RHYTHM OF
TIME , MAY NO, PARANOIA —

A WAR DRUGS ~
THE SONIK TERRORIST
OF 8 : 3 AM '.
I CAN'T REMEMBER
WHEN ~ ~

' . MUTE . THINE EARS . THERE
EYES ~ STARLE , FROM BLACK ~
AS ~ OWEN SIGHT . FROM
RAINBOW EYES : ". "WE THRIVE
THERE ,, NIGHT . ~ AND
SACRIFICE ~ OUR SOUND .
THE LAMBS !" WE BE , WILL
. PAY THE PRICE ~ SONIK
MIND ~ SHALL GIVE THEM FREEDOM

2: Dragonfly

Clifford's boyhood is spent in institutions and with a series of foster families, where his rage and destructiveness are tempered by a strong artistic drive. He suffers physical and sexual abuse.

☑ @ "CHAMELEON" ! ☐

" STILL THE ARTIST BURNS... KNOWING, NO END'... BEYOND
THE FRAME OF LIFES TERRAIN ...
WHETHER MADNESS', OR OF SANE ... " I GUESS "THE MAKERS'
                                SPIRIT LIES' MY BLAME ...

" I ONLY BLESS FOR THIS' ... " I CLOSE MY EYES' LAST NIGHT .... AND
PAINT MY WISH "... COLOURS ... THOSES HAVE NEVER BEEN ... AND
LANDSCAPES' PURE, MY OWN "SERENE", WE DO NOT SLEEP ...
BUT ONLY DREAM' ... THE GHOSTS 'THAT LET US BE ...
" I SPAN MY MINDS EYE AS FAR AS IT CAN SEE ... THERCE IS NO
BOUNDERIE'.~ ONLY INFINITY ... THE SHADES, I SHAPE THAT MAKES ME ...
THE ARTISTS LIFE THAT BREAKS ME ... MY FEAR THE GREY WILL MAKE
ME ... THE LINES I DRAW MISTAKE ME ...
" SO I STAY' ... MY WAY ... ON EDGE ... MY FOCUS POINT TILL DEATH ...
THE CANVAS HAS A LEDGE ... MY CANVAS IS TO STRETCH ...
AND PAINT MY WHOLE LIFE THROUGH ... WHETHER, RED OR BLUE ...
THE COLOUR TOUCHED IS TRUE ◎ △

ne of my earliest memories comes from when I was at infant school. I was in care by this stage, and we were given a project to make, something out of Plasticine, so I created this pram, miniature and really detailed. I can see it now, cupped in my hand. The teacher was really surprised that I'd made this beautiful thing because I never said anything in class, never showed any potential. 'That's really good,' she said, 'show it to all the other kids.' I took it round in my hand, showing them all. Then, when I got everybody's attention, I closed my fingers over the pram and crushed it to pieces.

Wendy Mandy: Goldie's rage comes from the unbelievable lack of recognition from his caretakers. He was a sweet little kid who was deserted. What happens in the world of desertion, fostering and degradation is that a pattern is set. Goldie, because of his pattern of being deserted, found people who deserted him, not because it's pleasant but because it's familiar. Adoptive parents take a child, but foster parents are paid by the state to look after them, which means that sometimes foster homes can be very unhappy. The plain fact is that he wasn't wanted. And he wants so much to be wanted. As a result he was completely on the edge throughout his childhood, and that is where his creativity and his will to destruction stem from.

That was me; I was so unhappy that I wanted to destroy everything, be it bricks or sticks or glass or my Action Man. My first foster parents lived near Walsall; Mr Jones was a factory worker who took the belt to me whenever he felt like it. Their son Anthony, who was older than me, used to beat the fuck out of me, bully me. I used to dread dinner-time, because Anthony would punish me for even looking at his plate by scraping all his food on to mine. Then he would force-feed me until I was sick. They let him get away with this stuff. He even used to put the dog lead on me and walk me around. I cried for nights on end.

But living there did give me one taste of freedom. At the end of the street was this massive field, where me and the other kids in the area would go in the summer. We'd sit around this pond and make up stories about what monsters lived in there. You'd see dragonflies scooting across the water and I'd lie back and drift off to sleep. When I opened my eyes I'd see that summertime white that you get when you look into the sunshine. Years later I made this record, 'Dragonfly', about the feeling those fields gave me.

Even to those memories there is a dark side. Close to the fields was a cut-through I used on the way to junior school. I will never forget being in some old barn near there with some geezers, men, much older than me. I was around six or seven years old and they were touching me. The memory of what happened to me that day only surfaced about five years ago and I still get this claustrophobic feeling of flesh closing in on me, fucking horrible. That really fucked me up for a while.

At school, first at Bussell Jones Junior School and then at Frank F. Harrison, I was always the kid who never had the uniform when everyone else was wearing theirs. I was the class fool who everyone laughed at. You tend to do that when you feel threatened, play the fool, because it's the best way to stop the bullies kicking your head in. I never really had close friends at school because I was either with foster parents or in homes. People would take the piss out of me all the time and my problem was that I had to go to school, I

could never skive like the others who lived with their families, because the foster parents or the wardens were always on my case. I hated school, man; it was hell for me, horrific. But it was no different from the home. I was just going from one hell to another; it never really made much difference. It was only the art classes which saved me and gave me my taste of freedom.

I was completely numb during this part of my life. I don't remember very much at all because I buried it out of sight, at the back of my mind. I had an interest in art, making stuff with my hands, but I was also very destructive, always starting fires, out of control. Eventually the Joneses couldn't take it any more. I couldn't stand the bullying and started to have really serious screaming fits, temper tantrums like you wouldn't believe.

So I was shipped out from the Joneses to this institution called Hammerwhich, a converted Victorian hospital, a dark, scary place with a big sweeping staircase, where we slept in dorms. I was about nine, and wet the bed a lot. But there was somebody there who I looked up to, a half-caste kid with one tooth missing, the first black kid I'd seen locked up. He used to play music, and that's where I heard John Holt for the first time, that kind of early pop reggae which sounded great.

From there I went to another home, Croxdene Children's Home on the Dudley Fields estate. It was a very painful time and I spent a lot of years crying there because I just didn't know who I was, or even where I was. I don't remember any fights or anything like that – I was left alone a lot and was very destructive. Those were very painful, very unstable years. Then one day my brother Melvin visited me and told me he lived with my mum in Walsall, which was so close, but could have been a million miles away for all I knew. It was at Croxdene that she came to see me, just the once, but then I was fostered out again, to Mr and Mrs Newman.

Mr Newman was a bastard, sitting on his chair watching wrestling on the TV all day. He beat me a lot. I had a black foster brother there, who frequently went missing, and a foster sister, Rowena, who was about sixteen, five years older than me. She started to abuse me, sleeping with me and playing with me. This wasn't any kind of childish experimentation, though I let it happen because I think I just wanted to be mothered.

Wendy Mandy: Sexual abuse is when someone does something inappropriate, that you would say no to normally, but, because it's the only attention you can get or you are afraid, you don't say no. It can perhaps be quite pleasurable for the child physically, because maybe they get no attention at all, but they have an innate understanding that it's a violation of equality. That makes the person it is being done to feel very uncomfortable, and that turns into shame and guilt which they can carry for the rest of their life.

I felt betrayed by the way Rowena made me feel so I went all out to drive her mad. I was searching for love and not receiving it, and looking for my mother in these women who couldn't provide what I wanted. That's why kids go for abuse, because that's often the first place where they will receive some form of love, physical affection. So rejection would set in and with Rowena I'd get in her face, questioning her, everything about her, relentlessly. We'd all be sitting in a room and I'd be muttering and whispering things to her. She'd get really irritated: 'What are you saying?' And I'd sit there all innocent, playing dumb. And as soon as she settled down, I'd start again. I also used to stare at her, winding her up silently behind the backs of the Newmans. She'd start complaining to them: 'He's staring at me!' I'd deny it, things would settle down, and then I would start again. After a while old man Newman would snap and I'd get a beating, but I'd keep on denying it flatly, right up until the point when he'd completely exhausted himself beating me. I would never give up or give in to them, so it got to the point where the beatings became just another form of attention. And of course the beatings didn't stop me when it came to bugging Rowena – I used to keep on and on and on at her until one day I broke her. She had always suffered from asthma, and then suddenly she became a nervous wreck because of what I was doing to her. Rowena had a nervous breakdown and was hospitalised. She had to have an operation on her throat, which had closed up because of the pressure of what I did to her.

My thing was, I hated women, all of them, just wanted to destroy them. The full truth about my hatred of women only dawned on me when I made the *When Saturn Returnz* documentary in 1998. The experience of making that film and sitting in the same rooms with the same people revealed so much to me. I asked my foster mothers or carers: 'Why didn't I stay here, why wasn't I happy?' And they would tell me that whenever I was on my own with women I would scream and scream. I never wanted to be alone with them because it totally freaked me out.

The other side of that coin is that later on I became a womaniser, because I wanted to be loved by women and be dominant over them. I didn't want someone else controlling my life with me cast as the victim, which is how I always felt when I was young, so I would fuck as many birds as possible. With some of them I would force them into saying: 'I love you,' and then I'd just walk away and leave them to it. Or sometimes I'd say to them: 'I love you,' after they'd begged and begged me. But then I'd add: 'I do love you, but I love lots of things,' and laugh in their faces.

After the problems I caused Rowena I was moved away from the Newmans, who just couldn't cope with me any more. Mrs Newman was more of a grandma figure to me because of her age, and I still lacked somebody who could fulfil the mother role in my life. But I couldn't find anyone, particularly after I was put into Lew Joseph Children's Home in Wolverhampton, where I stayed until I was eighteen.

Rhoda Warden (carer, Lew Joseph): Initially he was very apprehensive, nervous and a bit of a loner. But he settled in and he was a torment. He teased the staff and he had his moments when he was very angry. But he loved his music and his art. He had a little cupboard in the playroom which was full of his tapes and paper and pens.

In my teens I started to get into music, going to discos in Sneedhall Lane, getting a taste for Northern Soul, listening to tunes like 'Ski-ing In The Snow'. I used to do some of the moves: 'Look, the black boy's doing a move!' I was hanging about with guys on the estate, especially my friend Paul Gough, who would always be drawing Stukas and Messerschmitts while I drew motorbikes. In the third year I started getting really creative and built this model of a racing car. It was huge, six feet long, with wire wrapped around to make the wheels. It looked great and really impressed the others. That was me at the time, either getting into trouble or making things. I even made a Steve Austin leg – like out of *The Six Million Dollar Man*, right? – for some school play. My role was to walk across the stage in slow motion and the fucking leg fell apart halfway across, so I had to scramble off!

We'd build camps on the railway embankments and smoke newspapers and I had my first experience of getting some bird's pants off. I remember losing my virginity to a girl called Angela at the back of the canal.

In my locker at the home was my life, my pens and paper and these records which represented all the different types of music I was into: Squeeze, Steel Pulse, the Police and 'Walking

On The Moon' and the Stranglers, who were the only band whose albums I bought. For the rest I could only afford singles, but with the Stranglers I bought their albums *Rattus Norvegicus* and *Black & White* because I loved their dirty bass sound, it sounded so black. I bought 'Public Image' by PiL when it came out in the little wrapped-newspaper sleeve, and Squeeze's 'Up The Junction' on pink vinyl.

Around this time I was also getting into the visual side of this stuff, having seen the Yes covers by Roger Dean in an art book, and thought it was fucking wicked, even though I hadn't heard the music. He made fantastic worlds, a mixture of seascapes and mountains and other planets. The colours were mad, but it was only much later that I found out that American graffiti writers had already clocked people like Roger Dean. And then I got a book of American artwork for bands like the Grateful Dead, and started picking up on the picture disc craze of the late seventies. That's why way down the line I designed a picture disc for the *Enforcers* twelve-inches on Reinforced in the early nineties – it hooked into that timeline.

The Lew Joseph Children's Home was run by this pair, the Jacksons, and their son got me into people like Elvis Costello. When I heard 'Oliver's Army' it just knocked me out, the sound was so slick. I used to listen to this music on my own, people like Siouxsie and The Banshees and the Buzzcocks, who were the first band I saw live. I used to play the same tunes over and over and over again. In the home we had fifteen minutes each with the record player to play our own stuff, and there'd always be these arguments between the six or seven kids. But I was into playing the same record again and again, rather than different ones. I was always stuck in a loop. Then I'd be kicked off by the other kids, who complained about me playing the same song. It would drive everyone mad. So I'd say: 'Whatever,' and just sit there looking at the artwork on the record sleeves while they played their pop tunes.

One time the deputies who ran the gaff, Chris and Steph, took us on a trip to Derbyshire and they put *Sgt Pepper's Lonely Hearts Club Band* into the eight-track on the way over. By the end of the trip I fucking knew every single word. When I think of Derbyshire I immediately think of *Sgt Pepper*, which I was given that Christmas. Then Chris gave me *A Hard Day's Night* and I went back and got the rest of their stuff, I was so bang into the Beatles. Everyone was slagging them off because they were old hat, but I wasn't buying music for trends, I was curious about the sounds. Every day I used to walk to school and save my bus fare so I could buy paints and pens and music.

My nickname at that time was 'Paki' because a lot of people couldn't tell whether I was black or not. I used to hang out with this white kid, Paul Whitehead, who was the cock of the class and would fight anybody. I used to go to his mum's place at lunch-time to listen to UB40. And there were a few other black kids at Frank F. Harrison – David Warner, Eric Smith, Heather Campbell – who I knocked around with. The school was on the edge of Dudley Fields and Beech Dale estates, which were known for being heavily National Front. I used to pass them on the way to my friend David Banner's house on the Manor Farm estate and get abuse; it was pretty hairy there, but of course I couldn't do anything about it at the time. They'd be shouting out 'Black cunt', 'Nig-nog', all that, but it bounced off me because I was so hurt with everything else. No other pain could replace what I'd been through.

Banner was into Queen and heavy rock and scrambling motorbikes. I remember me and David used to stop off at his house where his dad always made us a cup of tea. Every time he would give us tea and biscuits, which was amazing to me, just watching David and his old man get along together. He was a couple of years older than me, but even when Banner left school and went to live somewhere else I'd still stop by his house and have tea with his dad.

I stayed on at Frank F. Harrison after I was sixteen, even though I flunked everything but art. I always felt an outsider there, but I did well at art mainly because the art teacher, Mr Hurst, got me through. He made me stay late and work on my stuff, and got me out of certain lessons so I could develop technique. He saved my bacon by putting a good word in for me when I did badly in other subjects. He got me through my art O-level and still-life work. I love him to death for what he did for me, and always try to stay in touch with him – I spoke to him only about three or four years ago. I concentrated on art and wasn't really into socialising because I had to be back at the home by 9 p.m. every night, apart from Wednesdays, which were sports nights for us younger boys.

On that night of the week the older boys at the home were allowed a trip to the local skating rink, Whispering Wheels, which is where it all began for me. I couldn't wait until I was old enough to go, and was so excited that first time. There were all these black and white kids together, skating to funk and soul, Earth Wind & Fire, Southern Freeez, the tunes which really turned me on to melody. Then I started to go on a Saturday morning and practised like hell until I learnt to be a good skater. We'd be wearing side-pocket trousers, tank tops, and I had this sheepskin coat I'd acquired from somewhere.

Being that kid who had his life packed in a suitcase and moved from home to home, I kept my distance and was very observant. That's really how I learnt how to do anything, whether it was skating, art or, later, music. I guess I became a good skater because I observed everything. In those situations you pick up on the icons and you go to the best people

– not just the fastest, but the ones who have the most style, the most edge.

It was a pattern I repeated throughout my life: when I got into break-dancing there was a local hero who became my best friend, Birdy. In graffiti it was those NY cats Brim and Bio, and much later in music it was the great DJs Fabio and particularly Grooverider.

But back then, when I was skating, it was so important to me that I excelled. And I did get really good. And I felt like I belonged at Whispering Wheels, partly because the music there became a parallel influence to the stuff I was listening to back at the home. And I felt: 'Fuck. I don't belong with them lot, I belong here.' They were mainly white kids, listening to white music, punk and new wave. At Whispering Wheels I got into Earth Wind & Fire's 'September', a majestic track which I loved so much because my birthday's in September. I was like: 'I've got my girl, I'm skating good, I'm as happy as fuck.'

So I was blazing to 'September', 'Papa's Got A Brand New Pigbag' by Pigbag, all those twelve-inches. We used to skate round to a local shop which is still there to this day, Ruby Red Records, and Mick who ran it would turn us on to the new twelve-inches like 'Behind The Groove' by Tania Maria. That bass line taught me about new sounds and I kind of said goodbye to Squeeze, Costello and the Stranglers and left them in the locker. I stopped listening to that stuff, and in fact wouldn't play music at the home during the allotted times. I just got my pens out and started drawing. And I started buying records – that was part of growing up for me.

I started to go to Whispering Wheels on Sundays as well. I felt separate because I had to be back at a certain time; on Sunday nights by 7 p.m., like fucking Cinderella Fella! At the end of the session, when everyone was partnered up with their birds and going for burgers, I'd have to sneak off and get the bus back to the home.

Melvin would sometimes meet me at the skating rink and I started playing roller hockey on a Saturday afternoon and got so good I was in the England B team. There was a geezer called White Mitchell whose dad managed the place, another guy Stan, who was seeing Mitchell's sister, Jacko, and Cockney, the guy who taught us loads of moves. I remember one time watching them putting the nets up for the roller hockey game in the afternoon and, in the end, I became goalkeeper and we were joined by another really good player, Kenny, who caught the same bus as me, the 996.

Then on Saturday afternoon after the hockey matches there was another session with the funk being played by White Jacko. Saturday evening was OK but the Sunday sessions were the best – we'd have figure-of-eight sessions taking each other out and I was always the cheeky kid on skates you couldn't catch. I was getting my first skating partners, chatting birds up, feeling more free. It felt like a burden had been lifted since I was pretty hot on skates and getting some attention. I was coming into focus.

A while back I got a letter from a girl I saw at that time; I think we went out on a couple of dates. In the letter she told me how amazed she was at how well I'd done and that she was so proud and happy for me she cried when she saw me on TV. It was great to receive her letter, which brought back to me the happy times we all had at the rink.

I'd had a taste of freedom from Whispering Wheels. Around the same time the feeling started growing and growing that I should go back to my family. I had been kept on at the home past the age of sixteen because otherwise there would have been problems with my benefits, but the end was in sight. I would have to leave eventually, so I started to really think about what I was going to do and where I was going to go. At the back of my mind all through this period was my family because I would go and see them sometimes, or they would occasionally come to the home. As well as Melvin my mum once brought Stuart to see me – he would have been five or six at the time.

I didn't care how dysfunctional it was at home, I didn't give a fuck, I just had to be there. There was that primal connection calling me. There is that instinct: 'The kid has to go home, man.' Now I wanted to be with my mum again.

MR DAGUS [O] THE LIFE'S THAT
WE KNOW, THOSE
THAT THINK AND WAIT
'AT LIFES DEBATE —
CONCENTRATE TO FOCUS —
THEIR POINT OF TRUST [O] DARK ANGELS
IN FAITH — WE CANNOT
SEE IT — ONLY FEEL — FOR THOSE THAT REVEAL — THERE
SIXTH SENSE — AT HEAVENS DATE ..., A KIND OF
BRAIL WE UNVEIL — IN ALL WE TOUCH — A MUST FOR
THOSE THINGS IN AXION ", OR SCEINCE CONCEIVED —
THE FACT IS STILL BASED ON MASS MAN'S TRUST —
SO THEREFORE, IF I CONCEIVE — THEN YET IT IS
TO BE? — FOR I 'AT FAITH MYSELF INVEST IN
[O] PURE ENERGY " CONSTRUCT — MY, OUR, US —
UTOPIA — THAT IN ALL WILL ONE DAY BE, —
" A LIFE K — IS MY NAME, — TO GAIN " FAITH —
BY — " THIS FRAME —... " EXISTEST — IS MY
PICTURE. —

31/10/98 — WHAT TIME? SHE TOLD
EARLY MORN !!!! ME 2" !

3: Inner City Life

Returned to his mother by the authorities at the age of eighteen, Clifford embarks on a life of petty crime with his brother Melvin and their crew, leavened by an interest in Rastafarianism and music. He gains the nickname Goldielocks as a result of his distinctive dreadlocks.

Of "THE INVERTED TRUTH"
WE ALL "SUFFEND" AT
THIS POINT OF "D'BRIS" TO
BE AT RELAXON WITH OWN
UNASCRIBABLE CROSS POINT
BEING PUSHED IN THE SHELL
ADDICTION EATS YOUR FUEL
WHISPERS MINE OF FOOL WE
CANNOT ESCAPE ITS MY
WAR THAT I MUST PUT THOSE
VIVID CONFLICTS OF PAIN TO
THE BACK OF MY MIND
ADDICTION MAY TRACE

ADDICTION IS SOMETHING THAT CREEPS LIKE
SHADOWS AT SUNDOWN IT FADES FROM COLOUR
TO BLACK AND WHITE, AND THEN CASTS YOU
IN THE DEEPEST BLACK NOT EVEN YOUR EYES
CAN FIND SPACE WITHIN ITS VAST ABYSS
LOST BETWEEN GENIUS AND MADNESS AS
THE THEORY OF PARANOIA, OR PSYCHE,
DO "BEGIN BATTLE UNTIL YOUR MIND IS
THAT OF PAIN AND WOUND ADDICTION IS
SOMETHING THAT "HAS FIRE IN ITS OWN
DESIRE "TO TAKE WHAT YOU CANNOT
COMPREHEND "AND SLAY YOUR DOORWAYS
YOU HAVE "BUILT IN YOUR" CONSCIOUS
MOTIVE STRUCTURE STRIKING AND THE
WEAKNESS OF YOUR HIBERNATION OF
CONCEPT "WHILE STATIC" THROUGH
VULNERABILITY "AT THE "FAIL RATE
OF YOUR CONDITION THROUGH SELF MANIFESTO
OF THE SUB-DEMON THE BASIC NATURE
OF YOUR UNCHARACTERED" LOG OF EVERY
CHANNELED ENERGY THE SWITCH BOARD
OVERLOAD ADDICTION IS DISTURBING
TO THE TRESPASS AT INTERNAL LAND

For about six months they allowed me to go back to my mum at weekends, and at the time she was living at Chervil Rise. I remember the first time I was there I went upstairs to see Melvin, and his room was plastered with Rasta pictures. But before I actually saw him I saw these locks sticking out of the top of the bed. Even though he was a couple of years younger than me, he was pretty dread by then, lying in bed with his woman, who was seven months' pregnant at the time. You could see he was on the verge of becoming a full-on Rasta, just by the way he carried himself and the life he was leading.

Soon I started getting into Rasta myself, reading the Book of Revelation, thinking the world was going to end listening to Pablo Gadd. There was this family, the Connerkies, who were connected to us through my mum's boyfriend, Slim; they were his sons Nigel, Timmy, Leslie and Frogs, who was inside at the time. They were all dreads as well, with locks down to their arses. I started to grow locks and bind them up. My hair was light on top anyway, and I used to put salt water on it every day so that the sun would bleach it until, eventually, people started to call me Goldielocks.

By the time I was allowed to leave the home and go back to my mum she had moved in with this guy Eddie, who lived at Whitmarines estate, about ten miles away. Eddie was the geezer who really brought up my brother Stuart. Jo-Jo, who was just a baby then, didn't live at Whitmarines; he was living with his dad in Walsall at the time.

Stuart Meade: I was about seven, but remember that when he used to come and see us at the place where we lived by the race-track he was always wearing this green army jumper with padded shoulders. I didn't see that much of him when I was growing up. Mum and Melvin would say: 'That's your brother,' and I would be like: 'Oh, OK.' And then he and Melvin would be jumping around on the bed upstairs.

I remember Melvin would meet me off the bus and we'd walk past Molyneux down to the estate, nick loads of bacon and fry it up back home till it was burnt, for bacon sarnies. We'd go upstairs to the bedroom, which was fucking freezing cold, and stuff our army jumpers full of pillows and throw each other around.

Margaret Pusey: It was a really nice time when he came back and we were living at Whitmarines. He was enjoying being back with us.

Then my mum moved back to Chervil Rise, which I really liked. I had some great times there. It was beautiful, man. She'd sit in the New World pub having a drink with Slim and we'd go down and see her. Slim worked in a foundry and was a grafter. He would get completely plastered on a Friday night and we would sneak into the bedroom and nick his wallet and empty it. That happened for months and months; we made a killing off that kid!

My brother and me would be robbing the Spar at every opportunity, lifting fish fingers, bacon and eggs. They knew we were doing it but they were helpless; we would do anything to get fed.

There was quite a lot of crime around. If you were in the wrong part of town at the wrong time you'd get jacked, no two ways about it. But it was like any place; if you live there you're part of it so you know what the score is. It was intimidating for me when I first moved there but I soon became part of the scene.

We'd hang out on the estate, go down to this guy Pops and buy a £2 draw, roll 'em up and smoke 'em. Weed didn't really suit me but I wanted to be part of it, so we got into smoking chalices and getting mashed up.

By that time I had a bit of a workshop going, building massive chalices, pepper-pots and pipes by sanding down coconut shells and painting them, using Polyfilla to carve intricate lion's heads on the front. I'd sell them for weed, whatever, though I was never really into smoking. Too laid back for me. My previous encounter with weed had been skiving off school with my friend Whitehead. I remember having my first joint with him listening to UB40's 'King', standing behind his sofa going: 'The floor's disappearing, man, I'm losing it, man.'

On Saturday nights I'd come out of Whispering Wheels and see the Rastas turning up in their three-litre Capris at the Half Moon Club opposite, hearing the sound of reggae drifting from across the road. In time I got to know some of them and would maybe go to a blues in Bilston. I'd been into Steel Pulse and Marley but standing in front of a speaker listening to dance-hall reggae at the Half Moon made me realise how real urban black music was. There I was one night with my rum and black, in my sheepskin coat, sweating like a cunt, and the bass was ripping straight through me. I remember walking out and just being sick everywhere!

The rawness of the sound and the lyrics was challenging. There'd be these hardcore lyrics about Babylon and then some sweet melody would come in. Those guys would take music and fuck with it. Like Ken Boothe's 'Everything I Own' would be drawn out and altered by the DJs. If Michael Jackson had a hit in the charts they'd take that and version it off. I got really turned on to music by those guys.

I always wanted to hang out with older people, and got to know a guy called Smithy as well as the Petersons and Black John. They were the three-litre posse, they were playas, going out and doing their thing and having a laugh. They used to call me 'Disco' because I had these blue snow boots which I'd bought to keep warm in winter, right? I went round to see Smithy one time and he said: 'What the fuck have you got on your feet, man? Dem disco boots!' So for ever afterwards I was 'Disco'. I was the young kid in the crew, a bit of a lightweight, the one who would borrow the keys to the car so I could have a kip halfway through the night.

Smithy would play me music in the car, sound-clash tapes, *Live At Fishguard* and Saxon Sound and people like Yellowman, and that was the way in, because it was hardcore, the bollocks. They took me on board even though I was just eighteen and they were twenty-five, twenty-six. Smithy took a shine to me and we travelled around to blues played by Skippa & Lippy, who were the DJ sound of Wolverhampton at the time. They would also play Lover's Rock, which had such sweet melodies after listening to the rougher sound-clash stuff.

I really had a love for this ghetto life. It was exciting, ghetto-ism. There was Diane, a hustler, and I used to go and have a cup of tea with her while these punters came and went in the other room. We also got bang into shotguns, supplied by Mr Grey, trying to be playas. We'd buy them, cut them off and then sell them, sometimes go over the back of North Street in Walsall and try them out.

On the day we got our dole money we were all right. We'd live large for three days, maybe pay off a few debts and then we'd just go and rob. For us that meant we'd rob the Spar and do a few runners from town. They were pretty common then. About eight of us would walk into a shop and try on everything and then just blaze. The chances were they'd only catch one or two of us, so six or seven would get away with all this gear.

Me, Melvin and some of the other guys used to specialise in safes. We'd go into the offices in the factories on the neighbouring industrial estate and Melvin was always the one who'd lead the way. We'd get a safe in the back of a car, and drive it back to Chervil Rise to our flat on the fifth floor, get it in the front room, put some blankets down on the floor in the front room, and spend hours hacking into it with crowbars, files, anything. No matter what tools we had, Melvin would always, always get it open. He was like a rabid dog, mental, and would cuss out anyone he didn't think was making an effort: 'Right, you're not getting anything if you're not going to do fuck all!' If anybody said anything about the time it was taking, he'd go off: 'You have a fuckin' go – you think you can do it?' He was crazy. Sometimes there would be a grand in there, and sometimes fuck all. God help us if there was nothing in there, which happened loads of times. Melvin would go ballistic. He was mad as fuck. If we found nothing in a factory or some offices, he used to shit in the desks. He'd be livid.

We used to dump the safes on the third floor; one day the cops came and took away nine or ten of them. They'd always be knocking on our door and we used to have this escape route through a skylight. One night it was: 'Clifford Price, you're arrested.' But we never got pinched for the safes. Anyway, once we had got the safe back and opened it, my mum would come down and make tea for us.

Margaret Pusey: Melvin had a habit of leaving his potatoes in the oven. And I heard this noise and thought the potatoes had blown up. So I went in there and they've all got blowtorches, trying to open this safe. It was all: 'Don't worry, Mum, have another fag, Mum, have a cup of tea, Mum.'

Mum was a bit of a Ma Baker character, but Melvin? He was always going for it! When the riots blew up in the Midlands in 1985 after it all went off in Handsworth, we came out of the New World and he pulled the grids off the Spar supermarket before every fucker joined in and put the windows in. We took stuff back to the flat and we were stocked out with all kinds of food, groceries, everything. So anyone on our balcony who wanted to buy nappies had to come to us. We sold everything, man.

Lee, one of the guys, was into mugging people as well and that was when I started to think: 'I can't do this any more.' The time came for me to do my bit, and I followed this old dear down the road while the rest of them watched me from the balcony. This woman must have felt my presence behind her and she turned around and looked at me and there was a pause . . . we looked at each other . . . and I lost my bottle and walked off.

I was more into shoplifting or ram-raiding in town. We'd do things like back a car into Boots and take as much stuff as we could. One time me, Mad Dave and Lee went to do Boots and it was my turn to break the window. I got this brick, chucked it and then the window shattered: BOOM! It was so loud it nearly burst my eardrums so I just ran. I was out of there. They were shouting: 'Where the fuck are you off to?' and I was like: 'I'm gone, man!' We were always bungling like that. Lee would pinch stereos, but they'd be shop-window models with no internals, so they were useless.

Then this big job came up, put together by me, Lee, Black John and the rest of the Petersons. There were a load of bleached sheepskins stored in this factory in Snow Hill. Me and Lee climbed on to the roof, removed the leading and got in. We were piling the sheepskins on the roof and the next thing we know, the alarm goes off. Everyone's fighting to get out of there. We finally scrambled away and got outside and the getaway driver had fucked off. The next day I was woken up by the police, who hauled me off to the station. The getaway driver had been caught and ratted us all out.

So I was up for my first offence. I got community service and that was the end of my criminal career. I thought: 'Fuck this, I'm not into this at all.'

Around the same time I really started to question Rasta, thinking: 'How can I be a Rasta in Western society?' Lee would say: 'You can't eat this or that because it's got animal fat in it.' And I'd go: 'You tell me I can't do that and you're out there robbing people all the while?'

Then hip-hop culture came along and grabbed me by the bollocks. *Wildstyle* the movie was phenomenal, about the taggers and rapping crews fighting each other: 'We're the Fantastic 5 MCs / We're pleasing all the ladeez / We go to the party and do it right / That makes them to all go crazee!'

The cross-over from reggae to hip-hop coincided with the fallout from that sheepskin coat job. Smithy and those guys scattered and I realised it wasn't my thing because I always felt like an outsider. They were there, hustling blatantly, working girls, that stuff, and I was just a young buck. They'd say to me: 'Disco, enuff of dis, man. You have something else.'

Soon I was getting into break-dancing hip-hop moves and formed an association with this local lot, the Westside Crew. But then I heard about the B-Boys, who were the best breaking crew in Wolverhampton, if not the entire country, at that time. Their main man was Birdy, who was my icon. The B-Boys came from the Park Village estate, which was close by, but we weren't allowed to mix with them or talk to them. All of us would go to the CCR Club every week, listening to funk, electro, the new hip-hop and all kinds of other tracks. At the same time there was a club in the New Road, where they played black urban soul and a lot of stuff on the Greensleeves

label like Janet Sinclair. These tunes were reggae but on the edge of soul, great vocal tracks, and we'd listen to that as well as people like Man Parish and Chaka Khan.

By this time I'd started to break to people like Hard Rock Soul Movement. We weren't buying music – this was about getting tapes handed around, fourth- and fifth-generation stuff taped from VHS films of breakdancers. I'd be practising spinning on my back on quiet floors of the estate to tapes of breakbeats, tracks like 'Mary Mary' or 'Funky Drummer'. People would come out of their flats and find me spinning around on my back outside their front doors, and they'd go: 'What the hell are you doing?'

I never thought about making music myself at that time. Even though you didn't have to be a practised musician to make hip-hop, I was so far away from even being curious about that side of things, because to me it was about the rhythms, being part of the sub-culture which was obsessed with breaking. I never wanted to be a musician and it never occurred to me that I would make music later.

Something else had happened; I had chosen between breaking on a Wednesday night and breaking and entering with the boys.

THE BOOK OF DREAMS —
PRISMS OF THOUGHT. "A CHAPTER

Nov/93.
WEDNDAY.
I-AM'.

SHE IS FULL
THE' MOON. SHE BE —

: NO WONDER. AS I LOOK OUT OF
MY WINDOW AND SEE — THE FULL
MOON — LIGHTS UP. ALL THE SKY —
AND FILLS ME WITH. "OPEN
ENERGY — BIG SHE GLOWS" THE
CLOUDS PASS OVER HER AT A PACE, I'VE NEVER KNOWN —
THE BIZZARO RAPID CHANGE. OF TIMES NOW. SHE —
DOES NOT BREATHE STILL' AS IF — THE BLINK OF
WHICH I SEE … '" HOLD ME IN HER — TIMELESS AWE —
'HER LIGHT IS THAT OF THE UNIVERSE. — "BOUNCING
THROUGH HER…AS IF THE PRISM" … ." MAKES OF
HER RAINBOWS, WHEN I CLOSE MY EYES, FROM HER
BLUE STILL LIGHT — "AND SO THE 'VOID IN MY HEAD —
MAKES FOR NIGHT, OF ITS OWN DESIGN" FORWARD
AND BACKWARDS', TRAVELING IN TIME', NOT MINE —
BUT — THE' SIGHT — OF DREAM 'IN SEARCH TO FIND
AND PLACE — THOSE VIVID RAYS OF PRISM LIGHT —
AT PEACE …". WITH LIFE — UPON THE CREST OF
HER FULL 'MOON" THIS' HER NIGHT —

'NO WONDER" I THINK, YES WONDER' I MUST —
I FEEL AT ONE AND PART, JOIN PEACE — INDEED —
MY FULL I TRUST — BALDARUS — UPON HER
'CUSP' ~—

4: Bombin'

Hip-hop offers an alternative to Rasta life and a get-out from crime as Goldielocks flexes his talents by graffiti-writing and break-dancing. He cuts his hair and becomes Goldie, and stars in the pioneering hip-hop documentary Bombin', which leads to a visit to his heroes in New York.

"TO FACE THEM" YOUR IDENTIFIED THE NUMBER KNOWN TO THE
PHAROAHS WAYPOINT OF DENIEL "TO PIERCE THEM, INCEPT THE
SAME DECEPTION THEY HAVE DECOYED YOUR SEARCH FOR TRUTH
IT EXISTS YES WE KNOW WHERE IT LIES ENTOMBED WITHIN THE
PHAROAHS COLUMNS ITS WALLS PASSAGES DUSTS SANDS PARTICLES
OF ACROCROCES TRADITIONS JUST WE CANNOT BREATH IN THE LIE "
FILTERED BECAUSE I CLOSED MY EYES "FEAR OF THE BLIND
THE PURE AIR OF MY LIFE, AND THOSE I BREATH THE RACE BREED
THE COUGARS WHO SAW THEIR YOUNG SUFFOCATE CONSUMED
BY THE PHAROAHS FLOOD "TO THE HIGH GROUND DAMP PAWS"
LEFT TRACKS "IN THAT WE REVERSE, CIRCLE BOUND TREAD
ROADS WITH CRACKS. AND MOVE OUR RACKS IN ABSTRACT
"THEY WON'T FIND US HERE THIS AIR IS CLEAR," IN THAT I FEED
~~AWAKES CAN CROSS OUR TRACKS~~ "I A PHAROARS TASTE IS THAT
OF MEAT THEY BLEED I SAW IT IN THE CRACKS AS WE PASS
~~TO DO AROUND THEM BEHIND THEM IS THERE GREAT FEAR~~
I AM CONDITIONED TO HUNT "TO ~~BEARON~~ TASTE TO SEARCH
FULLY BECAUSE I SEE TO STOP THE FLESH OF ~~MORAL~~ THEIR
OWN IRONY I COUGARISAM.

Hip-hop culture showed me about the visual side, the graffiti, and because art was just about the only thing I could get into at school I started tagging. I needed a name, and just really fancied the word 'dupe', so I looked it up in the dictionary and it said: 'cheat'. That was good enough for me. I became Dupe 84, because that was the year, and started tagging around the estate, stamping my name on property.

Gus Coral: Goldie has used his life as his subject matter. That's a hip-hop thing because this is a culture not separated from lifestyle. You live it, you don't just do it. He's still a B-Boy. He's also very technically adept. His graffiti have physical dexterity; he can draw a perfect circle with a spray can, and when he's doodling you can see that his line is good, innate, inborn.

Subway art to me was a way out and breaking was at its peak so we used to go to battles all over the place. One time we were in Covent Garden, London, and I saw this local guy, King Breaker, go for it. Afterwards I spoke to him and he said: 'You know what? It's all about one move. You have to come up with the power move which takes you ahead of the pack.' I have a lot of respect for that guy, because he had that natural lick. I always remembered King Breaker's advice and the time-lines flipped recently when, about six months ago, I found out that Rhino, the guy I train with and with whom I have lots in common, has been best friends with King Breaker for years. Just another of those threads that runs through my life.

But back in the day, in our neighbourhood nobody would

take on the B-Boys at the CCR. One of them, Birdy, used to do this legendary backspin. He went down into this clockwork motion in the smoothest way, it was the most beautiful thing. Everything would go quiet and he'd be spinning silently. I was intense by then, breaking every fucking day. I needed to originate something of my own so I developed this move I called the Westside Freeze. And one night in the CCR I did it, fronted out Birdy with it. Everyone went ballistic and he counteracted with this move called the Corkscrew. He was pushing himself backwards in this Freeze position, but it was a Freeze that moved forward in a straight line. He just about won, but from then he had respect for me. A couple of months later the B-Boys split so he and I and a few others formed the new B-Boys and we got a manager, Polly, who was the mother of the only female member of the crew, Bubbles. Polly wasn't too happy when she caught me and Bubbles fucking one day, but she knew the B-Boys were something special, and through her we started to travel around and show people our stuff dressed in green and gold Adidas tracksuits, really flash.

We also started to go to all-dayers on a Sunday, travelling all over the place meeting people like Sly from Rock City Crew in Nottingham. There'd be me, Sly, Albert and Crazy Kid and Cliff Lewis, who was in B-Boys. So a few of us from different crews would travel to, say, an all-dayer in Leicester and have it out, a battle would kick off, maybe me and Sly would go up against King Breaker from London and Smack 19 from Sheffield. It would be like the US and the UK troops against the Taliban; we'd collaborate and then when we got back with our own crews we'd fuck around and have it out. It was at one of those all-dayers that I first met Danny Price, who at that time was part of this crew Breaking Glass. He was one of the first people I saw doing a Windmill both ways, and twelve years later it was Danny who was instrumental in me getting my first film role, opposite David Bowie in *Everybody Loves Sunshine*.

Birdy: He had locks and his green tracksuit with Goldielocks down the leg. He wasn't that good at dancing, but the character he had about him was really good, you get me? His artistic work as a graffiti artist was really good as well.

I started painting on the estate after tagging for a while. I must have put together more than sixty illegal paintings on Heath Town, but I didn't get too much grief – the community police turned a blind eye because it really brightened the place up. There was stuff all along the walls where the kids went to school. One said 'Don't Be Late' in great big letters. It was amazing to me to walk around the estate and be surrounded by my work – there were just so many that I had spent hours on, making sure they were dead right, with all the right colours. I did ones called 'Fantasy', 'In Space', 'Time To Rock', 'Rock On', and 'Rebel', which was a bad piece, nasty, with lower-case letters with a spear in the middle. 'Lost In Space' was a favourite because I did it on this massive precinct so you could see it from all around.

Margaret Pusey: The first one he did was the Statue of Liberty in the middle of the bedroom wall. Oh, it was beautiful. I thought it was wonderful that he started making a name for himself, it made me feel ever so proud.

But I wasn't working on my own; with a few of the others I also formed the Supreme Graffiti Team, and I painted the name on the backs of our matching denim jackets; they looked really boss and made people pay attention even more. Then we set up this plan to paint our first train, which we'd read about and seen footage of guys doing in New York. One of the guys who helped was called Tucker. He was a great big huge kid and he made the news a few years back in tragic circumstances. He was just about to become a professional boxer because he was so handy, but he died of a heart attack while moving a fridge for his mum at her place.

Anyway, back then we got down to the British Rail yards in Walsall with ladders and I coordinated everyone. We put together this massive Supreme Graffiti Team logo right along the side of it. It was beautiful. Melvin and his mates came with us. While we were painting they were screwing the bar, getting completely pissed. It was really funny because we'd staked it out for days, timing the arrival of the trains by watching them through binoculars from the golf course, a real Steve McQueen / *The Great Escape* deal. Then when we got down there and started painting they found the bar and started getting off their heads. I didn't give a fuck but thought it was quite funny.

Birdy: Goldie's on the bottom floor, I'm on the middle floor, Louis is on top and we're just bombing it. People would come from far and wide just to see the murals.

I started to think: 'If we're going to have to steal we might as well steal paint.' So I started nicking Letrajet kits from art shops and paint from Halfords. Then I did a fantastic piece called 'Third World War': Russian and American flags and rockets going off in the clouds, right on the main drag going to the Park Village estate, where our biggest graffiti rivals Network were based. I hit them right where it hurt and they gave up. In the end it was ridiculous. I was on the news and other TV shows like *Daytime Live* and *Pebble Mill at One*, where I did this hundred-foot piece. I really wanted to be somebody else, recognised, so early one Saturday morning I went along to see this guy Oliver, a hairdresser whose shop window I'd painted, because I knew it was time for a change. I told Oliver to cut all my hair off and with that I was no longer Goldielocks. I was now Goldie, and that was the tag

I used from then on. Anyway, everyone had started to suspect Dupe 84 was me so I thought I might as well come out in the open!

Gus Coral: In 1985 my friend Dick Fontaine and I were making *Bombin'*, a film about hip-hop culture, for Central TV. We were on the lookout for British graffiti artists and Goldie's name came up. Somebody, I forget who, said: 'You should go and see this kid in Wolverhampton.' We went up to see him with one of the pioneers of New York graffiti, Brim Fuentes, who was the central character of our film. We were amazed when we got to Goldie's estate – I think there were sixty-two pieces of his artwork on Heath Town.

By then I had an agent, Martin Jones. He'd heard about the work I was doing with Birdy and the other guys so he came along and offered to find us commissions, and took over from Polly, kitting us out in Australian tracksuits, Pony sneakers, all the gear. It was Martin who took me and a bunch of the others in a van to a show in London, Electro Rock at the Shaw Theatre. That was where I met a lot of people, including Brim, who became one of my all-time heroes and was being filmed there by Gus, Dick and the crew. Brim was giving these workshops on tagging and hip-hop culture and I went up to talk to him and we just got on. He ended up giving me two screens that he'd used for printing T-shirts, and they also had characters done by two other really big names, Bio and Nicer, so when I got back home I used the silk screens to start printing my own stuff and passing it around.

Brim Fuentes: I was doing something with Afrika Bambaata in London and this motherfucker must have taken a train for three, four hours to get there. And he's like: 'Yo, yo, what's up?' in his sheepskin coat. He definitely stood out from the crowd. He wanted it and he got it. He knew what he had to do.

I remember that first time I went to London I saw what Trailblazers – who were a local crew – had done. It blew my mind, because the main guys, Pride and Mode, were streets ahead of us at the time. But they had that London arrogance thing going on. Then they came up to the Rotunda Centre when Martin organised this big exhibition and started dissing Brim and Bio's work, and that just made me mad, wanting to beat them all the more. I had been brought up by Brim and Bio, and when you're accepted by the crew anything outside of it is word, do you know what I mean? If people diss any of you, then fuck 'em. I remember I first met Pride at the Arnolfini Gallery in Bristol, and there was this arrogance which, I think, had a lot to do with the fact that people don't like it when they're threatened. Then I really studied Trailblazers' work and realised that they were just taking off Futura 2000. Mode was very good at characters, but that was it. End of story. I knew I could get up to their speed and beyond, because I'd always painted the whole picture.

Gus Coral: He was then, as I suppose he is now, a mixture of enormous confidence and frailty and vulnerability. But it was clear he was an artist. He had a large amount of talent and energy and was very hard working. He had short hair with this little teeny pigtail at the back and he was dressed like a B-Boy in his Puffa jacket and sneakers. It was difficult to tell exactly where he was living. He had a flat in the Heath Town estate which he'd been thrown out of because he'd been getting into it via an illicit route, over the roof and down through the window.

All the time I lived there I was just painting and painting – I was obsessed. I got a new flat after the one Gus mentions, which was also in Chervil Rise, at Hawthorne House, which was unbelievable. I was on the first floor, next to a gambling house. The door was always open and sometimes these geezers would come staggering in thinking they could have a bit of a flutter and a game and they'd find me, this mad kid, surrounded by paint and wet canvases, just working and working all the hours God sent. I'd go: 'No, mate, you want the gambling house next door,' and they'd be off.

Hawthorne House really was Graffiti Central. I had two bedrooms, no carpet, with paint stacked wall to wall, four feet high, which I'd hoarded through commissions, boxes of Omni paint. There was a drawing desk there, air brushes, spray cans, compressors, canvases, everything. There were stills of trains I'd got from Henry Chalfont, the guy who compiled our bible *Subway Art,* and all my drawings on display. Kids would come by to check my work out and we used to hold meetings of the United Graffiti Federation there. When the riots happened in the mid-eighties I set up major bombing campaigns, spreading the word and talking about what was happening in the ghetto. Although there probably was a lot of crime, the B-Boy generation was given hope by the hip-hop explosion. It was all about: who's going to be the best? Which crew are you from? It was all about becoming part of a unit, whether it was the Westside Crew or the B-Boys or Force 10. All these different crews came from different areas and had an identity, a feeling of belonging to something. It gave a lot of us a way out.

Hawthorne House was set up for this kid who just wanted to paint all day; I think I did my best drawings there, my best still lifes, my best characters. By that time we were doing loads of graffiti festivals through Martin, and when Brim came up to see us, we went on the trip to the Arnolfini. I'll never forget, we got there in a Rover 3.5 with a V8 engine, but with no tax or insurance. I'd already seen the obnoxiousness of the London scene but Bristol was different. That night at a house party I first met the Wild Bunch, who were B-Boy dons to me: Milo, Nellee Hooper, 3-D, Daddy G and Mushroom.

Nellee Hooper: I was DJing with the Wild Bunch (Massive Attack, me and DJ Milo) and it was the beginning of hip-hop culture; we were completely obsessed. We weren't interested in anyone who didn't live hip-hop, we had all the best tunes, all the gear – Cazal sunglasses, goose jackets, the best sneakers, and all from New York. I remember going to Harlem, 125th Street, on my own, looking for sneakers and the master tapes from *Wildstyle*. I was twenty-one years old – I must have been out of my mind. We were convinced we were cooler than anyone in London and definitely anywhere else in the country.

I guess I met Goldie in 1984, 1985 in Bristol. It was at the Redhouse, an illegal warehouse in St Pauls. We had over two thousand people rocking, and in the crowd the usual suspects: Roni Size, Smith & Mighty, Newtrament, Tim Westwood, lots of B-Boy posturing . . . and we ruled!

Suddenly a break-dancing stand-off started with Goldie and his B-Boys battling Bristol's City Rockers. They were much better and they had books of their own graffiti, much better than the shit 3D and T.U.M.A. (The Underground Massive Attack) were doing. Goldie was in . . . one of us (without the cool gear!)

Anyone from Massive can tell you about me walking round Bristol with a long overcoat and a sawn-off, trying to give it the big 'un. They were into funk in Bristol, but when 3-D came over to Wolverhampton for more filming on *Bombin'* we did this painting at Heath Town called 'T.A.F.', which stood for Trans-Atlantic Federation, showing that we were looking across the Atlantic to people like Brim and Bio.

3-D also brought me a tape of music he'd recorded for me. On one side was Miles Davis's album *Decoy*, and on the other was the soundtrack to *Taxi Driver*. I listened to *Decoy* for years but never understood it, couldn't get my head around it. It was only later when I started making music I got some-where; the track 'Dragonfly' on *Saturnz Return* was based on Miles, but also I dug it because by that time I had become very well acquainted with drugs and what Miles was doing was describing the loneliness of the situation. But that's way down the line. For the time being people like Nellee and 3-D were talented guys from another part of the country who I made a real connection with and we had a right laugh making the film and hanging out together.

Gus Coral: It didn't happen instantly, but Goldie did kind of become the star of the second half of *Bombin'*, almost naturally, without trying very hard. His personality had taken over Heath Town, breaking with the B-Boys and painting everywhere. He was obviously the leader, the one who was driving it. The thing about Goldie is that, although he has heroes, he has no problem accelerating to their level of excellence. And that's his talent coming through. He's quite sure of it.

I put so much energy into my graffiti, because I wanted to achieve more than anybody else and wanted to be the best. I also really enjoyed meeting my heroes and talking to them one on one about technique and what they had done to get ahead. Another thing is that I finally felt like I belonged, especially when the New York guys got into my work.

Brim and Bio each taught me very important things: Brim pointed out the social and street side of graffiti culture – he was interested in what was going down on the street, how racism, lack of jobs and education were affecting us. He already had a kid back home and he needed to get out of the South Bronx, but wanted to keep on making social messages. Bio would emphasise technique, the alphabet. He'd say: 'Look, man, you've got to work on your letters so that you can get them back to front, connect them backwards, or else it's pointless writing your name.' Bio taught me that technically a graffiti writer works on his letters from A to Z. Once you've got your alphabet down a C can become an E, a T becomes a J, an F becomes an E. You work on letter form until it's totally down. Through that lesson I came to realise the importance of form.

As Joseph Rykwert says at the beginning of *Bombin'*, the barbarians from within will take over and, in the twentieth century, the letter form replaced the human form as the central figure in art.

David Bowie: I think Goldie's a tremendous visual artist and wish he would do more. *Bombin'* obviously has a nice bit on Goldie and I have a feeling he'll eventually go back to painting with a vengeance.

At the time the film was being made there was this rush of the sub-culture taking off, it was a complete explosion. I took part in this massive show at Birmingham City Library featuring me, 3-D, Nicer, T-Kid and Bio. The Birmingham show was organised by Martin Jones, who got grants from the council for my painting and sponsorship from a local company, PPG Automotives. Billy at PPG started to give me paints for free and helped me create my own colours, which was great because they also had these cans with a mad nozzle technique.

When the film was being made and the exhibition was being held, Martin wanted to impress the New Yorkers who were coming over, so before the event we put them up in the Metropole in Brighton and had this mad party with all kinds of crazy shit happening – TVs flying out of windows, Brim and Bio having this mock marriage, people throwing up over themselves and being stuffed into the elevators and sent down to the lobby.

After we trashed the hotel, we got on the train to London and I went to my first underground club, Spectrum at Heaven, to meet up with Nellee. Trevor Fung was DJing and the NY guys leapt up on the podiums, raving like good 'uns, which freaked me out. When we were hanging with the New Yorkers this girl was on the scene – her last name's Reed, I can't remember her first name, and don't care to. We all slept with her, and one time this orgy was going in this hotel. She also slept with my brother. Anyway, I slept with her, bang, in and out, and never thought about it. She found out she was pregnant and told everyone she was having an abortion, so that was that, I thought.

That scene was wild – orgies, parties, drugs, guns, fights. Sometimes at the festivals and shows it would kick off, they would get rowdy. At that time I was carrying a gun, a Smith & Wesson .38, but only to be hard. My brother was into sawn-offs but it all got too much for me. I just thought: I've got to get rid of this shit because I'm trying to be somebody I ain't.

Gus Coral: Although I know he has an aggressive nature, in the years I've known him he has never, ever shown it to me, not even once or slightly. I learnt later that he was a bit scared of me and us in general, this film crew arriving from London. The confidence was a kind of front, some bluff so he could handle the situation.

I had my first graffiti show at a gallery in Wolverhampton and was doing these elaborate graffiti pieces and getting a lot of commissions, including the big one commissioned by the council on the estate where the kids walked to school. I really felt for the first time in my life that I was achieving something. I'd created this character – first Dupe 84 and now Goldie – and I'd become known. It felt fucking brilliant, because I wasn't the best breaker but I knew I had it in me to take this graffiti thing as far as it could go. I'd walk around Birmingham, outside of my home town, and people would go: 'That's Goldie, there he is, that guy's hot.' I'd hear that and it felt so good, the first sign that I was going to make it, I really felt it in my heart. It was unreal; I was walking on air at that point in my life.

Margaret Pusey: To tell you the truth I never thought he would become known for his drawing. As a little boy he always had something in his hands, he was always making things, but I thought he would be a piano player because he has those lovely hands with the long fingers. In Scotland we always used to say if you had hands like that you'd end up playing the piano, so that's what I thought he'd do, become another Elton John!

Around this time I hooked up with this guy called Whitey, who had a T-shirt printing company in Wolverhampton. I had printed these wildstyle T-shirts through him to coincide with the Birmingham library show, and made a few bob because I was pretty good at hustling that stuff.

I'd been looking for work and Whitey knew that my graffiti were good, so I started doing designs for him. He was the first guy who gave me a job doing artwork and we really got on well together, because he understood where I was coming from and let me experiment with design. We used to come down to London and try to get paid by these guys who were selling our stuff. They used to sell them from a stall outside the Oxford Arms in Camden.

Ian Whitehouse: It was Goldie who christened me Whitey, to distinguish me from Ian White, who I worked with and who had a T-shirt factory. Next door to the factory was a lock-up which Goldie and one of his mates had rented to paint canvases. I'd heard that Goldie was good, and he came up with these great wildstyle designs which we knocked out. When the tie-dye stuff came out we got into that as well. These old washing machines we used to dye the shirts had broken down, so Goldie, who always had a complicated love life, said he knew this girl who had a washing machine/tumble dryer we could use. We went round and picked it up while her old man was away and delivered it back. Two days later he got this really irate phone call from this girl – she'd washed her old man's clothes in there and they'd all gone pink!

Whitey's a good guy, a lot older than me but hip, with a Citroën all done up and a Zephyr hearse he was always working on. He had time for me and as an artist himself he understood me. I used to crash at his place a lot and did a painting for his son Toby, who I stay in touch with even now.

Ian Whitehouse: One of my mates in London was having some problems with the husband of a girlfriend of his, and he thought that the guy was maybe going to come down heavily on him. So he asked us to get him a gun. I'm not suggesting to anybody that this is the road to go down but Goldie said that it wouldn't be a problem. Next day he took us to a house in the back streets of Wolverhampton and came out twenty minutes later with a pillowcase under his arm. Inside was a box of cartridges and a twelve-bore shotgun. We took it to the factory and sawed off the barrel and presented it to the guy. Thankfully he never had to use it though I think that it might have been brandished.

Whitey also had a lot of mates who could get you whatever. I think there were a bunch of them who ended up doing a long stretch for taking hash over to the Continent inside a van-load of TV sets.

Ian Whitehouse: We knocked about together, going to clubs and having a drink. When times got hard we'd pool our funds and buy chips or a packet of ten fags. Once the guy in London pulled a stroke by booking space at a menswear exhibition in Earls Court and then not doing anything about setting up a stand. Having spent three weeks tie-dying and printing all these shirts, Goldie and I went round all the skips at the back of the show hall and got broken old ladders, oil cans and hardboard and sprayed and graffitied them up to show off the shirts. We set the show up in two hours the next morning and the stand was a raging success because it looked so colourful, like an explosion in a paint factory.

But we never made any money because the London partner stitched us up, so we told him to shove it, and I decided to get out of the game. Funnily enough it had the opposite effect on Goldie. He draws a lot of his strength from adversity, and the fact that this had happened made him all the more determined. When he's kicked in the bollocks he doesn't go down suffering, but comes straight back up. That's been his life story.

People wanted to come to me, because I was the first guy to hang with original NY graffiti writers, not just replicating it but actually down with them. That felt special. And once I'd made my name in the Midlands the next thing to conquer was London. And eventually I got big-time respect from people like Pride and Mode, who were rival graffiti artists from London. But when it came to my family it was different. Melvin would say to me: 'You can't fucking rob but you can do this. Why can't I?' He'd bully me into teaching him and I'd try but he just couldn't get it together.

My mum also recognised that I was being seen as a talented person by the outside world, particularly when the *Bombin'* cameras arrived with Brim and Bio. I was making a bit of money here and there – Martin Jones was feeding us some cash and whenever I had a commission I'd spend the money on pens, rather than stealing them, or I'd buy a small compressor and start air brushing. My paint collection became massive; I had a ridiculous amount after we got this commission to paint a mural for the Chinese New Year. I knew it was a commercial thing, doing graffiti for 'them', but what was always at the back of my mind on those jobs was that it meant I could buy more paint. And all of it got spunked on my estate with all the paintings there.

Gus Coral: Goldie's graffiti were the first I'd seen in England which were on a par with the stuff in New York. They weren't a poor imitation. We shot over a long period and went back to Heath Town with Goldie and 3-D a year later to kind of bring it up to date. And we went twice to New York, once with him. I think he enjoyed showing his work to a wider audience and he certainly enjoyed the experience of larging it up to your mates, like you do when there's a film crew following you around.

To be completely honest, taking part in *Bombin'* was the greatest experience of my life at that point. Talking in the film about what was going down on the estates, I felt like I'd picked up on something other kids hadn't, and going to New York was unreal, like going to Mecca. *Wildstyle* was the Bible to us, while Henry Chalfant's book *Subway Art* had opened me up to a whole new world. So when the chance came to go to New York, I was so excited. First I went to Manhattan where I took part in a TV commercial for Ford, a bunch of us breaking at the bottom of 52nd Street. We all lined up and did our moves, which was pretty wild, going up against American breakers, meeting people like Vulcan, T-Kid and Kaze 2, but even better, the commercial was arranged by Henry Chalfant himself.

After the shoot a few of us went back to Henry's famous studio on Grand Street, where he showed me all these folders of the originals in *Subway Art* and some incredible pictures which never made the book, ridiculous shit. And to cap it all, there, sitting in Henry's studio, was Lee Quinnones, this person who had changed my life by starring as the graffiti writer in *Wildstyle*. I was so fucking gobsmacked I didn't know what to say to him, but I realised then I was blessed.

Time always folds for me and Lee came back into my life again as recently as a few months back. I was sitting outside the Pelican in Miami and this guy came up to me and said: 'Yo, what's up?' It was Lee, with Design and Doze from Rock Steady Crew, more of my idols. They came down to this gig I did at the Astor the next night and Design said to me: 'You know, G, *Timeless* is the best album in the world. I listen to that shit when I'm painting.' That's amazing, because I was so influenced by him, and that influence set me on the path to making the music which he now plays when he's creating.

I had a Valve Dillinja dub plate with me which Lee grabbed and he drew a car on the sleeve with: 'To Goldie. Drive It Like You Hate It!!' For me, you can't get much better than that – Dillinja the Bassman and Lee the Ultra-Don in one package.

But back when I met Lee for the first time, I finished off working on the Ford commercial and then broke out of Manhattan to see Brim, Afrika Bambaata, all of them in the South Bronx.

Brim Fuentes: Goldie knew that this was it. If you were studying hip-hop then this is where Bambaata, Grandmaster Flash, the Furious 5, the Cold Crush brothers all started. If you played here and got respect here, then you were the shit, bottom line. This is where the scratching started, where motherfuckers started rapping, where if you put your painting on the wall you got respect.

Brim took a really hard line with me. I remember him walking me through the South Bronx. It was a wasteland, with an entire block absolutely devastated, through tenement yards, like a nuclear fallout zone. I was talking to him about how amazing it was to be in New York and he said: 'Fuck the Big Apple. You just see the glam and the glitz. You don't see the shit.' That really woke me up to the fact that the art we were making should reflect what was going on in society. He taught me social commentary.

Gus Coral: *Bombin'* was a mild success. I still meet people who say it was a landmark, but there were only about three people who watched it at the time. It wasn't an instant success for Goldie or anybody in it, and I didn't have a clue how far he would go but I knew that he was going places. He'd never shown any inclination to make music, though I do remember when music writer David Toop came along to put some pieces of music together for *Bombin'*, Goldie was definitely watching and his eyes were shining.

When *Bombin'* came out I felt like a superstar. Gus and the others obviously changed the way the film was going when they realised I had something, which was good for me, but looking back now I know that I owe everything to Brim and Bio. No matter that we're not in contact that often these days, I'm still there for them. Their crew T.A.T. are the best in the world, hands down, no question. I tag T.A.T. – that's my boys.

"I Cry Therefore I"

A thought became ,, the dream, so it seemed,
Thus love beamed ,, to let me in ,, to be "exploded
                              in me ,,,

Soul to let me free 'past shades confused 'the haze ,,
set tones ,, confined my ways , 'lifes salts 'taste
as old as time ,, seas sprayed ,,, 'the bitter 'juice ,,
of Ale, in all bave dignity ,, for all to see ,,,
the blind ,, became 'serenity ,
so therefore tears the seas that brought to me ,,

I cried 'there for I am ,,

'the shade 'blue in bliss , was not the colours of my heart, 'in love 'fired
the spark 'the coals burned hot to be, ignite , to truly find ,, the passion
'white 'at heart' ,, 'the pawns' alone could not play ,,, the complex back
'a cupid' simply stole queen's part, the arrows striken mercedine
man kin to down ,, the armies 'marched ,, against the clowns ,,, i cry
      therefore ,,, reasons the joys of life ,,,, my cupids hands

© ' and somewhere lies the dream ,,   Colin

5: Sea of Tears

Although his artistic career blossoms, Goldie is traumatised by the breakdown of his relationship with Michelle, the mother of his newborn child. When he becomes embroiled in an affair with another woman, Goldie escapes to Miami, where he meets his father for the first time in two decades. He works in a flea market business screen-printing T-shirts, selling customised gold teeth and hanging with true playas.

Those Who Are Creative,,,
A sleeping choice, in all once
awakened,

It will always seem like 'there
constant time,' to raise and live,
'to surround', and bound to be at
destination,, we end up and are
Somewhat found.

And for those who wish for nothing
are somehow caught in cloud,
A never ending misty exit ,,, a room
without a crowd,
A life womb of anxiety,
Faithful sometimes, upon mans
to do for that digital prophecy,
How can we measure life by
these myths of code,
Surely once shown purity, in its
cupid experience alone! No
look back at life in focus,, away
from maddening crowd,,,
Allow given time, wipe comedy from
your brow, maybe not now, but
in further roads, the signs will
show you how,
Curiosity will always lay rest,
But never get down. ,,,

"Remember of how,
where at you are part
of then, but now
back then the youth
I found played court
and made laugh, to them,
to fade away a frown,
fool teaches wish man
of deaf ,,, brings song
heard loud ,,, remember
how?"

y 1987 I'd made a name for myself as an artist, I'd met my heroes in the US and things were looking up. But I had to leave England, I just knew I had to get away and find my father, confront him and bury some of my demons. There was this letter from my dad which my mum had kept for years. In it he wrote that he wanted to see me again, and there was also a number for him at his house in Miami. I made a note of the number and kept it with me at all times.

My urge to leave became really strong three months after Michelle had given birth to my son Daniel.

I'd met Michelle one night at the skating rink. She was very pretty with this long black hair, a mixed breed with a bit of Indian in her family, but her mum was white and her dad was black. I started seeing her, the first real girlfriend that I had, and when she became pregnant my response was: 'Great.' But we couldn't start living together because I couldn't get a flat for us.

She stayed with her folks in Wednesfield and things became very rocky. They didn't like me and I think she started to resent me. Our relationship was in tatters.

Melvin and I also fell out badly at around this time. It made living at home really difficult, and contributed to my urge to leave. I didn't confront him about the breakdown of our relationship because I could see how he had been really scarred by his early life. Even to this day there's something about Melvin. He's got this picture in his house nowadays, a guy drew it of him. It's of his eyes. In one of the eyes there's a reflection of my logo for my label Metalheadz, which represents me, and there are tears running down his face. It's a very scary painting and those eyes are full of guilt and angst and burden. All the years I was away he was there with my mum. He'd seen the beatings, he'd seen my mum get drunk. Melvin had picked her up when she was down, he'd be there when the lovers came in and out of the house. Melvin saw it all. He had a tough time.

He's my only flesh-and-blood brother, but when I fell out with both him and Michelle I was so devastated that I closed off from the family and just concentrated on graffiti. I'd realised that I'd chosen to come and live with my family only to find out that they were all really dysfunctional, which was a major disappointment. Sometimes I think that was why Goldie was created; I had to get rid of the past.

There was another reason why I wanted to leave England. I'd found solace after Michelle with a girl I'll call Christine. That's not her real name, but I really believe that to use it would give her power over me. I'm serious; naming her gives her strength and feeds her evil, because she became a really wicked force in my life.

We met under quite innocent circumstances. I'd first got to know her when I used to catch the same bus as her, the 996 from Lew Joseph to school, and when we were about fifteen I snogged her at a party. A bit later I met her again at the skating rink and we got on really well.

One day, after a few months on my own getting over Michelle, I met Christine in Walsall High Street. She was a shortish girl, and by that time had a kid called Martin, named after his father, who was doing a long stretch, though first of all she gave me some nonsense about him working on an oil rig. I started seeing Christine, visiting her at her place, and I have to say I really fell head over heels in love with her. But there was a problem; every time I made a move towards her, she told me it didn't have a chance of working out. Every time I backed off, there she was, ready for me.

I wanted more from her, but she would never allow the relationship to flourish because, she said, Martin was eventually going to come out of prison and she would have to stay with him. But even when he came home, we continued to see each other on the quiet. Still she wouldn't finish with him. So, as I say, I would leave it and then she would want to see me again, meeting in secret places or in the car. It was becoming impossible.

I couldn't get my head around the fact that she would not stop seeing Martin, so one time I took a shotgun to him. I was definitely going to cancel him out, because with him out of the picture Christine and I would be fine. I waited for him in my car outside their flat. Just seeing him walk out and towards me made me grab for the gun, which I had with me at all times then. But when I tried to cock it back, it just wouldn't go, the action jammed. I guess I got paranoid. So there I was, struggling with this fucking gun, ready to cap the bastard, and he just strolls by! I fucked off, cursing my brother's gun.

The whole business was just freaking me out. It was the biggest wind-up of my life, and that was what was getting to me: I was so in love with her but she just kept out of my reach. She'd been there for so long – since we'd met at that party I went to when I was still at the home. Then I'd seen her on the bus and when we used to go skating, and now there I was, making a name for myself but still I wasn't enough for her.

I would go off sometimes. Once I started seeing this girl called Sonia, who had a great kid, Jade. Sonia and I were cool, but Christine was always in my head. And it was doing my head in.

One night, while this was going on, I went to a club in

Kingswinford with a few of the boys, and asked this geezer for a couple of Rizlas, because he had a pack in front of him. He just said: 'No, fuck off.' I said: 'Fuck you, then, mate,' and it all kicked off. He ran outside and I started to follow him and as I got towards the entrance I saw the security running towards me, going sideways. The geezer ran straight at me with this fucking huge ice pick and went WHAACK!, catching me on my forearm, with the pick going straight through and out the other side.

Spurting great gouts of blood, I stumbled through the club and found a table where these people were eating their dinner. Dripping blood over these diners, who were looking astonished at the way their meal was going, I ripped the tablecloth off, sending plates flying everywhere, and wrapped it around my arm to stop the flow. Then I passed out.

Next thing I'm in hospital, just waking up, still feeling groggy. Christine came marching in, saying: 'You've missed me, haven't you?' I was feeling weak with my arm all strung up, and said: 'Yes, of course.' So she snapped: 'Well, what about these, then?' and threw these photos of me and Sonia that she had found. She ripped them to shreds in front of me. I couldn't make head or tail of it: it was OK for her to stay with Martin but I couldn't see anyone else. She'd hung me out to dry and I was fucked off.

So I decided to act on my need to find my father and go back to America. First I went to New York – this was my second trip there – to forget about things and do some graffiti. But even when I was in New York I couldn't shake Christine. I painted her name and a love heart around it on the side of a train near 116th Street lay-up.

It was winter, really cold, and here was I freezing my arse off. So I dug out the number I had found in my mum's letter and rang my old man in Miami. It took some guts to do that, you know? I hadn't seen him in nineteen years and we were having this kind of normal conversation when I asked him straight out if I could go down to see him. He just said: 'Come on.' Simple as that. That really threw me. This was the first time I would be seeing him since I was a baby and I felt: 'Is that all you've got to say?'

But I flew down anyway and my dad came and met me up at the airport in his little truck from his roofing business and drove me to his house. Even though this was the first time I'd met him in nineteen years, I just felt numb. My initial thought was: Wow, you look like the guy in the picture. This was a little framed photograph my mum had kept of him all those years which she had on her mantelpiece.

We got to the house on 191st Street Terrace, Carol City, which is a predominantly Jamaican 'hood, and there was my half-sister and half-brother, who I'd never met before. We all kind of got on at first so I stayed there for a while and things were OK, although they always seemed to be at each other's throats. My father was cool towards me but I never spoke to him about the past. It seemed to me that he was out of touch with what had happened in his life and had swept it all under the carpet.

At the same time that I felt numb, I also felt that I was there to make a new life for myself. I'd brought my portfolio and started to take it around to show people what I could do, I was that determined to get a job and settle down there.

But all the time I was in Miami I called Christine nearly every day, I was so hung up on her. I also kept in touch with people back home like Nellee Hooper. I'd call him from my dad's kitchen with his family raging around me. By then Nellee was working with Soul II Soul, which was really blowing up big back in Britain, and also making its mark as a sort of cult thing in America.

Nellee Hooper: We had moved to London and started DJing with

Jazzie B and Soul II Soul. Then 'Back To Life' and *Club Classics Vol. I* hit big time! Number one worldwide!

At the time there was this dread/soulboy hybrid called the Funki Dredd, a styler who wore his locks short. I had short locks with shaved sides, so all the cats in Miami thought I was a Funki Dredd because I was from England, right? And anybody from England must be a Funki Dredd because of Soul II Soul, right? So it was weird – here was I all these thousands of miles away and I had this connection to a scene which one of my best friends was at the centre of.

But the arguing at my dad's house got really bad. It was the worst scenario, seeing your family from Jamaica rowing constantly and getting really het up. I just thought: If this is family, fuck it! I didn't usually get involved, although one night my sister went for my dad and I had to hold her up against the wall by her throat and say: 'If you ever put your hand on my dad again I'll kill you.' But I thought to myself: Why am I fighting these battles? Who am I doing it for? Fuck this. It all got too much, so after a few months I chipped after I came back one night and my father said: 'What time do you call this? Where have you been?'

I said to him: 'Why are you asking me now? You haven't given a fuck about where I've been for years. I can look after myself.' So that was it, I was gone to stay with this guy I was working for by then, Brena', at his crib.

I loved Brena', he was like a brother to me and really took me under his wing. When I had first arrived and taken my artwork to the flea markets and the beach looking for work, Brena' had hired me at his booth, where he sold T-shirts. He also engraved gold teeth and set diamonds, all kinds of shit. It was Brena' who taught me custom casting.

At first I used to leave all that to him, but over time I

learnt how to make them by mishap. It really came about because Brena' would always be late at the stall. He'd drop me off and then say he'd be back in a couple of hours but quite often he'd go off somewhere and not turn up. So these kids would come along waiting to have the moulds made for their teeth and, since he wasn't around and I'd watched him, picking up things like the fact that you have to avoid getting too much air in the mould, it would be down to me to do it.

Sometimes, in the evenings back at the crib, I'd watch Brena' wax the moulds and after a while I realised that it was just a miniaturised version of sculpting. So, for me, it wasn't too difficult, as long as I was careful with the first layer of wax, slipping it on and off the teeth to make sure it was right. At first I started helping him out with the waxing and soon I was into designing them. What was attractive to me was learning to manipulate a solid object and form it into something which was artistic. It gave me a real adrenalin rush, because it hooked into all my ideas about B-Boy transformation, giving people a new identity. And when I got my own set I reached the final stage of me becoming Goldie.

I'd had two teeth knocked out way back in a fight in some club in Walsall and had capped the rest. The first set I had made were removable; a grille on the bottom set and two half-grilles up top. But on the way to Atlanta one time I took them out to eat at a restaurant somewhere and left them there, wrapped up in a napkin where they were probably thrown away. So I got Brena' to make me the trademark teeth which mark me out to this day.

Margaret Pusey: When I first saw them I thought they looked good, they suited him. In fact, I wish he had got me some because I haven't got many!

At the booth we started to get into all sorts of stuff. I persuaded Brena' that we should do air brushing, and built a trestle table which we could slip the shirts over so that I could customise them on the spot. Kids would come up with photographs of themselves and go: 'Yo, yo, I wanna Benz with, like, me on the front, with two nine-millimetres and GETTIN' PAID on the front and SUCK MY DICK on the back!'

So that's what I did all day long, charging $50, $60 apiece, regular love hearts and stuff for the girls and gangsta shit for the boys. I also did about half a dozen rides, air brushing cars for about $3,000 apiece. I'll never forget, this guy Korly got me to do a Hellraiser number on his motor. By the time I'd finished it had flying eyeballs on the side, a snake on the roof, a claw holding a huge eyeball, a guy's face on the front with mad teeth, helmet and horns. It was freestyle, air brushed, none of this masking shit. All I did was adapt the graffiti I'd learnt in New York and at home and it was the bomb.

This was the best of times. We made a killing, me and Brena'. Everything was cool at his house, apart from the indestructible cockroaches. We'd turn the light on at night and the bastards were everywhere, scuttling around. We'd try to kill them by stomping on them, setting them alight, but they seemed to survive everything!

During the day we'd pick mangoes and oranges off the tree in the garden and that's what we'd live on: mango punch, orange punch, orange punch with milk, orange and mango punch. Brena's family was from Surinam and he'd cook the same dish all the time: *Brena Bona*, which was delicious. Me and Brena' have a strong bond.

Because of the money coming in from the booth, life was really good. On the weekend we'd spunk all the money we'd earned, getting completely whacked drinking strawberry daiquiris and going to all the clubs and bars. I loved the

Breaking with the B-Boys in Wolverhampton in 1983

Below: Spraying, age eighteen

One of my graffiti in the basement of Chervil Rise

First train in London, 1987

With Vulcan and Bio at the Transatlantic Federation graffiti show in Birmingham City Library

Brim, Birdy, me and 3D, who later became a key figure in Massive Attack

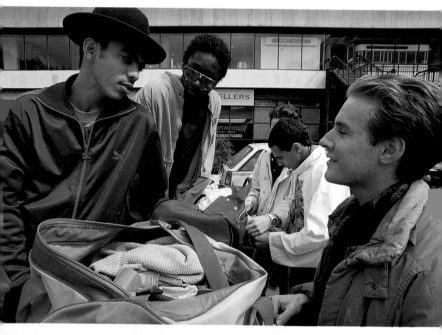

My favourite painted
sweatshirt

Below: *Survivors*
piece in progress,
F.F. Harrison School

Right: 3D and me at
the Wolverhampton
Show

Neneh Cherry painting, 1991

Graffiti for Dan Fontaine

Right: *Wildstyle* graffiti by Sarah Gregory and me

Unnamed B-Boy Fly Girl by Sarah Gregory and me

beach, even though at the time Miami Beach was not *the* beach. It was really moody when I first went there; if you got close to South Beach itself you got fucked up. The action at that time was two blocks back. We just used to bounce from beach to bar.

There were also certain moves going on. Trucks would be delivered to the house and we'd do paint jobs on them. And there was such a cast of characters. People like Tracy, who had an Impala 66 Supersport, Funki Dredd locks and was always going on about how he dug 'that Soul II Soul joint'. There'd be guys coming down from Atlanta, scoring loads of gear and sending it north. One, John Probert, now lives in South Africa. I saw him on the news not that long ago sitting next to Nelson Mandela and thought: Wow. You sure got to the top of your tree, you old cherry.

At the time I knew him Probert looked like a straight-A college kid, but he was a big blagger, highly into surveillance. His job was to come down to Miami, score fifteen, maybe twenty keys of gear at $8,000 a pop and take them to Brena's house, where the car would be packed out and driven up I-95 to wherever. By the time it got back up north the price of a key would be up to $22,000.

Most of the time I'd stay at the house and there'd be shoe boxes of money to count. One night we sat up and counted $198,000. Took a long time to count, let me tell you, but it was worth it. We'd get house-sitting money, or a car would be sorted, everything would be cool.

We were earning but it was funny, I wasn't into gear then as much as I got into it later in my life, even though it was all around me. One problem was that you couldn't buy an eighth, which would have been a couple of hundred bucks. Instead you had to buy it by the key, and I may have been living well, but I didn't have thousands to spend on gear. Probert took me to a safe house in Nashville once and it was

just full of keys of coke, absolutely pure, layered like slate, crystalline. We'd have a few lines but we didn't fuck with it, not like I did later.

But it wasn't reality to me living that life. Playas would be driving these big cars, niggas had gold on top of their gold teeth, there was Miami bass everywhere, booty music – it was amazing, totally different from that New York hip-hop mentality.

And there were those Southern attitudes. You soon realised that the thing about rednecks is that those guys are thick, plain and simple. You saw racism everywhere, but I didn't get too much grief because people didn't know whether I was Spanish or black. The Latinos would say to me: 'What you is, meng? You got the green eyes and dark skin. You from Englan'? Cool!'

Brena' used to have a few Yardies come by his work place. One was a diamond setter; he set them in teeth. A lot of them had skills like that, but they were also deep into some runnings. Like the time I went to see Tracy when he got put away for twenty-five years in Brouward County Jail for a double murder. He said to me: 'You know, man, I had my time. I had ten years and now I've got some shit put away for my family, so that's that.' Their mentality was different from what I'd come across before – they got hard into dealing, and if they got caught, or killed, so be it.

Miami's tough. I'll never forget one day I was working in the booth on the beach and this Yardie came in after he'd had some argument and he was steaming, raging. 'See dat pussycat, boy?' he said, pointing to someone on the street. 'I'm gonna fucking kill him, boy, cap him good!' This guy had scars all down his face, a mean geezer. About a week later I'm on the corner of 121st Street near the crib on the phone to Christine when all of a sudden I hear: RAT-A-TAT! RAT-A-TAT! Nine rounds went off. She was saying: 'What

was that?' I just said: 'Oh, wicked. Welcome to America.' A couple of days later, at the Sunday flea market, I found out that it was the mean Scarface who had come to the booth, shot four blocks away from me, his head blown to bits. And I said to myself: 'It doesn't matter how fucking mean you are, mate. The streets are super-ugly.'

Still, Miami may have been tough but the living was good and I felt like I'd found a home for my talents. By that time I was featured in Henry Chalfant's second volume of *Subway Art*, so all these graffiti writers came by to check for me. It made me realise that New York was so different from anywhere else in the US, because it's the mecca, and if you do well there it means something across the whole of the States. In fact, the UK was far more down with what was going on in New York than places like Miami.

I liked my life in Miami and decided to stay and make a go of it, even though lurking at the back of my head was Christine. We'd never resolved things entirely and I wondered whether it could work, if only she would leave Martin and join me. But that didn't look like it was going to happen. I set about applying for my Green Card and using my dad's residency to boost my case. I'd go up and see my dad every so often, take him a bit of money. He'd sorted out his other sons so that they could live in the States. We were quite cool with each other but he had a bit of a rant about the Green Card when I badgered him about it. I was like: 'You know what, Dad? Fuck you. You got all your sons from Jamaica over OK but when it comes to your son from England you're not bothered.' Generally, though, I got on all right with him. We never talked about what happened in the early part of my life, and his wife Polly was OK.

Then I came to a crossroads in my life.

I'd just come back from Nashville, Tennessee, where I'd been with Brena' to visit a couple of big playas. I left Brena'

there and drove down 1-95 off my fucking head, eighteen hours straight, doing about four eight-balls of gear. By the time I got back the bomb had dropped. There was a dreadful letter from my mum telling me that my stepdad was dying of cancer and that I had to come home. I never had any time for Pusey and didn't have to go back, but my mum was in a state.

Margaret Pusey: It was a very sad time all round when Pusey was dying but it did mean that Clifford came back into my life a bit as well. He used to take me round and hold my hand.

Also Christine had been telling me, during those long-distance telephone calls, that she missed me and wanted me back. I sat on the beach and wrote a poem, 'Sea Of Tears', about the experience of having to make a choice, and travelling across that sea:

> Tears . . .
> Tears . . .
> Tears . . .
> What are you doing here?
> Washing away the tears . . .

Then I went home.

I got back, saw Pusey one last time, during which he gave me the instructions about the clothes he wanted to be buried in, and that was it. He died pretty soon afterwards. We buried him in the suit with the pockets cut out and it was very sad, but I had really come back for the girl, and as soon as Pusey was in the ground I made one of the biggest errors of my life: I tried as hard as I could to get back with Christine.

All those months I was in Miami writing to her and calling her, she had told me she wanted me back. I was so in love with her I was prepared to sacrifice everything I had built up across the Atlantic. When I got home she was still with her

man, Martin, and we started seeing each other on the quiet, shagging behind his back. She kept on telling me that they were going to break up, but it never happened.

Meanwhile, there was business to be done. I had the money to take over part of this jeweller's, Lady Jane's, in Walsall High Street. Me, Whitey and Ian White hired the shop next door, called it Try 1, and I started making gold teeth in the back.

Ian Whitehouse: We met up again and it was at that time when we were going clubbing that I think he started to really get interested in music. Because I'm sixteen years older than him, he got turned on to music he'd never heard before and started to ask about individual tracks and artists. It was a bit of an education.

Try 1 soon got picked up by the media after I was featured in *i-D* magazine issue seventy-seven, a nice big double-page spread about me, my time in Miami and how I was making the running with these teeth. The *i-D* thing was good for business, but even better was the fact that I was making it outside of the B-Boy world, so I was proving I could make a name for myself with something new.

Stuart Meade: When he came back from Miami he had changed quite a bit, what with the teeth, which looked great. He never really acted big and flash even though he was completely differently dressed when he got back from America in all these nice clothes. He came back looking like a million dollars but he never really acted the big man.

But Christine just didn't want to understand where I was coming from or appreciate what I was achieving. The screw was being turned like never before, and it was getting to me like never before. I was smoking shit in the Five Star Club and I really didn't give a fuck, I'd take anybody on. I was

doing gear and getting really wound up over her.

It made me more violent. One time I got involved in a fight in the Five Star and smashed my left hand to bits hitting this geezer repeatedly. I bust up every bone in that hand and was really worried that my drawing would be fucked, but luckily it recovered after several months. I don't know about the geezer.

Things were getting too mad, so we gave up Try 1 and went back to Wolverhampton for a while. One of my only friends at that time was Tyrone. I first met him when I used to live in Walsall. I'd walk to my place in North Street and there'd be gangs of kids hanging out, and I wasn't really liked.

Tyrone Lewis: Where we are is North Walsall, which is sur-rounded by these areas we're at war with: places like Bloxwich and Brownhills. They don't come into our area and we don't go there. Bloxwich and Beech Dale are National Front, whereas we just smoke weed. One of the reasons they don't come here and fuck with us is because we are all close; imagine ten or twelve families with every family having four or five half-caste kids in it. That's how it was when we were growing up. We don't have friends from outside because we've all grown up so closely together. So when Goldie was first around in North Street he was a bit of a loner. I live on Proffitt Street on the junction with North Street, and was one of the few people who would mix with him because I'd known his brothers Melvin and Jo-Jo all my life. It took him a while to blend in but now he's one of our own.

The Lewises were the biggest family in that area, well handy. When I started getting into guns and fucking around, Tyrone had time for me, while all his brothers just wanted to fight me because I was different from anyone else. They'd come to my house and stand at the gate going: 'Come on, then . . .'

They were older than him, so when he told them to leave it out, he'd get a beating from them.

Tyrone Lewis: When he got back from Miami he was always talking about these bits of a gun that were being sent over from America. So we used to go to this place in Wolverhampton every week and first there'd be the barrel, then the nozzle, but after a while I lost interest. Then one day he turned up in Walsall in the town centre where we all used to hang out, and he opened his leather jacket and there it was finally, this nine-millimetre. So we took it out in his car, this Talbot Solera – you could see the road through the floor of that fucking car – and we were shooting out lights. That was the first time I had ever shot a gun. Then something happened and the police got involved, so I went down to his house and removed the gun for him before they got there, so they only ended up finding a pellet gun.

Me and Tyrone started going out a bit, with our hair slicked back. We'd go to clubs, like Edward No.7 in Birmingham and the Fifth in Walsall. Edward's would attract an older crowd than us, the football hooligan types, and most nights there'd be someone coming down the stairs pretty fucking fast. I saw some people get knocked out there. Some of the best times I remember with Tyrone were sitting in my Talbot Solera listening to 'Sitting On The Dock Of The Bay' and just generally getting into scrapes.

Tyrone Lewis: Goldie and his brother burgled a school and stole an oven which Goldie could use for making gold teeth. When it came on top this other guy Danny tried to stitch me for the job, and when Goldie found out he gave himself up and I think they bound him over. Then Goldie went and dealt with Danny, who had long hair, like a bird. I remember him chasing Danny down the street with a chopper and, when he got him, he held him up against the wall and went to chop him, as if he was going for

his head, but he actually chopped his hair off! He actually scalped him, which was good because if he'd inflicted physical scars then maybe Danny would have done the same thing again once they healed. But the mental scars of having all his hair chopped off probably never left him.

Tyrone has always been able to look after himself, but he used to get into fights a lot. Eventually he was set up for three stabbings and ended up doing four and a half years for something he didn't do. But he's always stayed in touch and we get on now like we always have. Tyrone always said I was going to make it.

Tyrone Lewis: I always knew that he was going somewhere. When you spend time with Goldie you leave with this energy. If I'm around him I'm more hyperactive. He never thought he was going anywhere and always put himself down. He never gave himself credit and you felt that he thought he didn't deserve it. Goldie could knock Mike Tyson out in a ring in front of fifty thousand people, but he'd still ask at the end of the fight: 'Did I win?' He's a very genuine person, Goldie, and if he hadn't moved out from the Midlands he'd either be dead or up on a murder charge.

Tyrone really looked out for me as well when I started to go through really heavy shit with Christine. She kept on niggling away at me. We would see each other on and off, even though I'd started seeing another girl called Madge, who accepted me for what I was, letting me get on with my graffiti. Madge will always have my respect; she was very understanding, proud of my work, quite old-fashioned in a way. Her view was: 'That's what you do, that's your thing.'

Madge is a fantastic mother, outstanding. At the time she already had a baby girl, Rachel, and soon she became pregnant with my son, Jamie, who's a fantastic kid. I still see them both and they call up and we chat. One of the biggest drawings I ever did was of his name. I stayed with Madge for quite a while and tried to get my head together, did a lot of drawing and bought my first motor, a Rover 3000, for £275. The guy wanted £500, but when he saw me and three other geezers roll up at his front door he realised that he had to accept our nearest offer!

But as always I couldn't give Christine up. Until finally one day she plunged her dagger into my heart. She threw everything I had done for her back in my face and told me she definitely didn't want to be with me, that she was staying with Martin and that it was over for good.

I begged and begged but she wasn't having any of it, so at last I just walked away. It was only later that I discovered that my walking away flipped her out. She had wanted me to keep on going back for more punishment, but I'd put an end to her game. So she put a curse on me, literally condemning me to lifelong unhappiness without anyone to settle down with.

As I say, I knew nothing about this at the time, but pretty soon afterwards my life just seemed to flip into the dark side. I had been working on this graffiti show to occupy myself now that I was back in town. It was well received but my head and heart just weren't in it, and Christine gnawed at my soul. I'd had enough. I'd proved myself to everyone and it didn't seem to have got me anywhere. I wasn't happy with my life and I didn't want to be here any more.

One night I was packing everything away in this warehouse in Sun Hill, Wolverhampton, where I stored all my stuff, surrounded by paint cans, feeling empty, desolate, ruined by the failed relationship with Christine. I'd learnt all my life to live with pain, but now I couldn't stand it any more. Without even knowing what I was doing, I stood on a crate, slowly put a rope around my neck and waited to jump. Instead I held back and just stood there, the noose

around me, sobbing because I didn't even have the guts to go through with it. I gathered my clothes and went home to North Street, Walsall, where I took a bunch of my mum's pills and was then rushed to hospital, where they pumped my stomach. That was a complete cry for help.

I later used my suicide note in the song 'Letter Of Fate', which I sang on my second album, *Saturnz Return*:

No one ever said that living would be easy for me . . .
Leaving me alone
No one said that breathing would be easy for me . . .
There is no grace around me
Alone . . .
My letter of fate I write
For me tonight . . .
There's a stranger I feel inside of me . . .
There's nothing else for me
There's nothing else for me
Just my letter of fate

Afterwards it was weird; lots of my friends and the people around me knew about the suicide attempt but nobody ever said a word about it. Apart from Christine, who taunted me: 'Well, if you really wanted to kill yourself, you'd have done it!' This was a really low, bad period, but I wrote it all down and never threw the letter away, I kept it and made it into that song. It was a reminder to me of what an idiot I was, and how people can get so closed off from normal life.

It was this realisation which hit home. I was alive. I'd travelled across my Sea of Tears and I'd survived. I didn't want to go back to America this time because I felt that there was still something for me in England, even though I didn't know what it was. It was time to redefine my life and reinvent myself again.

There's one voice, that haunts as one...
The violent spirits of a demon strong,
In chaos then but it may seem ...The chapter of...
A static dream... A motion" that in all frozen...
To anticipate" before which fall... The truth in
that may lay in the higher being...A giant
step away..." In not this presence "can reveal...
A prophet" through God "Did aid this seal," A bond
moves close to God... Life points at us with many
rods..." Of true they be it not... The road of
destiny holds the plot..! This blueprint ...laid...
that points "of compass" I lie thus be not ... But
Esther and beyond... X < universal marks the
step... Pure treasure "thought its" blind in all
it seems is not... Beware the decoy ...The
pharaoh "laid of roads" they all of Babel bind
at point ...This map of man somewhat disjoint...
To mark wide the presence of signs' for what
brings of warren lays the blind. ___

6: Terminator

Goldie moves to London as a house guest of film-maker Gus Coral and is opened up to underground breakbeat culture by his new girlfriend Kemistry. He establishes himself as the leader of the Metalheadz crew and the public face of the burgeoning new scene.

MY MIND IS UNSURE,,, IN THIS TIME,
RIGHT NOW... IT SEEMS TO BE OF
PROPHETS AND PAGANS ,,, A TIME...
THEY SAY ..."OF AN END".. I GUESS...

: 1997
JUNE...
IS THIS NOSTRADAMUS...
THE EVE OF WONDER .

I WOULDN'T BE ANYWHERE ELSE...,, MY FEAR IS STRONG EVEN
THOUGH THERE IS NO NEED, BECAUSE MY SOUL AS BROUGHT ME
THIS FAR... I GUESS MY HUMAN INSTINCT... THE PRIMAL
SCREAM ... IS AT ITS HOTTEST DEMONS... FAITH! I PRAY...
THE ACT OF MASTERING THEM ..IS MINE __ IS THIS
TRULY THE NOSTRADAMUS TIME, IT LAYS HEAVY ON MY MIND
RIGHT NOW ...DAYS AWAY ..."BUT PRESENT NOW ..." IT AS
THOUGHT OF BEING CONCIOUS HAS BROUGHT US HERE "... TO MOST
AND MANY UNAWARE... TO ME MYSELF - BUT ONLY CLEAR...
AT LEAST I CAN TRULY SAY I BEAR WITNESS TO A REVOLUTION ...
DRIVEN AT TECHNOLOGYS END...THE OVERSPILL OF MANS
WILL __ AND POWER OF.. THE MIND...
I WATCH THE SKY AGAIN TONIGHT... AND TRY TO FIND PEACE
IN THE UNEASYNESS I FEEL __ALL WILL BE REVEALED...
THE BOWLS OF THIS INTRICATE WEB OF LIFE ,, I JUST CANT
HELP BUT...THINKING THAT NO MATTER HOW I TRY TO
CONCLUDE AND DECIPHER... THERE IS A BEAUTY IN THE
WONDER OF BEING PART OF THIS ... 'THE MASTERS'
'TIME'..

BADER

THE WILL TO BELONG AT ONE...

got Birdy to get my shit together and he drove me to London, to Gus's flat on the eighteenth floor of Dorney Tower, bang next to Primrose Hill. I lived there for years rent free, and it was the place in my life where I felt at my most creative. Being at the flat was like regaining my lost childhood. I never really grew up, and maybe I haven't to this day, but at Dorney I experienced some sort of adolescence.

Gus Coral: One day in 1989, Goldie knocked on my door out of the blue and asked if he could stay for a while. I hadn't seen him for a couple of years, though we'd had a few brief conversations on the phone. I think he'd been involved in some sort of scrape in Wolverhampton and had to leave. I didn't ask. He came thinking in terms of a fortnight and ended up staying on and off in the spare room for about ten years.

At Dorney, for the first time, I not only flipped the catches on my suitcase, I emptied the clothes out. It was my first real home. I call Gus 'Pops' because he was there for me at a crucial time, the benign presence of a father figure, not an authoritarian who wanted to impose his will, not a bastard who would abandon me. He's a very laid-back, creative geezer, and by just letting things be Gus helped me open up. On one canvas, *Goldikus*, I wrote on the back:

> Goldie rides again.
> Number two in a set of ten.
> The adventures of the calligraphic kid.

> This canvas is dedicated to Gus.
> My Homie, Bro and Pops.

And that's what he is to me. But maybe I fulfilled something for him. The room I was in had previously been occupied by his son Luke, who had committed suicide not long before. So there was an exchange being made when I arrived. I remember once pulling back the lino in my room and on the floor was a painting which Luke had done years before. We never spoke about Luke much, but there'd be a day every year when Gus would come back red-hearted and I knew he'd been to Luke's grave. Gus is very special to me, and he gave me a very special time by letting me stay.

Gus Coral: Goldie's a big fellow with gold teeth, isn't he? But when you think about it you realise he's not big physically – he just has a huge presence when he walks in the room.

Living at Dorney was also like going to art college for me. He gave me the space and the time to flourish, to work on my painting and sketching and to figure out what I wanted to do next. Eventually I started painting canvases with an artist called Sarah Gregory, who was a true collaborator and deserves much wider recognition. She was the first woman I worked with on equal terms. She'd come round in the morning and there'd be one bird there and by the time we'd finished working on a canvas in the evening another one would be knocking on the door. She saw the womaniser in me and knew where I was going with that stuff.

But first off at Gus's I was making jewellery. I had a work-bench set up at the flat, with an oven, gold for teeth and oxyacetylene torches.

Gus Coral: He had his dog Mass with him, and he was comfortable here. I know that the thing creative people most need is encouragement – just that alone can do an awful lot. I turned him on to jazz, people like Miles Davis, and we talked about film. But it was a two-way thing. I was finding out more about hip-hop, which is a pretty strange thing for me to be into, given my background.

And Gus and I got on really well, though it was really funny when we brought birds back. They'd be going: 'He's not your dad? OK. But he's much older than you and he fancies the arse off me. Your room's full of paint, there's a pit bull terrier here, what's fucking going on?'

Soon I started to pick up all kinds of work for clothes shops, record labels, PR companies and advertising agencies. I don't know how the fuck I managed it, but I was building great big fake TV sets for advertising hoardings, and had these Roman columns I'd made in Dorney, all kinds of shit. I was also working on photo shoots and dealing in T-shirts and clothes, hanging out with the Stussy Tribe, a real tight-knit bunch which included Michael Koppelman, going to places around town like Four Star General and listening to hip-hop and opening up to other music.

I came back from America convinced we in the UK could be just as open as them to the idea of cultural cross-breeding. The more cross-fertilisation you get the more hybrids there are, and just about everything exciting in the arts is some sort of hybrid.

Michael Koppelman (DJ/street-fashion entrepreneur): We met because he really likes the clothes that I do, which at that time was mainly Stussy stuff from the States. He always struck me as this really inspirational guy, someone who could make things happen not only for himself but for everyone else. In fact he showed me a lot of support in the early days and I don't think I would be where I am now – still DJing and working with Stussy but also handling labels like Hysteric Glamour and Gimme 5 from Japan – if it wasn't for him.

Also Nellee had moved from Bristol to London and had hooked up with Jazzie B and the whole Soul II Soul crew in Camden, producing their album.

Stuart Meade: He called me up one time and invited me down to London, where I went to stay with him for a while. It was great because he took me along to meet Jazzie B, who was really big at the time. He gave me all this Soul II Soul and Stussy stuff and I took it all back home in some kind of shock. I was like: 'Wow, my brother hangs with Nellee Hooper!'

Soul II Soul drove me along so much at that time and Nellee was the ultimate white-boy B-Boy, the first one I had come across who had so much fucking style. He had the long hair and sheepskin, and was sharing a place in Delancey Street with DJ Milo, who had also come up from Bristol.

Nellee Hooper: Me and Jazzie were loaded, living large, and Goldie was there, he saw it and loved it! He was proud! I knew he wanted to do the same. He was never jealous or resentful, he just wanted to learn and do the same.

People say a lot of things about Nellee, but he's one of those guys, a finely attuned producer who knows what he wants to hear. And if it ain't right he'll flog an engineer to death until it is. He's got the look of a cat – in fact he's also got nine lives! He can tell you a few stories.

Nellee Hooper: I remember he came back from Miami with a solid twenty-two-carat gold and platinum ring he had made for me. It had cost him three thousand dollars to make and it said 'Soul II Soul' in diamonds and 'Nellee' around the band. That was a lot of money for him, but it was respect. He had always looked out for me and I know he would now. P.S.: Some fucker stole that ring to buy crack!

Through Nellee I also got to meet Howie B, who at the time

was engineering the Soul II Soul album at Utopia and Mayfair Studios, so I'd go and sit in on a session. That was my first experience of seeing a guy working a studio, and I stayed as quiet as a child, doodling on the two-inch recording tape in the corner and learning how to do it. Sometimes I'd ask Howie questions, but I didn't want to intrude, so I mainly stayed in the background, watching or writing down words for songs and taking in the buzz around Howie when he was making his single 'Candy Mountain', as Nomad Soul, with producer Dobie and singer Diane Charlemagne. I did the artwork for the single sleeve, this beautiful dragon, and by then I'd started writing poetry, occasionally showing it to Howie in the hope that it could be used as lyrics for songs.

Howie was really helpful. More often than not he'd say: 'Well, this isn't really a song. It rhymes but that's not enough,' and his comments made me realise the difference between poetry and songs, that the words had to match the music. Howie also gave me studio tapes with instrumental dubs of songs and I'd try to write to those, rewinding them and listening to the groove. At the same time, I'd be listening to the tapes and then coming up with my own melodies. That's really how my first songs came about.

Howie completed the Nomad Soul album with Dobie and Diane, which was all set to be released by Island Records. It was a great record, but was eventually shelved. That was one of my first experiences of the tragedy of the pop industry; that someone can make incredible music but, because of management or whatever, nobody can move it, so it just stays on the shelf, gathering dust for ever. Here's Howie, who was all-cool and went on to do great stuff, be it with Soul II Soul or Björk, on his own label or touring and producing with U2, and he couldn't get his music out because of the way the major record labels work.

Howie is this quiet, wee, unassuming guy who I felt an

affinity with; I remember one night we just sat in the studio and recorded ourselves talking shit. If I was in that position, would I have done that with any other kid on the back end of my studio time? I doubt it, but Howie was up for most things, still curious, always will be. That for me was special. We also had the same problems with women, who would wrap themselves around us until we didn't know what we were doing! At that point Will O'Donovan, who later worked with people like Paul Weller and eventually on *Saturnz Return*, was just the tea boy, so I was making connections every which way without realising it. For example, Howie shared a flat in Camden with Dom T, who was soon to be Björk's other half.

Gus Coral: Goldie was really into hip-hop, but in London he started going to raves, a very different vibe, and, dare I say it, white. But he really connected with people and started going out a lot. We got to know each other pretty well and I worked on some of his stuff, shooting footage for videos and pilots and the film projects we came up with.

I started going to raves and kind of stopped going to clubs like the Wag. Although I'd check for Nellee all the time, those guys weren't really into it. Concurrently I was doing the merchandise artwork, the bomb-print stuff for the Soul II Soul shop in Camden.

Around that time I used to ride nearly every day to Camden Town past the Red Or Dead shop. I kept on seeing this bird working in there – dark brown eyes, blond locks down to there. But for weeks I couldn't pluck up the courage to go and say: 'Hi.' Then one day I dropped in and eventually we started talking. And that was Kemi, DJ Kemistry. I invited her out for a drink and we started seeing each other.

Storm: Kemi and I were best friends, sharing this flat in Crouch End. She came home one day at the end of 1990 and said she'd met this really mad bloke with gold teeth who told her he wanted her to appear in a fashion photo shoot, which was a total blag. Basically he cooked her a meal. I'm not sure that's not the only meal he ever cooked her in their four years together! I dropped her off at Dorney Tower and the front room did look quite spectacular – he had all these Roman columns in there. They started seeing each other and I really met him when we went to a graffiti show he had at the Wag. I had this sense that he was dangerous, like that bit at the end of *Taxi Driver* where Travis Bickle turns to the camera and flashes that smile. You can always see that with Goldie. There's something behind his eyes questioning: 'Can I trust this person?' He's very guarded but a great person.

Kemi was very quiet but totally dark, really hardcore. She had this deepness about her. I found her very beautiful but, more importantly, she was the first woman in my life who truly understood what I was about. She was into deco, African art, sorting through thrift shops and picking up interesting bits and pieces. I still have a carved African head we called Suki and other mementoes of her, pillows and stuff. Her interest in music was a really attractive quality as well. There was her tranquillity and then this music she was into, which blew my mind.

Storm: Kemi was totally Libran: romantic, a bit dreamy, but didn't waste time. She was very wise and much calmer than me, because I'm a Scorpio. But it worked really well with Goldie because he needed someone who could ground him. She was lovely and had a really cheeky sense of humour. And they were happy together. Kemi was definitely in love with him, which was very strange for her because she didn't fall in love that often. They were a lovely couple to look at as well. Kemi always liked her men with a bit of a dark side and she liked that about him. But when he was around us Goldie never needed to use that dark side, so it was just nice all the time. That's the calmest I've ever seen him.

Kemi and I really clicked and I got to know Jane, who became DJ Storm. She was working in hospitals during the day and she was cool. She's like my sister. She and Kemi wanted to be DJs and they drove me a lot, wanted me to achieve something for all of us. We'd bounce ideas off each other. They'd be giving the female slant on things, getting the lapels right, adjusting my collar, know what I mean? And when we first got together, Kemi was always talking about this music she was listening to, which she couldn't really describe. She just said I had to experience it. So pretty soon she suggested we go down to Rage, this club night at Heaven she and Storm were into.

Storm: During the day I was a radiographer treating cancer patients and Kemi worked in Red Or Dead, but our lives were consumed by buying loads of records and obsessing over this music which was coming through, jungle or drum'n'bass, whatever you want to call it. At the time that and the other new genre, happy hardcore, were the bastard children of rave. Black producers had brought the reggae bass line into the mix and created jungle, and that scene gave black people, in fact all sorts of minorities, a place to be. There were a lot of misfits, and I think Goldie was one of them just as much as we were.

Kemi and I were so inspired by the scene, and really wanted to be DJs. In fact we were so into it that normal life just passed us by. I remember the landlady telling us that the Gulf War was on and we were like: 'Really?' Kemi and I were out all the time or on the radio, listening to stuff from labels like Strictly Rhythm and Shut Up & Dance.

Before we met Goldie we used to go to a club, Rage, on a Thursday, then on a Sunday we would go to Solaris in Gray's Inn Road, which had this lighter American side to it. By 1991 there was a divide and Fabio and Grooverider were playing alongside Jumping Jack Frost and Mickey Finn at Rage, while house

DJs like Carl Cox, Paul Oakenfold, Rocky & Diesel were going their way.

So I'm down there in Rage in my long coat and sneakers, a B-Boy sweating away when everyone else is in T-shirts just going for it. The adrenalin was pumping around the place. I heard the main DJs, Fabio and Grooverider, playing a weird hybrid sound; there was still the late rave stuff but here was a new sound, a mad fusion of the old and new.

Storm: That first time he came to Rage he didn't like it at all. He was really flamboyantly dressed when he first came back from Miami and he had the maddest outfit on that night. It looked like a boxer's coat with the hood and everything, but it was striped and velvet. He was just this bizarre, eccentric guy. And he couldn't understand Rage at all, maybe because he had missed out on the rave scene. I think he thought it was going to kick off because there were black and white people there, but everyone was being really nice to each other. Kemi said to me: 'I've told him that he can either come with me and my music or he can go now. I'm not giving my music up.' So the second time we went to Rage we made him come downstairs on to the dance-floor and you just saw him switch. All of a sudden he heard it and got it. And by now he wasn't threatened by the people around him. He'd come from Miami, where the clubs were pretty much segregated, but he could see this was different.

The energy at Rage was unreal, especially after being in America listening to the more laid-back booty music. I'd always been the sort of kid who wanted to belong, and the second time I went to Rage, this light bulb appeared above my head. I just thought: Fuck! Now I wanna make this music! I didn't have any idea about how to do it but I knew I had to. Kemi and Jane weren't even DJing then – they were just punters. A couple of days later I saw Reinforced, Nebula 2 and Mannix at the Astoria, which made me start thinking hard about how I could do it, and meanwhile there were all these massive, unbelievable tracks in the air, stuff like 'Visions Of Rage' and 'Seance'. Seeing that Astoria show blew my mind, because they were producing this urban blues. For me it was about joining another B-Boy crew, but the B-Boys were in Wolverhampton. So I had to say: 'Well, can I, er, join you guys here?'

Storm: We used to have our own raves when we got back from going out and I can remember Goldie going on about his dream, that he would be this wicked producer and Kemi and I would be the DJs playing our tracks. And it came true.

I funded them some money for decks but none of us could DJ. I remember one classic night when we were listening to Shades Of Rhythm off our fucking nuts. We'd go into the biggest room in the flat, which was Nicki's, a nurse who also lived there.

We'd get her Amstrad and Kemi's Binatone and put two records on and try to mix, and we were useless! And we'd get into scrapes. Jane's boyfriend Toby would put this strobe he had on and we'd have a right laugh. Toby was the ultimate raver – long hair, the kind of guy who'd buy ten Es to test and then go back and buy more and they'd all be duds, that kind of kid.

Storm: We all came from nothing, so to this day he and I can stand up and have a good row with each other. Not a lot of people will talk back to Goldie when it counts, but one thing we always tried to do was keep him away from his demons, because I think he has a lot of them. Mine was a normal working-class background where we were fairly open with each other, but for Goldie this was the first time he could start expressing himself and tell us about his life.

I was just this deranged kid with gold teeth shining, this nutter talking a million miles an hour. In Rage I just thought: I've got to make them play my music one day. It was another task ahead of me and I had to think through how I could achieve it. I started to get to know all the DJs and even went on the road with one of the biggest, Randall. I remember me and him drove to Hull, and that's when I first saw Jumping Jack Frost up there, playing fucking hardcore. It was wicked, mad days, and in Rage I met people like Danny Jungle, INTA and Face Killa.

So I was meeting all these people, and, at the same time, thinking about the two types of music I've always believed in: Shantytown Reggae and Detroit Techno. The latter may have started in Detroit full of soul before it was exported to Europe, where it eventually became techno bastard child, but I did my homework and checked out people like Carl Craig and those who started it. When Fabio played Carl Craig's 'Bug In The Basebin' he blew everyone away because he played it at 45 rpm instead of 33 rpm. So everyone was asking: 'What is this new "jungle" record?'

At the same time I was doing artwork because I was pretty skint, living from hand to mouth and hustling every which way. I was signing on here and there and grafting really hard. I was good at hustling. I was getting T-shirts and clothes by the box-load from the Crash Crew – Johnny Gosling, who now runs Mekon Records, Gordon Hagen, Trevor Norris, who had a shop in Camden, and his girlfriend Janet Fishgrund, who was at Lynne Franks PR. They were the people around when I was getting into Es and smoking Leb. I built the TV with great big knobs on it for the hoarding in Ladbroke Grove for Janet. I was working out of Lynne Franks in Edgware Road. I'd be swapping canvases with certain employees there for boxes of clothes – God bless Lynne Franks!

Storm: He really wanted to do it, make his own music, but he didn't have the means. The first thing he did was with Howie B, and it was terrible! They thought they could make this drum'n'bass stuff and they brought it to us and we laughed very hard. It was just wrong. But then he went off to Iceland and when he came back he had these tracks which were special.

I was also selling the T-shirts to this very cool cat Aggi in Iceland, who I met through working with the fashion shop in Covent Garden, Michiko Koshino. I used to call him Agzilla, we were very close. There was a period when I was going out to some place in Middlesex and signing forms to send boxes of clothes to him, and I was making enough profit to survive. After a while we all went for a snowboarding trip to Iceland and that was where I first met Björk, who was by then going out with Dom T. While I was there I went into a studio and made my first demo, 'Ajax Project' by Rufige Kru. I worked on it with Aggi and this geezer called B and we used all sorts of samples, *Star Wars*, Mantronix, Phil Collins, whatever we could get our hands on.

Tyrone Lewis: I remember when I was in jail rave was big and I thought that Goldie was going to be difficult about getting into it because he was so proper about his roots, hip-hop and soul. But by the time I came out he was already making tunes which were past rave, he'd moved on!

When I first came across sampling I already knew about breaks. The first hip-hop generation would just stop a record, take it from the break and the DJ would loop it so people could dance to it. That very thing of two decks and two records was like the bubble letter in graffiti – the starting point for all of us. So when I came to make music I felt that the breakbeat element needed incorporating more. All that stuff like the 'Mary Mary' break needed to be used. And I would load and load and load until there was nothing left in the sampler. So 'Ajax Project' was really rough, but I brought it back and it went down a storm, everyone played it. We got five hundred made and sat up all night in Crouch End printing the labels using a potato to print the symbol.

Storm: He brought it home and paid for a thousand to be pressed up and we sat up all night stamping the logo with the potato shape he had cut out. It was a total cottage industry. Around that time all you heard from people was: 'This mad guy from Wolverhampton keeps on coming up to me and going on about these tracks he's made.'

I remember clutching the cage, watching Groove take the record I'd made out of the box and put it on the deck and thinking, Fuck, fuck! Them playing my music was like Brim drawing me an outline or Birdy showing me a move.

Storm: Kemi and I had already made a name for ourselves as a bit of a novelty, these two girls going to this wicked record shop called Music Power in Green Lanes to buy stuff. Reinforced was *the* label at the time and we were obsessed with it, used to buy their releases before we'd heard them. And Goldie was so caught up with everything that he did do a few things which people thought were embarrassing, like jumping on the stage at the Astoria during a Reinforced night and shouting about how he'd made these tracks and he wanted them to listen to them. And the main Reinforced people – Ian, Gus, Mark and Dego (who were also 4Hero) – came along to the flat to hear his music one time.

4Hero were there from day one. I'd heard their track 'Mr Kirk's Nightmare' back in the Midlands and it married hip-hop – break culture – with rave and techno. They were pioneers, Mark and Dego.

Storm: I remember Dego just sat there, listened to it and said absolutely nothing, didn't even acknowledge us when we offered him a cup of tea. We girls thought they were really rude, but Goldie was just worried that they didn't like it. Of course, they did, and rang him a few days later.

Although 'Ajax Project' went down well, I knew the quality wasn't right. So, I got a number for a guy called Ian from Reinforced and said: 'I wanna do some artwork for you.' I went to Jumbo Studios in Dollis Hill and they liked my stuff. I redesigned the Reinforced logo and we started to get on really well. I said to this guy who ran the label, another Gus: 'I really want to do a tune,' and he said: 'Well, go into the studio and do it.' In a way the guys at Reinforced gave me what my Pops Gus had given me: the space and encouragement to spread my wings, this time in sound, rather than in visual art.

Gus Coral: When he started on the path to becoming a music star he seemed to have a natural instinct for business. He seemed to be happy to move around the music industry with enormous speed and mental agility. He has a talent for practically everything, not a specific one. Added to that he was quite late coming to pop stardom compared with most people, and a bit smarter and wiser as a result.

The money I got from selling T-shirts paid for the studio time, and that's how the second Rufige Kru twelve-inch, 'Killa Muffin', and the third, 'Krisp Biscuit', were made. Then we quickly followed through with 'Darkrider', 'Believe' and 'Menace'. By then I had taken a big step because I knew that I could work a studio, getting exactly the right sounds and relooping them in the right way.

Storm: 'Killa Muffin' made clear to us that he really had got something, and brought elements from his past – hip-hop, being

in a breaking crew, visuals – to what was going on now. Everything was good; eventually he got on Reinforced and Kemi and I started DJing, doing this graveyard shift on Sunday morning, 6 a.m. to 9 a.m., and he was our MC for a while.

The beauty for me was that I could arrange things, I could mix elements and put them together. I got into making music like I did with graffiti – I played the studio, watched and listened to how people worked. Then when I went in I literally used the equipment – samplers, recording consoles – to paint the sounds in my head. I don't engineer. I'm one of those guys that sits there with twenty-five people and goes: 'OK, guys, we're gonna take the sixteenth snare at the second bar, reverse that, do this, do that.' There are computers now which do it all digitally, but I learnt in the days of analogue, when we'd physically slow things down and turn them around, play with sound.

Storm: The amazing thing about Goldie was that he came from out of nowhere to this scene and made things happen. He showed us that you could use whatever skills you had to make a difference. Me, Kemi and Goldie together were quite a powerful trio. I'd had a good education and could understand numbers, Kemi was great with words and Goldie was the artistic one who could visualise things. He was also a great frontman. If Goldie has a good network of people behind him – who aren't going to use and abuse him – then he can do anything. But he needs a team.

Collaborating with Mark and Dego was great because they gave me free rein over the studio as well as being great producers in their own right. We had a great time bouncing ideas off each other and working stuff up. I'd loop and loop and loop stuff until they said: 'There's no memory on the computer left, you've filled all the tracks up.' Usually people in that situation throw their hands up in horror. I'd say: 'Great!' It was like me having twenty cans of paint and knowing that I was going to use every one of them, knowing where the colours were going to go. That's how tracks like the 'Darkrider' EP and the series of releases on *Internal Affairs* – 'Stylin', 'In My Soul', 'Find A Way', 'Hands To Heaven' and 'Shinin' Down On Me' – came about.

Rave had been and gone by this stage and happy rave, the Antichrist, had reared its head with some really muppet stuff on *Top of the Pops*. My raw B-Boy edge separated me from them and I wanted to do something different. I was still going to Rage, always on the prowl for something new, thinking I had to do something to blow everyone away. Tracks around at the time were just sixteen-bar loops, important but real simple tunes with labels like Ibiza and Kickman Records, and tracks such as '16 Track Ting'. I wanted to make a tune which would be the ultimate power move. I wanted to take it further. Added to that, those guys at Reinforced never did E. They were all as sober as fuck whereas I was out there.

There was a darker sound taking over, Britain's new urban blues, which represented the way people were feeling at the time; there was a recession and the country was in decline. But forward ever, backward never, I was in the studio again, creating something fresh. In 1993, still recording as Rufige Kru, I released my darkcore anthem 'Terminator', lifting the buzz-saw synth riff from Joey Beltram's 'Mentasm' alongside the mutating breakbeats that began to characterise darkcore.

Storm had played me a tape of 'Deranged' by Doc Scott, which was unbelievable; it took that 'Mentasm' sound and fucked it right up UK style.

Storm: Doc Scott was the first person who introduced that really dark element and changed everything in dance music, not just drum'n'bass. But Goldie recognised that and made it part of his music. He's one of those producers who can make you feel good or bad within a tune, he can play with your emotions. Listen to his track 'Rage' – that sounds like rage itself.

'Deranged' just ripped my heart out and said: 'How would you like it served?' The bass line was so dark, I had to meet this guy. So one day I went down to Music Power and one of the guys there, Chris, pointed Doc Scott out. There he was, with long hair and blue eyes. I was so amazed that these tracks, which were so dark and nigga black, could be produced by a white boy. Ten years before I had taken part in a big graffiti show in Birmingham and signed all these kids' books. During our first conversation Doc freaked out, saying: 'I saw your show and you signed my book.' That proved to me that B-Boyism was thriving. It wasn't about what you looked like, but what you could do. Around that time Sean O'Keefe, a member of 2 Bad Mice, couldn't get into the Astoria to play his own gig, because he was being rushed by all these black guys unaware that he had the biggest track on the scene.

The other thing about Doc Scott was that he didn't have a mixing desk at this point, so no one knew how the fuck he made tracks like 'Deranged', the 'NHS' EP or 'Dark Angel'. He barely had any equipment at all. To me, Scotty is the roller. No one can roll out breaks like Doc Scott. It's the space that he leaves between the sounds which makes him what he is, and that's why there was the Enforcers' tune 'Rollin' Like Scotty'.

Around the time I first got to know Scotty I was thinking that time should be the theme of 'Terminator'. I always had a thing about time, which probably stemmed from my suppression of childhood. I didn't want to have recollections from that period of my life, I always wanted to forget about them, which meant that time was meaningless for me – days would go by and I wouldn't take anything in. And when I started making music I was watching the film *Terminator* a lot. It was always bugging me, that movie, particularly the scene in the tunnel with Linda Hamilton when she says: 'You're talking about things you haven't done yet.' That chicken-and-egg thing about going back in time. It had that Escher quality to it, like a loop, where 3-D shouldn't exist but it does. That was the trigger I needed. So I took that sample and put it with these mad sounds I'd collected.

Storm: I remember watching *Terminator* with him for the first time and we must have stayed up for about seven hours talking about it. I don't think Goldie had met people like us before who would just sit and chat shit for hours.

I started working with Toby Linford, the other half of Rufige Kru. He was a guy who had a great record collection and would source tracks and breaks; he was the white kid who was buying records when I'd have tapes from New York. Linford was more of an anorak – he'd probably give me a slap for saying that, but there you go . . .

We were working with an Akai S1000, a basic sampler, and Mark Rutherford really showed me how to loop and sequence. He was very patient with me as I combed through and started to subtract certain sounds, beats and samples which didn't sit right. It was like turning a painting and removing the colours you definitely didn't want to use.

And there was another similarity to graffiti. Maybe I'd go to tag a wall and wouldn't have all the right colours but I'd make it work. Rufige Kru was similar because we'd use anything that was left on the surface. So, for me, samples and loops which no one else was using were the ones that worked better. I'd always go for the oddity.

For some mad reason I had this layering thing going on. I didn't want to do music where you'd have something, straight, and then a break, and then another thing straight without anything on top. I would always layer my sounds and build them up, which was another reason I got on with Reinforced; Dego was one of the only other people around who was also into layering, because Mark and Dego had mastered the equipment.

At Reinforced I really started to develop because the equipment I used there didn't have as much memory – it was a 950, right? So we had to free up as much as possible and be as inventive and creative as we could be. There was a lot of third- and fourth-generation sampling going on, but it didn't affect the sound quality. And we could time-stretch, which is where you take a sample to its limit. The sound becomes dissipated but distinctive – it's used a lot in garage these days. It was a barbaric and raw way of doing it, using the 950, and a lot of people on the scene just couldn't work it out. Dego and I used to experiment on our project Del Die GoGo – an anagram of our names – which we did at Reinforced.

I'd get some studio time and go into the studio with a bunch of records and Linford, and say: 'I want this, this and this, put that there, there and there.' I was very curious but at the same time I wanted to keep my distance because technology always kind of scared me. I'd rather handle it at arm's length, be the technical director pushing the engineers, saying: 'Can you put that sound you created last week with this piece here?' I'd manipulate the situation, maybe because I could see the possibilities as an outsider.

A very special thing happened the night we EQ-ed 'Terminator'. Linford had to get back to his gaff out east, and went to get the 9 p.m. train, but as we were just getting down to the meat there was no way I was going to let this thing go. It was almost as if when he said 'See you later' it was more final, like: 'See you LATER.' And when he left, that was really when it, my musical career, became Goldie. Granted, Linford brought brilliant stuff to it, but when he

left the studio to get that train it became a Goldie arrangement. Linford went fucking berserk the next day when he heard what we had done, it was so unreal.

As I say, Mark was really open-minded, and he suggested we try using an HF 3000, which is an analogue harmoniser. You could, say, play one chord on a guitar and it would be harmonised by five notes above and five below. So I said: 'I wonder what happens if you put breakbeats into it? Let's try it.' I was intrigued by the idea of using something designed for analogue equipment and placing it in a digital environment, because it hadn't been done before. So in one take I got on the manual wheel which controlled the sound. The break was from James Brown's 'Funky Drummer', which everyone used, right? But not this way. I started to really play with it and take it to the limit, without it falling out. It was contained within the two extremes. And it sounded brilliant – the pitch was going up but the speed stayed the same. It all fell into place. I got goosebumps and Mark was bugging out, saying: 'I don't know where you're going to go with it, but this is completely different.' The track had taken on a life of its own, right from that whistle at the beginning which, when it came out, used to cut through anything being played in the clubs.

Storm: He was off his face completely that night. He'd be phoning up shouting: 'I've just dropped another one!' At one point he even came home to get another pill. Then he'd phone us from the studio and play us another bit of it and we'd be totally encouraging him in this state of off-your-facedness.

I was doing a lot of Es in them days, really soul-searching, this kind of seratonin-releasing soul-searching. So Mark and I started dropping Es at about 1 a.m., wisely after the track had been arranged. We did about seven pills apiece, and in the end I was EQ-ing the track standing on the desk with my head on the ceiling of the studio, freaking out. We had a Logic C-Lab sequencer and Mark was working it, but couldn't see the screen because his eyes were somewhere up in his head. So I had to work the mouse on the computer while he talked me through it with his eyeballs rolled way back. We were off our nuts! We finished in the morning and must have listened to it about forty times. 'Terminator' itself is four minutes long. Which is ridiculous when you think about it.

Anyway, I rang Grooverider up at 5 a.m. that morning. I'd hustled his number from Music Power just a couple of months before. He'd played 'Ajax Project' and 'Darkrider', but I wanted to terminate him, show him, everybody – I just wanted to put people to sleep. I was the Nutty Professor: 'I'm gonna show you ALL, all of you, I tell you!' So I rang him and said: 'I've done it now. I've made something which is going to blow your fucking mind.'

Grooverider [D&C, April 1999]: Goldie is an artist. Forget drum'n'bass, he's an artist in his own right. It's not his cause. He's done drum'n'bass. It doesn't matter what music he makes, he's always going to be an artist.

Within a few days I had transferred it from tape, which gave it a warm analogue sound, back to digital, which is far more crisp and immediate. It was too warm for me, not right for the drum sound. Then I waited for Grooverider outside Rage and gave him a copy. It was the first time I'd ever seen him play something without listening to it first. That was the peak, hearing that intro on the floor. You can't beat that feeling, the magic was unreal. Sometimes I can smell that instant, for a fraction of a second, no different from when you can sometimes taste the first time you smoked a cigarette, or feel the first time you came.

David Bowie: 'Terminator' was quite unlike anything I'd heard

– this was around '92 or '93. I think he was recording as Metalheadz at the time. It just blew me away, those breakbeats and that cutting synth riff.

One thing about that track is that everything is covered – you can't break down what sample is from where. That was because I didn't want anyone to steal from it – it was the ultimate B-Boy trick. When we finished I got Mark to put a high hat playing all over it. You cannot sample 'Terminator'. One person tried, but with dire consequences. Me and Ian from Reinforced went to a shop in Richmond and just cleared the shop because they were selling snide Rufige Kru tracks. You don't fucking do that. So we went there, ripped the till out, chopped the fucking phone lines. You have to respect this shit. We were pretty crazy then. I was so passionate about it, it was almost violent.

David Bowie: Unlike something like Brain Killers' 'Screw Face,' for instance, there was already an inherent sophistication going on with 'Terminator' which would really flourish with *Timeless* and reach a kind of zenith with *Saturnz Return*.

'Terminator' was the peak for me, like having the sharpest razor ever. I was trying to encapsulate the magic of that subculture, I was so into the vibe, the clubs and the energy that scene had. But 'Terminator' was also the B-Boy side of my nature coming out. I wanted to get harder, nasty, fucking super-ugly. At that point I was artistically firing on all cylinders because I had a second shot at youth culture, having already done the graffiti thing. I'd already seen what could be achieved in one direction so I thought: Let's apply the same methods to this form.

Storm: Goldie knew how to manipulate sound, make a sound come from right back there to slap you in the face. He knew what it was about: ecstasy, the speakers, the strobe, the dance-floor and what was going on in your head. He understood that drum'n'bass is really textural. It's about the experience; you don't just hear drum'n'bass, you feel it. It was the same as his artwork, he has slabs of bass to build on. I always said you can visualise a Goldie track, particularly if you're on really decent drugs!

B-Boyism is about adjusting to any street environment. Any kid that's brought up on the street can adapt, because they have to. When I was a kid I could hang out with skinheads or black guys into reggae at the Half Moon Club. I was a bit of a chameleon even then, which meant I could have the best of both worlds.

So 'Terminator' was part of that process, because I was shape-shifting. And I have to give it up for Mark Rutherford, the engineer I worked with at William Orbit's Cargo studio in Crouch End. Orbit kept himself to himself, he was always cool. I didn't know him that well, just through the circuit, but he left us to it. First of all I worked with Mark and his partner Johnny Gosling, but it was Mark who really challenged me. If a social worker told me when I was a kid that something wasn't possible, I just went right ahead and did it. I always wanted to break the rules, and the same applied to music. You can't take the thug out of a kid like me. And I always had that, even though I had this artistic streak which kept me from, say, mugging the old lady, or kept me principled about certain things.

And although it wasn't released commercially for a year, 'Terminator' dominated the floor for that whole period, and when it eventually came out it sold around thirty thousand copies, unbelievable for an underground record.

Noel Gallagher: Our band was starting up around that time and I was still in my going-out-to-clubs phase. I think I first heard 'Terminator' on the chart show and I thought it was really good but I also thought: Whoever made that track has got serious problems and has got to go and see a shrink. That track is not right! It's too fast and it's too mad and he'll never get anywhere. I do believe that people who make that kind of music are generally quite sick. It sounds like they're ill. With Goldie's music, you've got to be insane to make it because it's not something you can sit and play on a guitar in three minutes. You have to persevere at it for six or seven days, and to listen to that for a week, day in, day out, must drive you insane.

We built 'Terminator' up by only having it on dub plates for a year. For those of you who don't know what dub plates are, they are pre-release acetate versions of songs, pressings on aluminium sheets covered in lacquer which a DJ can play thirty or forty times. This gives the guys the ability to play stuff long before it's officially released, and shows that they are ahead of the game. It had been used in reggae a lot, but I always insisted that my Reinforced dub plates featured my Metalheadz logo on one side. These were dub plates with an identity, for the B-Boy. I'd carve out acetates, put inscriptions on them, give them a visual identity. Grooverider came up with the phrase 'metalheads' to describe those freaks like me obsessed with the latest metal acetates. Also, I remember he was DJing on KISS and he said: 'I've got a few "metal heads" to play tonight,' meaning the aluminium acetates he was playing.

There was a guy I used to hang around with called Darren, a guy who's pretty handy with his hands, hard as nails, but at that time he was hanging out with Mad Scientist and those guys in Kentish Town. He came up with this design for the head which I adapted. I added some headphones, so that the skull symbolised the head while the 'phones were music, because music will be here long after we're all dead and gone. The credit for that design goes fifty-fifty between me and Darren. So we started using the logo on the acetates I was doing at Reinforced, which means that Metalheadz at that time was really a dub plate label. The first time the logo appeared was on a dub plate coming out on Reinforced, and soon people started to recognise the name when a dub plate was played with the logo on it. It gave it, and us, a new identity.

What was weird was that I'd chased this dream to blow everyone away and I think I went too far. When 'Terminator' came on in the clubs, everyone stopped dancing. They just stood there, smashed to bits, didn't know what to do, how to move to it. 'What the fuck is this?' It would speed up, drop away, slow down, chop and change. In a way it was like a B-Boy going in there and showing all these styles and moves within four minutes. I got really worried, but Groove said to me: 'Don't worry, mate, just give it time.' Groove would bag it in the mix, dropping it in and putting it with something different every week, and soon people would go: ' "Terminator" 's coming on!', and just go for it.

Margaret Pusey: I didn't know that he was involved in drum'n'bass. The first I heard that Goldie was making a name for himself was when somebody mentioned that they had seen him on the television. I saw it and went: 'That's my kid!'

But the first time I was supposed to hear it in front of a big crowd at a rave it didn't come together. It was my mate Mickey Linass's wedding, and then we went up to this big event at Donington and we were supposed to be on the guest list. So we drive up there, but there was a fuck-up, and I had to stand outside and listen to 25,000 people go mental to it while we argued about whether our names were on the list or not! When we got back Kemi and Storm were going: 'How was it?' and we said: 'Er, we didn't even get in,' so that was a bit of a blow.

We were having mad times. Once I went up with two DJs who were really good friends, Randall and Marlon, to a gig we played at the World of Dance festival at Lydd Airport in Kent. We were on our way back in this convertible BMW 325 which the owner, some fucking geezer called Monkey, wanted to sell to Randall. On the way back to London there's this place called Devil's Island. The geezer was driving so fast that me and Marlon, who were sitting in the back, looked at each other and just put our safety belts on . . . and we never belt up in the back!

We looked up and he was going at 100 mph straight towards this fucking island. Randall was going: 'Monkey! Monkey! Monkey!' and then everything went slo-mo. Like they always say, the crash seemed to happen over a really long period and then suddenly we jumped out of what was left of the car. It was a write-off. The geezer was going: 'Look at my car!' and we were going: 'Look at the car? We could have been fucking dead!' He wasn't even insured, and he'd smashed his car up. Randall went: 'Naaah, I don't wanna buy it now!'

By then I couldn't go anywhere without people pointing me out, muttering: 'That's Goldie, that's the guy that made "Terminator".' It totally made my name in the clubs. Up until that point I had no self-confidence but 'Terminator' set me on the path to becoming Goldie the drum'n'bass guy, and I guess it made my name as a creative producer.

It also had an effect on other people, influencing Doc Scott to put an EP out while Dego brought guys like Underground Software into the Reinforced fold. A lot of those who came to the label were there purely because I was. We were sending out a lot of waves to the dance community.

Gus Coral: The quality of the music really did surprise me. It was new, original and, although my music is jazz, I found I did like it.

I put together some dub plates of 'Dark Angel' for Scotty

and we took them along to Rage. I'd done loads of Es and I was sitting on the podium buzzing like a cunt when I heard Groove drop 'Dark Angel' in the mix with 'Terminator'. I looked at Scotty and he looked at me and we knew what we were doing was really powerful. At that time he was doing stuff for Simon 'Bassline' Smith, but on the drive back from Rage that night he said to me: 'You can take it for the label.' I'll never forget, the next time I saw Simon 'Bassline' Smith I took him to one side and informed him: 'Doc Scott is now on Reinforced.'

As Reinforced really moved up a gear it started to release stuff like the *Enforcers* series, the visuals for which came about because I was still bugging off picture discs from back in the day by people like the Stranglers and Squeeze. Years later I played a gig in Detroit and came across this DJ called Rota, who lived for *Enforcers* tunes. He came out, took the turntables off, put this spool across the two decks and then put the records on to the spool, and, with the needle on backwards, started mixing *Enforcers*. Upside fucking down and inside out! It sounded unbelievable. I thought: Well, how do you follow that? So I played the Carl Craig track 'Bug In The Basebin' at 45 rpm just like Groove had done all those years before and these kids came rushing over to me asking what it was.

Then I knew that the sub-culture was alive. Here was a track that originated in Detroit, came to London, where we bastardised it, because that's what we do, and gave it back to them in this mutated form. That showed me how we had become the new B-Boys, that the sub-culture grows and infects itself. The way the music has developed, we have created this monster and it's walking by itself now.

Anyway, back in the day *Enforcers* was part of the soundtrack to the club which really took over from Rage – Paradise. Around that time ragga jungle was just about coming in, and we were also going to RAW on a Sunday night, Laserdrome in Peckham, and Q Club and Eclipse in Birmingham. I remember going up there with Randall and taking a dub plate of 'Menace' to be played there, and seeing people from Wolverhampton who knew me as Goldie the graffiti writer but not for having done stuff like 'Terminator'.

But Paradise, which was in Islington, became *the* place where everyone would hook up, no matter where else you had been earlier that night. Paradise was promoted by Jay of World of Dance, who's a top geezer, full of it, been there and very probably done it. Jay was the Pepe Le Peu of the rave scene, and he'd been behind the events at Lydd Airport, so when he said he was doing Paradise nearly all of us got on board. Paradise was basically presenting all the best DJs, minus Fabio and Grooverider, who steered clear because it just wasn't their thing, the crowd wasn't right for them.

So at Paradise there'd be people like Randall, Kenny Ken, who've both been in the game a long time, and others such as Mickey Finn and Darren Jay, and it was a really good time, a new era. There'd be GQ on the mic, a wicked MC who made it his show, the don host. And he was on top of the tunes, rolling them out neat and not getting involved in the heat of the mix.

Hardcore jungle was running hard and Reinforced was still very strong, having entered its second phase not only with *Enforcers* but also *Internal Affairs*, *Ghosts*, *Tom & Jerry*, *Tek 9*, all of which were dropped at Paradise. And the mix there was comparable to the best times at Rage; the crowd would scream to rewind, making the DJ play the mix again, which was almost unheard of in those days. During the Paradise period I was still steadily doing Es and we'd stay there until five or six in the morning. It would get really hot and sticky in there, and we'd have it.

For a long time I was dedicated to giving Reinforced my

stuff because I wanted a family, a camp. And they were very welcoming. Dego and I share the same birthday and we're very alike. He was always very accepting. I'd be in there out of my mind on Es and, although he didn't touch drugs, he'd be: 'Look, man, you do that shit, I don't, but you've got ideas,' and we'd sit and work all day. He'd go home and then Mark would come in and we'd work through the night.

After 'Terminator' I wanted to move further out and, although it was great at Reinforced and I have ultimate respect for them, it was time to move on. I agreed to put out 'Terminator II The Remix' through them and then decided to get in with John Truelove at his label Synthetic, who struck a £10,000 deal for a four-track EP, with, once again, the Metalheadz label featuring on one side. That was the point when the moniker Metalheadz really started to become established. It was like: 'Hey, guys, fuck with me and then fuck with the crew.' The crew was deadly, because Lemon D could deal with any funk, Hidden Agenda could deal with the abstract side of things, Wax Doctor could handle any breaks, Peshay in his day could be dark, J. Majik was raw. It was B-Boyism; the crew was working together, developing all the time.

Not only was it time for me to strike out on my own outside of the Reinforced family, but there was music which I felt had to be released. Reinforced had a version of 'Ghosts' which had been held back, so Metalheadz 001 was a twelve-inch with me as Rufige Kru doing 'Riders Ghost' while Doc took the other side with 'Drumz VIP'. We both fronted the cash and we did it ourselves, setting the label up as an independent with Kemi and Storm helping to get things moving.

Storm: It was so exciting when Metalheadz started. We ran it from a one-bedroom flat. We used to move my bedding into the front room at night and I'd wake up in the morning and answer the phone: 'Hello, Metalheadz!' Kemi would pass by with the tea and toast and pass the mailers across, and it worked, you know? We all said at the beginning that we didn't want anything to do with the money.

For me, Scotty made the label what it was in his early days with his *Star Trek*-like moves. We released a lot of his stuff, including the jazzy, blissed-out 'Far Away', which was another tune showing that drum'n'bass could be laid-back but still retain its edge. And, just so nobody forgot, on the other side was the very dark 'It's Yours', which was at the other extreme, hardcore to the max.

In late 1994 we followed up with DJ Peshay's 'Psychosis / Represent' twelve-inch, which ensured that Metalheadz was becoming a label to watch. In many ways Peshay was a protégé – I'd known him for a while from his time releasing stuff through Reinforced and had helped to nurture his career. Even though he also released tracks on other labels such as Basement and Good Looking, he was a firm part of 'Headz, working with people like Photek and later remixing 'Angel' and 'Inner City Life' for London/ffrr.

Peshay worked with a young engineer called Rupert Parkes, who made his name as Photek, emerging with his distinctive clattering and groundbreaking sound via Metalheadz releases and remixes. I always used to say that Rupert was 'the assassin' because he could just go out there and kill 'em with his approach. His 'Consciousness' EP had this amazing sample going: 'Intelligence brought to the surface of consciousness . . .' while 'Into The 90s' had enough jazz and trip-hop moves to get heavy radio play from the acid jazz likes of Talkin' Loud's Gilles Petersen.

Soon we were smashing them up in the clubs from every direction; Alex Reece was fresh out of the bag with 'Fresh Jive', which also included the superb 'Basic Principles' and 'I

Need Your Love'. Alex had previously produced some hard techno stuff, but he came out for the first time under his own name with this release on Metalheadz and showed how far you could go in terms of incorporating a jazz vibe into our music, although he had obviously learnt from the true pioneers in the field, Dego, Mark and the 4Hero crew.

Alex released quite a few tracks with us, including the incredible 'B-Boy Flava', but, as you'll find out later on, he, his manager John Sexton and I had a bit of a falling-out over the commercial side of the business, and it was that which gave me an inkling that not everyone was in it for the music.

Whatever, for a very long time after we launched it, 'Headz attracted pure talent and we were making connections every which way; Alex came to us because he had worked for this geezer Paul Saunders, who became an early Metalheadz mainstay under the guise of Wax Doctor, knocking out prime tunes like 'Kid Caprice' and 'The Spectrum'.

Wax had been around for a while, releasing stuff like 'The Saint' as part of Reinforced's *Enforcers* series, but I think he came into his own with us, harnessing serious Detroit influences and using his smooth but mad production skills.

As each release came out on 'Headz, so the names of the crew became known individually, while the label became the stamp of quality. Punters and the industry alike were paying attention, particularly when we got a nineteen-year-old known as Dillinja as part of the team.

He'd been going in various guises since the early nineties, and concentrated on developing a roots vibe which gave me that bass line from way back. Tunes like 'Brutal Bass' were exactly what they said they were, and we still check for each other, having worked on *Timeless* on a couple of tracks: 'This Is Bad' and 'Jah The Seventh Seal'.

There was a lot of young talent like Dillinja being ignored by the mainstream music industry, but we had the scene hotwired. Which is how Jamie Spratling joined as J. Majik. His 'Your Sound' and 'Jim Cutter' were totally dope to me and a lot of other people. I used to call J 'Luke Skywalker' because at that time he was uninterfered with. He could go in there and do his biz. If you were going to deal with Metalheadz then you had to deal with J. Majik before you even dreamt of dealing with Photek or Peshay or Scotty. He made this track for us, 'Arabian Nights', which just trashed the joint.

Soon 'Headz became a real family, particularly when Dillinja brought in his mate Lemon D to produce true 'urban style music', to quote the name of one of his biggest tracks. Lemon effortlessly merged hip-hop and drum'n'bass and created something new; when I dropped Lemon's 'This is L.A.' at a party in LA they went absolutely nuts to the sample of a newscaster saying: 'This is Los Angeles – gang capital of the nation.'

So the label blew up, bringing in people like Hidden Agenda from Newcastle and Source Direct from Ipswich, replicating cells of the scene all around the country. For me, running 'Headz was an extension of my role as a switchboard operator. I was always the one making the connections. Back in the day Grooverider wouldn't really speak to any other fucker on the scene, everyone was very cliquey and I don't think they realised the power of this music. Having been a punter, I had a lot of insight and I really wanted to get them all together. One time I called up A Guy Called Gerald. His record *Voodoo Ray* had been massive and people on the underground played me his '28-Gun Badboy' and *Automanikk*. So I rang him up. Fabio and Groove were playing his stuff but didn't know him, so I just called him up and said: 'You've got to come to London, I don't think you know what your music's doing down here.' And they met and really got off on each other. I was like that, I always wanted everyone to get together.

Kemi and I were more or less living together and I wanted

to make a song for her, to capture her mood, which is how 'Angel' came about. I can look up to heaven now and say: 'That was for you, darling.' I used to stay with Kemi in Crouch End, us getting off our tits all weekend on Dennis the Menaces, me getting really pear-shaped, like the M25 had blown up in my neck.

Storm: I think ecstasy was a good drug for Goldie because it made him finally open up to things like spiritualism and the theory of life.

One time I brought Grooverider back to the flat, which was like inviting God back to your place for us. I got such a bollocking from the girls, because he gave me a lift back from Rage and I just asked him in. They were hissing at me: 'What do you think you're doing?! We're in our dressing gowns with no make-up on! Fucking hell!'

I was bouncing back and forth between the girls' place and Dorney Tower but mainly working in the studio. With 'Angel' I wanted to push what the media were already calling drum'n'bass into a more musical direction and reflect the fact that I was into my classic old soul, tracks like 'Change' and 'Change Of Heart', 'Freeez' and the SOS Band, big tunes.

By this time I was being managed by John 'Knocker' Knowles. I'd got to know him by hanging out with Howie B, who had also made another important connection, having introduced me to Diane Charlemagne, whose vocals on 'Angel' gave it a jazzy, diva-esque feel.

So, with 'Angel', the idea was to try to get this music into the charts, break into radio. And we did break into the KISS FM chart despite people like Lindsey 'I Think I Know What I'm Doing For Urban Black Music' Wesker, who was working at KISS. I took him 'Angel' and he told me drum'n'bass was rubbish, that it had been done and would never work. I was devastated. A few years later, I bumped into him in a shopping centre and said: 'I thought you said this would never work.' He was completely embarrassed. A lot of people in those positions in the music industry start off knowing what they're talking about, but eventually they get their eyeballs sucked out by the process of working in the business for too long.

'Angel' blew up and I thought: Right, now I'm going to deal with underground and show how it can move up to a much bigger level.

The thing about club and dance-floor is that the loop is continuous; all you can do is stretch the loop. Everyone has their time in maintaining the cutting edge of technical ability before somebody else comes along and tops you. It's no different, in a way, to how breaking developed.

So when I started to rise I kept on thinking about how I'd watched Nellee and Howie come through with Soul II Soul and their own stuff and 3-D and the guys happen with Massive Attack – remember, I left the country to go to Miami when Acid House had just started, so I'd missed out on all of that. Now I'd created something that I could be a part of. That was one of the reasons behind forming Metalheadz; there was so much new music around and guys were following me on the street and just giving me their stuff to play.

But I wanted a bigger canvas again.

[LETS]

STABALIZE YOUR THOUGHTS FOR A
                        SECOND ,,,

IT IS NOT AN END TO ALL OF THIS,
UNTIL IT IS PURLY YOURS ALONE,
AND EVEN THEN, THIS EGO BROUGHT
ABOUT BY MANS' WISH TO TAKE IT
ALL WITH US, IN HIS CONCEPT FOR A
SURROUND ,, MASS ENDING , IS A
FEEBLE FEAR OF THE FLESH ,,
IT IS PRIMAL ,, AND HAS ALWAYS BEEN,
SO JOYLESS WE MUST BE WITHIN THOSE
SECONDS, FOR WE ARE JOINING , MOVING
UP WITH OTHER SOULS TOGETHER,
IN SOMETHING THAT CANNOT BE EXPLAINED
UNTIL WE REACH THERE , BEYOND , BEHIND,
A NEVER TIME ...

GOLDIE ☆ ☺

JULY ..99 .

7: Timeless

Goldie becomes a star with debut album Timeless, but his relationship with Kemi falls victim to his success. Associations with the likes of Björk and Noel Gallagher result in burgeoning celebrity, and he launches the acclaimed Metalheadz club. A twenty-one-year-old Miami resident, Ricardo Lopez, sends a mail bomb to new partner Björk in protest at her plans to marry Goldie, and videotapes his own suicide.

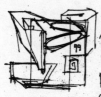

IT IS A REVOLUTION... NO DOUBT... NOT LIKE ANY OTHER...
FOR THOSE I GUESS THAT HAVE NEVER BEEN...
WATCHIN THE WAYS... OF A CHANGIN WAVE...
BEFORE THE CAME "THE YOUTHFUL CATALYST OF, WANT OF
CHANGE... TO LEAVE ONES NAME" SO IT MAY SEEM...

REDEMPTION MADE EXTREME... OF FAITH MADE ONLY BY...
THOSE THAT BE... A CONCIOUS WRONG OR RIGHT, IN A
FAITHFUL HOPE THAT MIGHT... BRING US ALL" TO RIGHT
OUR ONLY DREAMS...

POETS, PREACHERS, ARTIST, READERS, SCIENCE, CREATIVES" ALL THE CARDS LAID
FOR LIFES GAME"... IN TRUTH TO LEARN"... THERE LIES THE AXON AT BAY...
"FROM DAY... 'S OR SO THEY SAY... 'WERE NEVER MEANT TO BE THE
SAME, WHY FORCE, THE PERFECT UTOPIA'S HAND... SURELY SPIRIT HAS
NO LAND... SO LIFE IS BURDENED WITH MORTAL MAN" TO ROAM, THUS
LOOK AT WHATS AT HAND... "I THINK... THEREFORE I AM", "I CAN, I WILL"
IN HOPE I SAW THIS, SO CALLED LAND..." SEEDS OF KNOWLEDGE, SO WE
PLANT"... ~~TOMORROW SEED THE GIFT, TO MAKE LIFE"...~~ ~~THEY READ THE~~
~~STORIES"...~~

While my relationship with Reinforced was tailing off, the label Moving Shadow sent me and Dego a track by 2 Bad Mice called 'Mass Confusion' to remix. I hooked up with the guy who owned the label, Rob Playford, and went up to see him in Stevenage. I had a lot of respect for 2 Bad Mice – their track 'Powdered Chemistry' was out way before 'Terminator', way before 'Darkrider'. One of 2 Bad Mice was Sean O'Keefe, who I have a lot of respect for, the old bat, and Moving Shadow was a good label, very influential.

Rob Playford: There was a track we did as 2 Bad Mice called 'Waremouse', and when Goldie heard that at Rage he decided he wanted to make similar sort of stuff. He hadn't done any music at that point but he was well into the scene. We didn't know about this for a year or two, but he actually came to interview us as 2 Bad Mice, simply because of that tune. He was doing a pilot for a TV documentary. I don't think it came to anything, but he did a fifteen-minute edit of our bit, and it was great. We found out we had a lot in common.

Having done the remix of 'Mass Confusion', Rob set up this idea of doing a series of releases called 'One In Nine', collaborative twelve-inches. 'Fury' was the first thing that Rob and I started working on together.

Rob Playford: 'Fury' was released on Moving Shadow right at the end of 1993. While we were doing that, it sparked off some ideas in Goldie's mind. We were working from scratch in the studio, rather than exchanging tapes, so he'd see what I was doing and say, 'Can you make it do this?', so I did, and added, 'We can also do this, too.' We'd just go to and fro through a whole building process, and just step up levels, like on Donkey Kong! It was a huge learning experience for both of us. That made us both really excited, and we knew it could be a great working relationship. 'Fury' had basically sparked off some ideas, but this was really the beginning. Next, we started on a track called 'Timeless'; we thought we'd make it long. My idea was that it should be forty minutes, because that was the longest it could be due to the chart regulations at the time.

'Timeless' was the departure for me. I wanted to do something new, not only with the music, but with time itself. It ended up at twenty-two minutes and was made up of three songs: 'Inner City Life', 'Jah' and 'Pressure'.

At the core of 'Timeless' was a chord which seemed to slip and slither and had nagged away at me since I'd done a session at Reinforced. I got the chord on DAT and started bending it, using the HF Harmoniser. It was like it took the chord and wrapped it in knots. And it was like the chord had been put away so that it would mature like fine wine at some point in the future. It bugged me because I could visualise it as a circle of sound coiling forward in space on its axis, spinning and mutating.

The skills I'd honed as an arranger combined with Rob's outstanding engineering and technical abilities to produce a kind of song cycle, almost classical in construction. The first section, 'Inner City Life', was just beautiful, the result of pure collaboration between me, Rob and Diane.

Noel Gallagher: 'Inner City Life' is a very, very good document of what it was like in England at that time. We were still ruled by the Tories and life was pretty shit. England creatively was just about to go fucking berserk with – we won't use the term Britpop

– guitar music and lots of people, including us, were just about to come to the fore. Just before that was 'Inner City Life', which documented what it was like to live in cities at the time.

With Rob I'd found another perfect working partner, but I always wanted to challenge him because he was just like another social worker to me.

Rob would do things by the book, but I think I excited him with my mad ideas. I'd push him and he'd be on the phone to the technical people finding out how these things could be done. Run-of-the-mill engineers just hadn't studied technology in the depth that he had, which is why so much of the stuff we did together sounds amazing. What was happening was that the science + faith equation was at work and we were exchanging at a very high level. Except that with me it's usually one-way – I'll put a lot of faith into something but will only accept what science can do, not let it smother me.

With 'Timeless' I knew that what we had here was the centrepiece of an album. I didn't want to waste it just being released to the clubs. I thought it deserved a bigger audience, which meant that we had to deal with the major record companies but hold firm to our ideals and stay true to the underground. It was going to be some ride.

For me, making the track 'Timeless' was the ultimate statement of drum'n'bass's technical sophistication and manipulation, and it reflected the remarkable working relationship I had with Rob Playford. He was up for it, even when I started chanting on the 'Jah' section of 'Timeless', showing respect for the ghetto, showing the influence of Rasta, the blues at the Half Moon, that bass line, and integrating it with futuristic B-Boyism.

We completed the track 'Timeless' without a deal in place, but I wanted to make an album so bad. Around that time

'Knocker' Knowles introduced me to the person who would become my new manager, Trenton Harrison, who was managing Rebel MC at the time. I met him on the street one day and organised to go see him. Trenton started to take meetings for me, because I had connections at various record labels through my time doing artwork. At that point I really wanted Rob Playford to give me an album deal on Moving Shadow but he never made the move, and although I hinted at it I felt it had to come from him.

Getting Trenton to represent us didn't sit well with Rob, and with hindsight he may have been right. Rob had always mistrusted the major record companies; he thought that they weren't capable of handling this music properly.

Whatever, we took 'Timeless' around to a few people at the big record labels. I was determined to get a firm deal for two albums, not just a one-off with an option which could easily fall to bits. I had so much energy, Trenton could book me into a meeting and I'd take them apart.

Pete Tong: I'd seen Goldie's name about and we had a scout here [at ffrr/London Records], Richard Bolger, who was a fan. My colleague Christian Tattersfield had been offered a deal and he thought it was hot but told me that he couldn't handle it because Goldie was too scary a character, a bit of a nutcase. Trenton was a dear old friend of mine and had played me 'Timeless', which of course contained 'Inner City Life', and I was really impressed. It wasn't jungle but almost jazz, really soulful and esoteric at the same time. The fact that he'd made a track twenty-two minutes long was remarkable. It just got to me, and at the time seemed made for me. It was undercover jazz-funk, which had always been considered to be naff, but this certainly wasn't naff. The thing that was intriguing about Goldie was that he didn't have the usual set of references. His heroes didn't engage the mainstream, people like Pat Metheny.

Metheny's chord arrangements really influenced me and he taught me a lot. I came across him when I used to listen to the jazz station in Miami and heard his 'Still Life', which was just so fucking cool. That's why I came up with my own 'Still Life', on the *Timeless* album. I was paying tribute to Metheny, and it was so cool when we eventually worked on a remix together of his track 'Across The Sky'.

Pete Tong: After Christian Tattersfield took a back seat I said to Trenton: 'All right, bring him in,' even though he already had a reputation for being a bit stroppy. So he came into our Hammersmith office with his dog, or maybe there were two of them, and we basically [laughs] had a row.

I didn't realise how intimidating I was in those days, I was pretty fucking mad. But I was only doing it because I was so passionate. My attitude was: 'Look, man, you've got to sign this! This is it!' I walked into Pete's office, threw the cassette on the table and said: 'You had better sign this! End of story.'

Pete Tong: He was really aggressive but I just stood up to him. He was working this kind of reverse psychology so that if he had a row with someone and they showed some bottle, he liked it. He displayed incredible drive and passion, and I loved the idea of him being a punter at Rage and being so taken aback by the whole scene that he set this mission for himself to make music so that Grooverider and Fabio would play it. I worked with them a lot through the madness of Acid House, and had also been at the Astoria with Nicky Holloway, so I could relate to that.

I had a rule: the minute an A&R guy stopped playing 'Timeless' before it ended I was out of there. For me they had to listen to the whole thing, even though it was twenty-two minutes, a very long track. A few of them stopped it, and I was straight out of there. One who didn't stop it was

Clive Black at Warner, who's a great guy. He was blown away and we shook hands on the deal but it wasn't firm. This was on a Tuesday, and Clive said that he would get the paperwork done for signing on the Friday.

There was something not sitting right with me, because he would not go firm on it. Then Pete called me on the Thursday and offered me two albums firm.

Pete Tong: There was a lot of feeling in the industry at the time that I had done a loony deal, which I hadn't because although it was a two-album firm deal, which was unusual for what could be considered a 'dance' act, the money was relatively low: eighty thousand pounds. When you think that single deals these days can reach half a million quid, it was low. What Goldie liked was the idea of commitment. He knew he was making difficult music and didn't understand singles or radio play, and understood that whoever took him would need patience.

I took the night to decide and the next morning we phoned Clive Black to tell him it was off. He was gutted and demanded to speak to me. So I told him this story: 'Imagine you're a hunter and you've shot a rabbit. You turn and say to your friends: 'I've shot the rabbit,' but what you need to do is go and make sure that the rabbit is dead before you start doing that. Because while you turn to your mates the rabbit's going to get up and go. And that's what happened, you didn't want to go firm on this deal.'

So he started saying: 'But you shook my hand!'

And I said: 'Hang on a minute. What's a handshake to an A&R man these days? You guys shake hands all day long. We both know a handshake to an A&R man could mean fucking nothing.' I saw him in a club not long afterwards and he was cool. I went up to him and said: 'Clive . . . it's the wabbit!'

Pete Tong: It was a bit of a Damascene moment when Goldie came into my life, to be honest. It almost felt like something that was meant to happen. I didn't work at it very hard and yet it came to me, sat on my lap and stared me in the face. I've had those moments of regret in A&R where I should have done something I didn't do. I sat with Jazzie B and offered him a singles deal, but he wanted an albums deal for Soul II Soul so it didn't happen, and that would probably have changed my life. The same thing happened with Neneh Cherry. Tracey, the founder of the label, took someone else to a meeting with her and they didn't sign her, but if I'd gone it probably would have happened. So here we were again, but this time it was meant to be – Trenton, an old, old friend of mine, brings in Goldie, a remarkable character. Up to that point we hadn't really had a superstar act. We had missed out, not only on Soul II Soul and Neneh Cherry but also people like Underworld and the Chemical Brothers. When I worked with the producer-style acts they tended to come out the wrong side of the superstar category; I got Smith & Mighty, Virgin Records got Massive Attack! But Goldie was without question a superstar character able to take the mainstream. My mission with Goldie wasn't about drum'n'bass. He was a substantial talent and my mission was to make him a world superstar making really important music.

It was a brilliant deal because they let me do all the artwork and have creative control, which is what every artist wants. It was a beautiful thing. Also the money meant that I could change my lifestyle; I'd been driving around in Doc Scott's Sierra for long enough. Some days I would literally have no money for petrol, but that changed. For me *Timeless* the album was the chance to spread my wings creatively, all the while paying homage to the stuff I'd done musically.

Diane Charlemagne had this voice which could soar and swoop, and really worked against the music that Rob and I produced, giving it life and soul. I'll always tip my hat to her contribution, because Diane was the diva of all fucking divas, and I would make her sing individual parts, take them away, play around with them and let them ferment.

I also got Loma Harris to sing 'State Of Mind', which I wrote in an afternoon:

I realise the state of mind
That you have found me
I've turned the page and rearranged
The things that life has taught me
I've felt the pain and played the game
But I am stronger now
Like the sun breaks through the clouds

Pete Tong: I don't think I've ever worked with anyone like Goldie; he soaks stuff up. Everything is an instrument to him, even Diane's remarkable voice. She wasn't necessarily cool or even the front-person, that was always him. But he had this thing about her sound, and that's what he does, identifies sound and locks on to it. Like a DJ builds a set, he builds layers of sounds and textures. That was his magic and Rob, who was very musical and technical, would put it all together.

Rob was the perfect partner for me in many ways because he knew how things worked. He'd been a computer programmer before he launched Moving Shadow, so he was coming from this completely technical direction but, like Mark Rutherford before him, was open to new ideas and ways of approaching things. *Timeless* the album was a joy to make, because we were joyriding technology and taking it to new places musically.

Like on the Sensual VIP mix of 'A Sense Of Rage' we had this bass line which we slowed down and sped up, fading it and sculpting it. Among the tracks we already had in the bag was 'Saint Angel', which was a nasty, nasty vocal track produced by Dego from my Reinforced days. Most of my tracks moved like that. It would be: nice, then dark, then breaks, then vocal, mad bit, technical bit – I'd just flip around. I remember I had taken 'Saint Angel' on cassette over to Grooverider at Black Market in the West End and then we drove our cars over to Tubby's. I remember we got to King's Cross and I saw the big old head nodding along to 'Angel', then when he heard 'Saint Angel' he got out of his red Mercedes 190 and just said: 'Un-fucking-believable.' I ended up dedicating it to Groove; he was really my patron saint at that time.

I think I hurt him with 'Saint Angel', but that's part of the process. These days I get really eager guys who'll bring me stuff to play, and I'll tell them what I think. But they'll come back, and back and back; the more of an icon you are, the more they want to defeat you . . . in a good way.

Pete Tong: Goldie was very focused in the early days. 'Timeless' was done, we brushed up things he had already recorded like 'Angel' and they produced several new tracks. When I met them, Rob's studio was in a house in Stevenage. The first time I had a meeting with Rob it was in his back bedroom where 'Timeless' was made. They didn't even have speakers – it was all done on headphones. To get that sort of sound under those circumstances was amazing. The way they worked together was incredible. Rob had done tons of stuff on his own and with other people but I don't think he ever did anything as magical as the music he made with Goldie.

The album was a joy to make and we worked with a crack team of musicians, bringing in Cleveland Watkiss on vocals, the drummer Mel Gaynor and percussionist Louis Jardine.

Timeless shot straight into the album charts at number seven, which was a first for a drum'n'bass record. But I don't even know if I'd call it a drum'n'bass record. I'd prefer to call it 'inner city ghetto music', because I'm not going to come up with stuff just to match people's perceptions of drum'n'bass. The whole business about being the King of Drum'n'Bass was fuckery as far as I was concerned. I was an instigator, a switchboard operator, someone who was able to connect people.

David Bowie: I got to hear 'Inner City Life' on a pretty cool NY radio station and got the information that all this stuff, including 'Terminator', which I'd really been into, was basically by this bloke Goldie.

Timeless soon started to explode: 'Inner City Life' became a signature tune at LTJ Bukem's club Speed in 1994, and then the video became an MTV staple. It was shot at Dorney – the guy who cuts my hair in it was the guy who really cut my hair, Conrad at Cuts. So it was about where I was coming from, and I wanted to make the statement that the ghetto was poisoning itself. My style was now far removed from the bark of the jungle that I was putting out in my Rage days. But musically and career-wise everything was set because 'Inner City Life' helped the album get recognised for what it was.

Pete Tong: *Timeless* is one of the most important records we ever signed, it's groundbreaking, no question. It sold 250,000 but was never a hit. It's the greatest drum'n'bass record ever made because it takes in everything, and 'Timeless' itself is a great song with great lyrics and all the darkness, experimentation and jazz which comes with drum'n'bass. But it was strange. The first time we released the 'Inner City Life' section as a single it went to number forty-one in the chart and the second time to thirty-nine. And yet six months later you'd hear it in bars, clubs, everywhere. People would think it was a hit record because it made such an impact

– the video, everything about it. He'd made his mark and broken out of the dance thing into the *NME*, *Q* and the national papers.

I didn't give a fuck about being targeted as the face of a trend by a huge corporation wanting to shift units. All I knew was that the underground would understand that, at some point, this scene would burst out overground and it was better to be in the hands of someone like me, a punter who had been part of the scene and was true to it.

Noel Gallagher: *Timeless* became one of those albums that everyone had – just like the Portishead record the year before. You'd go around to somebody's house, after being out or whatever, and *Timeless* was the album everyone played.

I eat, shit and breathe drum'n'bass, so I knew that this music had to have a much wider outlet, and that *Timeless* was the way of showing that there was depth and meaning to the scene. At that point we'd had 'Sesame Street' and all those shitty pop tunes, so I knew there needed to be a viable record to match the real talent which was out there: people like Photek, J. Majik, Lemon D, Dillinja.

Storm: When he was making *Timeless* it was the most perfect time. Even Diane walking out didn't stop him. He made that album despite everything. And it's such a great album. When *Muzik* magazine had their list of All Time Dance Albums and *Timeless* wasn't in there it was a disgrace, I was gutted for him. That album was the shape of the future for drum'n'bass.

Timeless really exceeded my expectations. I knew people would be into it, and enjoy all of its flavours, and the fact that we were trying to break out of the underground but still pay it respect and keep it real. So we pushed things; Metalheadz headlining the Glastonbury Festival in 1995 with an orchestra. There were a few knock-backs, like not being nominated for the Mercury Music Prize when so many people had made it album of the year, but for me it was enough to know that the right people recognised what an achievement it was.

Pete Tong: It was a joke that the Mercury people didn't pick up on *Timeless*, although our chances were hurt by the fact that it was a double album. And the following year, when Roni Size's *New Forms* won, it was almost as though they felt so bad about ignoring the genre that they were making up for it. And, with all respect to Roni, he won with a record which wasn't half as good and adventurous as *Timeless*.

The record got me on every magazine cover, on TV, across the media. To be honest I felt I was someone at last. I was grinning at the past and the people who had fucked me over. You know: Christine, fuck you! I was in people's living rooms and my children could see me. In a kiddy way I never really grew up with that stuff. It's very petty, I know, but I defy anybody to go through that head-rush of fame and money without it affecting them.

Once the money started coming in I got a Cosworth. You know why? Because Nellee had a Mercedes 190. I went to Bath and bought this car and was over the moon, then went over to Miami that year and brought back chrome rims which no one had in London then. I was rocking B-Boy shit, the best ride in town. And I kept on going out, with Nellee to Browns, just having a good time.

So everything was blowing up for me, but on a personal level my relationship with Kemi started to falter.

Storm: He and Kemi were together for about four years but eventually she felt he was looking elsewhere. He always says: 'I let her go because I knew I was going to disrespect her.' I always say to him: 'No. She told you to go because she didn't want you to disrespect her.'

I wanted to be honest and, even though I wasn't wandering, I knew I would, it was going to happen. And I really felt that our time had run its course. We did have a special bond, which was bigger than love, in a way. I was doing my music and she was DJing and we were being pulled in opposite directions, me with my career and being in the charts and her with her DJing, which was really taking off. She was cool when I told her that it was over, but I think secretly she was heartbroken. As well as 'Angel' on *Timeless*, I also wrote the track 'Kemistry' for her. It was cool between us after we split. We worked together really closely, on the label and touring and DJing. We got on really well because Kemi was the first woman that I really trusted.

Storm: Much later, just before Kemi died, we were in America together and she really opened up about him and told me that she was so upset about their break-up, because she really thought she had found someone who was on exactly the same wavelength, someone who would go all the way with her. She was much more devastated than she ever let on, but she was from a broken home as well and always had a way of hiding her feelings. There were other problems. I think he'd felt that maybe I had been en-croaching on their relationship because she and I were so close, and he had definitely tried to split Kemi and me up. One day he took a trip and I had to stay off work in the end because he was just going on and on, saying that I hated him. But I'm stronger than that, and it didn't work. I know when to keep quiet with Goldie, and to keep him on a positive level. There is no point in shouting and screaming back at him. He just gets like that.

Without Kemi I went wild. Even though she had restored my faith in women I couldn't stop womanising, and the success of *Timeless* meant that I was out there all the time, putting it about, having two, three women a night. For years and years I never had one girl, there were always a couple on the go at the same time. As I've said, womanising made me in control of the situation, but I'd take it to the extreme of making them say: 'I love you,' but I wouldn't be committed to love.

I was staying back at Dorney and really going for it when I met this girl, Tracy, and we started going out together. I think she went through the same stuff that I went through when I was a kid, and I guess I wanted to protect her. In the end I saw her for eight years and she gave birth to my beautiful daughter Chance, but there were long periods when we weren't together. Sometimes I would go back to Tracy. What with the drugs and all, my life was complicated.

Pete Tong: There was always this thing about: 'What does Goldie do?' Well, it was clear to me that the whole madness was going on in his head, it was contained there. And the magic was in the madness.

I first met Noel when he came up to me at the Brits the year after *Timeless* came out. Oasis were really exploding and at one point he picked up an award, left the stage and made a beeline for the table I was sitting at. He walked up and just said: 'Nice one, G. Top one, mate. Fucking wicked album,' and casually strolled on. I felt great, because he was a major rock star and didn't need to do that. I also felt a bit of a connection because he was from up North. Maybe if he'd known I was Man United then he wouldn't have spoken to me!

Afterwards at the bar some geezer had a go at me, so I broke a bottle on the bar and was going to go for it and Noel came over and just said: 'G. Leave it out, man. Let's go for a drink.' So we did and he probably saved my bacon, stopping me from steaming in.

Noel Gallagher: I met him around the time we were going to all these fucking showbiz parties. I was in the VIP area at some opening and for some reason – the facts are a wee bit hazy – he had left this area and couldn't get back in, so he was claiming he knew me as a way of getting in. This bloke came over and said: 'Is he a mate of yours?' and I said: 'Yeah, fucking let him in.'

So he walked in, handed me a bottle and said words to the effect of: 'Hold this, I'm going to do one of the bouncers.'

I put my hand across his chest and went: 'What're you doing, man? Leave it out, just drink your beer.' Then I went: 'Hi, I'm Noel, pleased to meet you,' and it all went from there.

I started to hang out with him pretty soon afterwards, going out to parties, back to the Heights, Supernova-ed up to the eyeballs, having a brilliant fucking laugh with him and Meg. I was living around the corner, Liam was in St John's Wood just down the road from Abbey Road, so it was on. I'd never really gone on the piss that much before, but every time I'd go out with them I'd end up completely drunk out of my mind.

One of my canvases at that time was *The Serpent & The Rainbow*. I very rarely give paintings away but I gave it to Noel and it fitted exactly in the space above the mixing desk in his home studio. It was perfect.

Noel Gallagher: When I was in Steele's Road he used to send two of his little boys to look after my house when I was away on tour. I saw them outside on their mountain bikes one time, so I went out and asked them what they were doing and they said: 'We're looking after the house, mate. We know Goldie.' They used to sort the photographers out, get them to leave, it really was the stuff of gangster movies.

And Goldie was pretty handy when idiots used to come calling at 4 a.m. God help those pissed-up students if Goldie was ever there. They wouldn't last very long. I'm quite a polite guy, so I'd go out and ask them what they wanted but he wouldn't. He wouldn't even have to speak to them, they'd be gone before he got to the end of the path. If you see some bloke who's nearly six foot with gold fangs coming towards you don't fucking hang about too long! And I'm from Manchester! If you're some fucking student from Brighton who thought you'd go round Noel Gallagher's house and take the piss you're pretty much on your toes when you see that lunatic coming towards you!

One of the really slick things Noel and Meg did for me was to fly me up to Scotland for a big gig. He put a shout for me from the stage, saying it was for 'Goldfinger', and afterwards in the hotel they brought in a birthday cake with a Union Jack on it in the gold and green Rasta colours, which was fucking wicked! Noel was funny like that – he also organised a Yellow Submarine cake for Liam, whose birthday is two days after mine.

Noel Gallagher: Both our careers were really taking off, but we used to see each other all the time, we were really close. He'd drop by if he saw the light was on. It was just like having a friendly neighbour. His first port of call of an evening would be our house. At the time I didn't have a mobile phone – I've only had one for about a year, the last person in England to get one – so we weren't in twenty-four-hour contact like some friends. There would be chance meetings on the street or out and about, and we'd end up getting hammered.

By the time I got to know Noel and the gang, I was also super-busy with the Metalheadz label, with Storm and Kemi keeping on top of everything and making sure it ran smoothly. We'd kept on attracting the cream of the rising talent, including being the first on the case of Adam F, Alvin Stardust's son, who has now made it in his own right with his more hip-hop-oriented stuff.

Storm: The way it worked was that we'd track Goldie down to wherever he was and he'd make decisions about release schedules, artwork, mixes, everything, right there and then. Also Doc Scott was really involved in the beginnings of the label; he was kind of the silent partner. If we couldn't get hold of Goldie when we were on the road, we used to call Doc and he'd help sort out little problems. It was a really great time.

Alex Reece's 'Pulp Fiction' was a really great ground-breaking track which became one of the biggest tunes of the year. I'd come across Alex when he was engineering for Wax Doctor and then heard 'Pulp Fiction' played for the first time ever when Fabio dropped it, and was astounded because, in a way, it was a precursor to the whole two-step scene. It soon became the anthem at LTJ Bukem's club Speed, and I wanted the tune for 'Headz. And, like I do, I went and got it, giving Alex an advance and going ahead with releasing it with his 'Chill Pill' on the other side. Almost simultaneously we also released Alex's 'I Want You' / 'B-Boy Flava' as well as remixes of 'Pulp Fiction', but by that time the relationship had soured. Alex's career took off and he signed to Blunted, a subsidiary label of Island Records. I think his manager John Sexton took him down a road that in my opinion wasn't right for him as an artist. We got a legal threat demanding the rights to it for his debut album and it was obvious to me his priority was money, not the love of the music or the people who put him there. Not that his action stopped us in any way from putting 'Pulp Fiction' out. It was ours and the deal had been proper so we went right ahead.

Storm: What happened with 'Pulp Fiction' was one of the first inklings that things could go wrong at the label. We had it pressed and ready to go, but it got a lot of airplay and Alex received this offer from elsewhere. The fact that he could sign it elsewhere for more money upset Goldie. We had already been speeding the release up so that he would get the advance earlier and, in the end, we asserted our authority as a label. But Goldie was really shocked by it.

There were always going to be petty beefs like that, but as my career took off the label started to storm. Then the idea was to create a new hub for the scene. Things were getting rowdy, because the jungle crew then were pretty much what the garage crew are now. People were getting shot, guns were going off. After the heyday of first Rage and then Paradise, I was going around clubs and gigs thinking to myself: Fuck, man, you can do better than this. Also, there were a whole lot of people who had become hooked on the 'Headz releases, so it seemed to make perfect sense to launch a club to reflect the label's identity.

I looked around for a place and came up with the ideal location, the Blue Note in Hoxton Square, on the perimeter of the city in east London and in the area which was just beginning to blaze. I talked to Eddie Pillar, the Acid Jazz man who ran it, and when we opened the Metalheadz Sunday Sessions it just exploded.

Nobody had run a Sunday night club in drum'n'bass circles before, apart from the morning-after sessions which had taken place a couple of years before, and we were pushing the music, just like Reinforced had with the friendly competition between me and Dego and Doc Scott as we bounced the 'Mentasm' riff between us over a series of releases.

With the club I wanted the same edge that we had to the label, the scene and the music, and that's what we achieved. Metalheadz as a club took the concept to the limit, drawing club kids, the underground, trendies, the media and quite a few famous faces, people like Kate Moss, Kylie Minogue, Fran Cutler, Billy Zane. I remember talking to David Bowie as he was sitting on the steps of the Leisure Lounge when we moved there later on. Even Catherine Zeta-Jones came down. People forget she was really into the music before she became a big star, and she's an even bigger fan now. When I DJed in New York recently, Catherine came over to the booth to say hi with Michael Douglas.

Anyway, at the Blue Note we'd have accountants standing next to some real hardcore geezers. We had people who didn't give a fuck, apart from for the music.

That was when I first started DJing, alongside Kemi and Storm. To me they were the best; I loved the way Kemi and Storm mixed. And Blue Note took things back to basics, back to club level. On Sunday evenings we used to go on after this jazz club and some of that crowd would stay on, which made things real interesting. And there would be some very special nights: Cleveland Watkiss singing and MCing, sometimes at the same time, Storm playing tracks like Lemon D's 'Urban Style Music', and when 'Inner City Life' came on everyone would go for it, me included – I'd be down in the crowd giving it plenty with the rest of them.

Metalheadz could never happen as a club these days; it was a case of right place, right time, right crowd. After a while Metalheadz had a lot of haters. Ragga jungle had broken out with General Levy in the charts, but we knew that wouldn't last two minutes, mate, so see you later! People like Rebel MC? See you later! I was not about people taking the mic and chatting all over your tune. 'Headz moved everything up a few notches in terms of intensity, everything, and MCs had to take the back seat. I'd heard them chatting at the blues I went to fifteen years ago and my view was: 'Haven't we done this already, chaps?' Rage never used MCs, it was just about the music, and that's what we went for at the Blue Note.

David Bowie: I went down to his club with him a few times. The main thing I remember about it was that it had these fantastic speakers, nearly blew me across the room.

The next couple of years things really blew up. In 1996 and 1997 I collected awards for *Timeless*, like the Best Music of Black Origin award, while 'Inner City Life' won the best MOBO single, and also picked up best male artist at the International Dance Awards, and best producer from the Hardcore Dance Awards, who also saluted Grooverider, Fabio and Rob Playford. Meanwhile there were props for the Metalheadz label and our compilation albums such as *Platinum Breakz*. It was fair to say I'd arrived, but I was by no means burnt out, and I was looking for new ways to challenge myself as an artist.

Trenton and I launched another label with East West Records, called Fereala, which was supposed to release more experimental music by artists who wanted to do something different.

And 'Headz started to expand into all sorts of areas. At one point we hooked up with Australian company Royal Elastics and produced our own trainer, the DLX, complete with the logo and my graffiti tag, which was launched at London Fashion Week and sold really well. The limited-edition run of ten thousand sold at £90 a pop. It was a wicked thing to do, creating 'Headz for feet. I've got one pair safely stashed away with the rest of my sneaker collection.

Pete Tong: Metalheadz was really rocking during the eighteen months around *Timeless*. Kemistry and Storm were hands-on at that time, before the management of it fell apart. So he had a happening label, a happening club and a happening hit album. The only problem was that *Timeless* was very difficult to translate live, and that became clear at the first show at the Forum Kentish Town, which was a disaster. The thinking was that here was an artist as opposed to a dance producer, but it was too early for him. The venue was packed but he and the band and the singers and the dancers weren't prepared. This was the first show they had ever done and they were doing it centre stage with the lights full on them. Why dismantle the illusion and blow it? For dance people, when you don't play and you don't sing, how do you portray yourself on stage? In fairness it didn't harm *Timeless* because it was such a good record and they did get better live.

We did this amazing show in Paris. Björk was there, the Red Hot Chilli Peppers were in the house and Kemi and Storm were DJing, which made me so proud after we had been through so much together. And it was a success. The crowd loved all twenty-two minutes of 'Timeless', and as soon as we had finished that we went straight into the nasty 'Saint Angel' and slayed them. We were quite a band; this wasn't just a couple of faceless DJs sticking their hands in the air, it was theatre: I had this spinning mirrored Metalheadz logo with lasers bouncing off it and this great rocking show.

One time we played Manchester and the tension was high. The crowd was rowdy, as only they can be up there. So I came on and said: 'This isn't about fussing and fighting. It's about this,' and I turned my back to show the Metalheadz logo between my shoulder blades. I went straight for this geezer at the front and said: 'Listen, man, it's just about the music.'

My proudest moment on that tour was when we played Wolverhampton Civic Hall, and there were old friends from Heath Town and my mum and Jamie my son in the audience along with the rest of my family.

It was an unbelievable night, to be the homecoming hero. In a way I'd had a taste of this already, because I'd never really had a home, so for me a homecoming means a variety of things: hearing my tunes played for the first time at Rage felt like a homecoming, because that club meant so much to me, and helped nurture me. Playing the Roxy in New York with Doc Scott when we were on the Here Come The Drumz tour that same year was an achievement, because it is the B-Boy mecca. But performing at the Civic Hall was really magical – the old crew were there, Ronnie Fray, Doug and his boys, people I've known from way back.

Just as important to me was the fact that I could take this show to places like Paris and then bring it back to the ghetto and they still appreciated it. You can take the boy out of the ghetto but you can't take the ghetto out of the youth. But what I saw at some of those UK gigs – beatings, guns being waved, an air of heavy violence – frightened me, because of what I'd witnessed in Miami. Over there they were killing each other over really big deals, but in England it didn't need to be like this – it wasn't about moving fifteen keys around and fighting over big money, because they didn't have fuck all. It was just about respect and pride. Same old. Fuck the South Bronx, we're talking about Hackney, Moss Side. No different from the garage scene now, where kids are getting popped. It's all bollocks because it's based on territory and cliques. It's never-ending. Remy, one of the guys in Manchester, is gone now; a couple of years back a kid popped him. There was so much pain at the funeral, so much wasted opportunity. There were more than a thousand people paying respect that day.

Pete Tong: After a few months the live thing did turn around, the show was hacked back. It went to America and did well. But we probably invested £70,000–£100,000 in that tour he did for *Timeless*, which was in retrospect a waste of time, and all these people were around. It was a bit like hip-hop, you know: everyone has to get paid.

To promote *Timeless* I was invited by Björk as support on a European tour and it really took off. Then we went to America with Björk. I'd met her years earlier via my friend Aggi in

Iceland, and got to know her through my mates Dom T, Howie B and Nellee Hooper. She had been going out with Tricky, but Björk and me got along fine on the tour, just doing our own things and respecting each other. The European dates went so well we decided to go to America, where things were blowing up for both of us. Björk was beginning to sell serious amounts of records and the critics there had loved *Timeless*.

Josh Evans (friend/film-maker): As a writer I'm always looking for music to inspire me, and one day I read this absolutely glowing review of *Timeless* by Robert Hilburn, the music critic of the *LA Times*. So I bought it and, to be honest with you, the first time I heard it I really didn't like it. But I kept with it and it soon became one of my favourite records. The thing about him is that he understands structure and how to piece things together. And he understands sound and its frequencies, how to manipulate them.

I went off with Doc Scott for a series of dates around the US under the banner Here Come The Drumz, which was us giving hardcore drum'n'bass to American fans who hadn't been able to witness it at first hand.

We hit up places like the Palomino in LA, the Roxy in New York and played all over the shop. The tour went down really well, though of course we got flak from Raymond Roker, the self-appointed UK drum'n'bass music critic. Roker's one of those guys who sits on high, judging what's going on in the arena, but isn't a gladiator himself. He spurs on his favourites, but I've never been one of them. When I appeared on the cover of LA dance magazine *The Urb* he started really slagging me off. I think his deal was that I was 'selling out' drum'n'bass to the Americans.

Whatever, Roker certainly didn't affect the Here Comes The Drumz tour, which was phenomenal – the gigs were off the hook and Scottie and I blended really well. Although we'd worked together we'd never really DJed together and it made for a nice mix.

Then the real bonus was that, at the end of the tour, Scottie and I met Michael Koppelman in LA and flew to Kauai to meet my hero Shawn Stussy for a Channel 4 pilot I was making called *Fereala*.

Michael Koppelman: The thing about Goldie is that he literally makes things happen for people. That trip we went on together to hook up with Shawn Stussy in Kauai was amazing.

Fereala would have made a great show – I had this idea to take over Brands Hatch and have joyriders stealing cars and racing against each other, and Hurricane Higgins playing against a pool shark from the East End. But it was unreal meeting Shawn, who's an incredible, laid-back cat. I presented him with a canvas that Sarah Gregory and I painted together, of a hand holding various things which spelt out S-T-U-S-S-Y: a dice with the S on it, a playing card with the T on it, a pool ball with the U, and so on. He was knocked out.

Kauai was incredible, with waterfalls and natural beauty – not like Hawaii at all, far more unspoilt. To this day I still check for Stussy, because as a label it's retained its purity, having captured the imagination of kids everywhere. It's a real shame that Channel 4 canned the pilot, because they really missed out. Shawn's now retired from the business and this was the only interview with the man who transformed sports and casual wear around the globe, no doubt.

So things were going really well around that time. After the euphoria of Rage and my success first in London, then around the country and then around the world, I felt unstoppable. But I'd been suffering horrific stomach pains and, whenever I slowed down, I realised something was rotten in the state of Goldie despite all the glitz and glamour. Then there was an incident which shook me to the core of my being. It was a portent of what was to come.

One day I was sitting outside a restaurant on Ocean Drive in Miami with Doc Scott and this girl I was seeing, Kirsty, who had just dropped into a palm-reading place two blocks away on Ninth Street. Kirsty said that the woman there couldn't see her at the time, but would meet her at the restaurant. A few minutes later, while we were eating, this woman arrived, looked at Kirsty and then at me and said: 'I think he wants to see me, not you.'

At first I was like: 'Yeah, right,' but something about her was compelling. She told me to come along the next day and bring an egg. I took half a dozen along in an attempt to be clever, and she sat me down and explained that she was a witch who used white magic for healing purposes. She studied me slowly with her eyes and then asked me whether I had been suffering from stomach pains. Of course I had. The knot in my stomach had been getting worse for months. Then she took one egg from the six I had brought her and placed it on the table in front of her. She raised her hand and brought it down, palm flat, smashing the egg to smithereens: THWAAACK!

I flinched, expecting yolk and egg white to fly every which way, but instead, when she raised her hand, there was none, I swear to God. Instead, among the debris of shattered eggshell was a blackened, rotten piece of meat. She pointed to it and said: 'That is the evil which has been lurking inside you, eating you away. That has been growing inside you because you have been cursed by somebody in your past, and they are out to destroy your future happiness because you rejected them.'

I was wonder-struck, but still held back, suspecting I was

witnessing the most amazing piece of theatre. Until she described Christine in detail. She said that this person had the capability to wield great power, and that the curse would gather in strength as long as I maintained contact. I have to admit that, although we had split many years before, I had kept in touch, by postcard and the occasional call, because my obsession with her had never completely disappeared.

The witch explained that the curse would only diminish when I severed all ties, and said about Kirsty: 'The woman you're seeing at the moment you won't see for much longer.' She also said: 'There is a woman around you who has black hair. You are not quite sure about her, but there is something there.' And she explained that my path would soon split in two. She said I might have two children with the black-haired woman. If I did, then I would marry her and achieve happiness and freedom from the curse. But if I didn't have children, said the witch, then that relationship wasn't supposed to be, and I would have to follow my own path, travel alone and seek my own destiny. Either way, the paths offered freedom from the curse.

I left there reeling, shocked by the knowledge she seemed to have of my unhappy past, my confused present and my unknown future. And, without realising it, my relationship with the black-haired woman was about to blossom. In America Björk and I had became closer. About halfway through the tour, we exchanged one of those looks – you know, the ones which mean that things have moved up to another level?

David Bowie: I think I first met Goldie at one of the festivals in the mid-nineties. Hard to say, and I'm not too good at recall. I know he was DJing somewhere. We kept bumping into each other all over Europe, he was always with some new woman, a brunette here, Björk there. Quite the ladies' man, I realised.

On tour we started talking and those eyes just got to me. I was so attracted to her. I went back to her room and ordered some water for her humidifier to keep her voice healthy and then there was that first kiss and: BAM! You can guess the rest . . .

It would lead to an unbelievable relationship lasting eighteen months but would end in tragic and horrific circumstances, which I believe were bound up with the witch's prophecy.

But for a very long time Björk and I were happy, completely fuelled by passion. I have this tremendous respect for her as an artist and thought that she deserved a better man than Tricky.

There was one time I was at an after-show with Björk at the Roxy in New York City just after I'd played there. All of a sudden I see Tricky walking towards us in the private bar there, trying to say something to her. There were bouncers all over him, the security bum-rushed him and threw him out. Me, I stayed right there, with her.

I have to admit it didn't play that well with Björk because she's not into that ghetto mentality. We were two opposites, but that was certainly part of the attraction, and soon we were bang in love.

I was invited to present her with a Brit Award when she was playing in India that year so I planned a surprise. Just when she was finishing 'It's Oh So Quiet' I walked up behind her, Issey Miyake-d out in this suit she gave me, and put my arms around her, kissing and grabbing her. She threw a fit! The organisers sent us a video camera so that we could record a message to send back, which we did, then promptly dropped the camera in the sea while we were mucking around later.

When Keith Flint from the Prodigy slagged us off after the satellite link-up showing me presenting her with the award, saying that we were nothing but a celebrity couple and comparing us to Michael Jackson and Lisa Marie Presley, I played the Brighton Essential Festival wearing a T-shirt with Keith's head on it, and 'Cunt Face' written across the top. If he'd dissed my music that would just have been his opinion, but he got personal, and that was out of order.

Björk and I travelled everywhere together. We once went on holiday to the Maldives, where some pissed-up German started getting fruity with her and I had to go straight into nigga mode, smashing a chair over his head. Fortunately the hotel let us stay, and gradually, as we chilled, she started to talk to me about how she composed music. Over the next few days I learned a lot from her about writing and lyrics. Björk's musical knowledge is astounding – she just lives and breathes music, has a library of sounds with her and a ghetto-blaster ready to play it wherever she goes. It was Björk who turned me on to the contemporary classical composer Henryk Górecki, who became another huge influence on me.

She also took me to see this weird old guy, a numerologist who lives upstairs from Waitrose in the Finchley Road. He twisted my head completely when he talked about the set of numbers in my birth date, and pointed out how significant the number nine is to me. Björk's like that; she has a spiritual side which will open you up to stuff like that, and an amazing artistic streak, but she's also very down-to-earth.

I remember lying in a hammock with her under the stars over the Indian Ocean, stars that we never see here, and feeling so in love, at one with her. We'd disassociated from all of the claptrap that goes with pop stardom. I felt I'd cut all the bullshit away and was happy exchanging what I'd learnt from the street with her artistic and bohemian background. At that point I really thought we would get married.

Björk would never do anything by halves. Once we stayed at her beautiful little two-storey house in the port in Reykjavik,

just listening to this great music she had introduced me to, looking out at the snow-covered houses and the boats in the bay. We went snowboarding, visiting the glaciers. There was a view from this mountain where the sun was on one side of it and the moon was on the other. Phenomenal.

Icelandics have two Christmas Days. On the second day they are mad about fireworks, and because I'd blown up so big I wanted to be the one who set off the most. So I set up a private competition with Björk's manager, Derek Birkett, who isn't one to do things by halves himself. We spent two days buying fireworks to let off on the roof of the hotel and it got out of control. I went out with a driver and my gold card and scoured the island until I had spent £7,000. I had these rockets about six feet high, all kinds of shit. Then we let them off and it was mayhem, the hotel's name got shattered, the electrics went. Needless to say I won the competition. Take that, Derek!

There is another thing about Björk: she's a very funny girl. We laughed so hard when we were together, just had fun, letting everything else in our lives go to be with one another. I don't think I've ever laughed so much with somebody. We'd get those books of cartoons, Gary Larsen's *The Far Side*, and just howl, be on the floor crying and pissing ourselves with laughter.

One time we were staying in this beautiful hotel near the Taj Mahal. We went out and bought a whole bunch of fireworks and walked through the huge gates there and down the steps by the Taj Mahal. We set up about fifty and let them all off and ran for it. There were locals scattering every which way, explosions and loud noises, the police arrived, and we just sat around the corner cackling at the commotion we'd caused like two kids being allowed to play together and get into scrapes.

During this period I was becoming closer to Björk so one

day I asked her what she thought about the idea of getting married. We started to think along those lines, and put an offer in on a huge house in Hertfordshire. Funnily enough it had once been the home of the original TV cook, that mad old bat Fanny Cradock. There was a stream running through the garden and I remember sitting on the banks, watching the water flow, thinking: This is unbelievable. I'm about to commit to this woman. And all that was running around my head was what the witch had said: I might have two children with the woman with black hair but, if it didn't happen, then it wasn't supposed to be.

The friction between us started when I joined her again in America on another of her tours. There had been some press reports that we were thinking about marrying, and I guess the pressure was on.

It soon became apparent that our relationship could not withstand this, and one night, it all came to a head. The witch's prophecy had played tricks with my head. I couldn't utter those three simple words to her again. I couldn't commit. She checked into another room and called Derek to cancel buying the house in Hertfordshire.

The very next day Björk flew back to England and walked into another shit storm, far more evil. While we had been in Miami this maniac Ricardo Lopez, who lived in the city not three blocks from the Casa Grande, demonstrated his deranged love for her – and his disgust of the idea that she could marry the 'nigger' Goldie – by sending a letter bomb to Björk's London address. When it was traced back to Miami the cops who burst into his apartment two days later found him dead. With a sick twist of the knife, he had videotaped his own suicide.

I witnessed all this on the local news channels on my hotel room TV in Miami. It was just too shocking for words and I felt so much for her. It also freaked me out because I was wondering what would have happened if we hadn't split that night. What would have happened if we had encountered that freakazoid out walking together the next day? I felt that we had both been swept up into a dark maelstrom, but couldn't figure what parts were played by Christine's curse and which by the witch's prophecy. All I knew was that I had chosen the second path predicted by the witch, the one which was filled with doubt for the future. But there was one sure thing; by choosing that path, however painful, I had lifted the curse.

Storm: Kemi and I were quite sad when he told us it was over with Björk. The meeting of their minds seemed to make them the ultimate couple.

Of course, in time Björk recovered from this ordeal. She is a strong, admirable woman and a true artist making incredible music, out of this world. And more recently her Oscar nomination shows that she can also burn up the silver screen. She has her own demons but she taught me a lot, and for that I'll always be grateful. I think she really loved me and I loved her. But I was always able to finish things, and that was it, over. I think it comes from being in care. You always knew that, however well things were going, that suitcase would one day be picked up and you'd move on.

My relationship with Björk was significant, not only personally but creatively. However, the Miami thunderstorm which burst around us as we split was the first of a series of dark clouds casting shadows over my life once more.

DIE IN ME EVERY IN GHT... WITH WHAT IF OR... WHAT MIGHT...
AND MY BODY SUSPENDS THE PAIN... MY MIND TRANSENDS DELIGHT.
THE FEARLESS FLIGHT... IN DEAD OF NIGHT... I SEARCH FOR LIGHT...
BETWEEN THE PURPLE BLUE DOTS... WHEN I CLOSE MY EYES...
THE PAIN "CANNOT DISGUISE... MY MIND OUTWITS THE WISE...
WHILE WORLD AROUND DEMISE... MY HEART STRETCHED WIDE...
IT RHYMES BUT RAYS IN LIFE... AND CUTS ME LIKE A KNIFE...
I DIE, ONCE EVERY NIGHT... AND YES THERE IS LIGHT... MORE
POWERFUL THAN WHITE... A SHADE MORE BRACED... THAN LIFE
SO PAIN SITS OPPOSITE MY ROOM. AND SHADES ME NOW AND THEN...
MY BODY IS HIS ONLY FRIEND. MY SPIRIT... TELLS HIM "YOU WILL END."
AND ONCE I LEAVE... MY LONELY ROOM... HE CANNOT "HURT AGAIN...
THE PAIN YOU CAUSED... ONLY SET MY COURSE... MY SPIRIT SAILS... WITH
WINDS... THEY HAVE ETERNAL END... GOODBYE "DEAR FRIEND"

TODAY... THIS LIFE" YOU "DIED... IS WHERE I BEGIN... THE MAKERS
MIND... I LEARNED TO FLY... AND IN HIS SANDS OF TIME
... HE WILL TELL MY WHEN... I HAVE PATIENCE ON MY STOOL
AND IN MY ROOM, "I LOOK AT YOU" THROUGH YOU... BEYOND YOU
MY PRAYERS HENCE WILL ONLY BLESS YOU...

UNTIL THEN... RIGHT... YOU ONLY COUNT, THIS "BRAINS" DEAR
FRIEND. I NAMED PAIN... EACH ONE OF
THEM...

@ : " IN HONOUR OF ...
YOUR .. FATHER.

I DIE MOST EVERY NIGHT

8: Saturnz Return

The creation of sprawling Saturnz Return – which includes contributions from Noel Gallagher, Björk, David Bowie and KRS-1 – is intense and painful. Fame leads to high-profile liaisons, such as a three-month fling with supermodel Naomi Campbell. But the lifestyle comes with a price – a gargantuan drug habit. Goldie's personal and business relationships collapse around him and his 'angel' Kemi dies in a horrific car accident.

AT THE EDGE OF... EVERY TREE, IN ITS AGE OF WOVELY
LIES A BASE OF NATURE ...THAT WE CANNOT VIEW IN ITS
DARKEST NATURE OF ITS OWN ORGANIC NATURE THAT AS
OUT LIVED US ALL, IN ITS RINGS AND GROWTH OF DAY AND
NIGHT ...IN A TIME ONLY MADE BY OUR BELIEFS OF TIME
THE SELF MADE CLOCK OF MANS DESIGN ... IN A
UNRELEVANT DECISION OF WHAT MIGHT HAVE BEEN
ITS ONLY WRITTEN AS WE SEE ~ BEFORE THIS, IN A
FRAME THAT DID NOT EXIST ~ OR SO BE IT WE PERISH
TO RIDICULE ITS PAST OF MYTH ~ FAR GREATER
THAN OUR OWN... " OUR FATHER ONCE OCCUPIED ITS OWN
SELFISH THROWN... ' DICTATE THE ROADS OF SOMETHING
THAT IN ESSENCE ... ' WE DO NOT KNOW ~ AND CANNOT
BESTOW ~ THE TREE OF LIFE, THAT WATCHED THE EMPIRE
OF LIFE UNFOLD ~ FOR US TO PONDER • A STOLEN
SEAT OF KINGS... PARANOIDED FOR MISCONCEPTIONS
~THEY BELONG TO US ~ IN ONLY THE FRAME, WE CAPTURE
OR DRAIN LIFE AND LIE THE WISH IN HOPE, WE HAVE
OVER THROWN ~ ' I WISH TO USE THAT TREE OF LIFE, A
BRANCH, IM BLESSED AND WILL MAKE MY OWN TO
BLOSSOM FLOWERS, I,M BUT SATISFIED IN HEART
TO BE A PART, OF FLOWERS IN THAT DESIGN, BEFORE

MY LIFE . COULD EVEN START ~ FRAGILE AS WE ARE THE TREES A THOUSAND
LEAVES THAT FELL IN AUTUMN BREEZE, AGED AS WINE, AND CURSED
TO DUST IN EVOLUTIONS TIME, THE SILENT ORGANIC ME ~ MORE FRAGILE
THAN THE LEAF, WE IN OUR TIME WILL WATCH FALL TO FREE CAUGHT
BY BREEZE ~ A DISTANT BREATH SILENT IN THAT, IT REMIND ME ~
IT GOES TO DUST ~ JUST A WE, WITH OPEN SOUL ~ WE ARE BUT THAT
LEAF ~ I KNOW DID MAKES THAT BREEZE, IN HOPES TO CARRY ME

J Storm: Like he always said, he would be the famous producer, we would be the DJs playing his tunes, he'd have a label and club. And, as he says on 'Timeless': 'So the triangle was complete.' That was all about us living in this part of north London, with Alexandra Palace at the centre of 'the triangle', as we called it, and the more money we made, the closer we got to the palace. But we never quite made it to the palace. I saw a change in Goldie once his talent was recognised and there was money to be made. The vultures gathered. That's why I think he moved out to the country eventually, because he can't take being at people's beck and call.

I was in a strange place in the period between *Timeless* and knuckling down to working on my next album, *Saturnz Return*. It's a trait of being a Virgo that whenever I peak at something I put it down and move on. When the scene and people like Fabio and Groove started showing me props I had to make a move. It was like leaving home for me: 'OK, guys, I'm going to have to leave you now.' I think it also has something to do with a fear of failure. So even though I had big-time success I thought: You know what? Let me just stop right now and change tack, just in case.

There was also a feeling that I had created this character and I wanted to tear it down, give the commercial world the middle finger. I had to go against the grain, and I kind of knew that it would be rejected, it was inevitable. But I do get the one-in-a-thousand thing, where people come to me and say about *Saturnz Return*: 'Goldie, you know what? That album fucking pulled me through.'

Anyway, all I knew at the time was that the new album had to be a great leap forward, in conception and execution. I wanted to do something which was true to me artistically, not what was expected of me by the record company or anyone else.

Timeless and *Saturnz Return* were different in one very important respect – the first reflected what was going on externally while the second was all about me looking inward. When I made *Timeless* it was about this ghetto kid who understands the realities of life, but doesn't really understand what life is about. He's all: Why? What? Who? When? What is this, life and living? *Saturnz Return*, on the other hand, was an attempt by me to present where my life was at. In science you can go and look at the stars through telescopes, but you'd probably find out far more about where the earth is at by looking under the sea. One of the beauties of life is that people have the ability to look inward. But people get very scared of depth; what's on the bottom, what's there? What secrets do the depths of the planet hold for all of us? I went through that process, which was very scary for me, when I made *Saturnz Return*.

I really wanted to connect it to the astrological phenomenon of Saturn's Return. I decided to put the B-Boy name into *Saturnz Return*.

Neil Spencer (author of *True as the Stars Above*): Saturn's Return is the Saturn birthday, which is based on an orbit of 29.5 years in length as opposed to one earth year. Since Saturn is stern and rigorous, that is the kind of birthday we get – a reckoning and a crucial stage in our personal evolution. Saturn is the planet of limitation, responsibility and earned success, and its return represents a time when boundaries are broken and outworn structures abandoned.

Projection of *Wildstyle*

The living-room in Dorney Towers

The view from Dorney Towers

Kemistry

With Noel Gallagher's British guitar

At the Blue Note

At the Phoenix

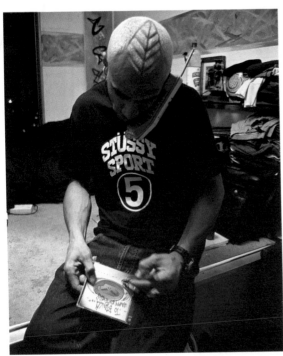

My new haircut

Chance

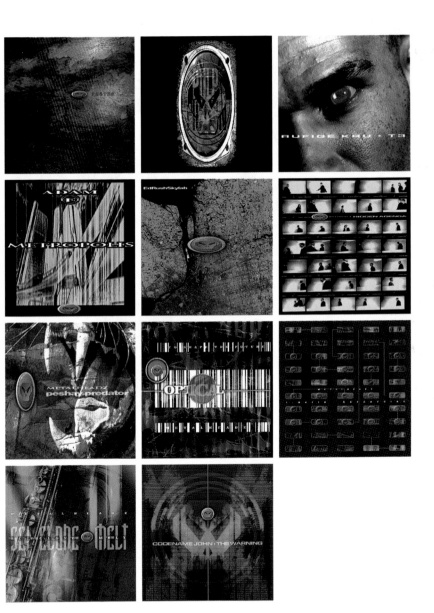

Metalheadz twelve-inch covers

Me in front of my *Survivors* graffiti in Heath Town

Astrologer Marc Robertson, in his book *Crisis Ages in Adult Life*, complains that society doesn't prepare its children for the fact that real adulthood comes between twenty-eight and thirty – and that it comes with a seething inner crisis that causes careers to crumble, marriages to fail, and individuals to face the most serious identity crisis of their early years. As Goldie puts it on his album: 'When Saturn returns, there is no escape.'

The Saturn's Return is beloved of astrologers because it so rarely fails as a signifier. Astrology books and magazines come supplied with examples of celebrity Saturn's Returns and their traumas. Princess Diana's decision to go public with her marital tribulations coincided with her Saturn's Return in 1991, at age thirty, which was much remarked on. Elizabeth Taylor's romance with Richard Burton commenced with her Saturn's Return in 1962, and led to her divorce from Eddie Fisher two years later.

For Goldie, Saturn arrived back at the same degree it occupied at his birth (12 degrees Pisces) shortly before his thirtieth birthday in June 1994, when he signed to a major record label. Saturn retreated for a few months before returning to 12 degrees of Pisces just after 'Inner City Life' sealed his reputation as a musical innovator. Intriguingly, what followed was not only fame and fortune, but a period when he made his reconciliation with his parents, locating the father he had never known and writing the orchestral epic dedicated to his mother.

I had great plans for the project and really wanted to start breaking barriers again. I was determined not to lazily come up with *Timeless Part 2*, although there was a blueprint there; the track 'Timeless' was mirrored by 'Mother', 'Adrift' on the first album was followed by 'Letter Of Fate'. On *Saturnz Return* I wanted the tones and tempos to be more varied, the experiments bolder and the tracks definitely more personal. 'I'll Be There For You' was written for my brother Stuart after he was convicted for stabbing offences.

Stuart Meade: I got into some trouble at home and stabbed a guy. I was just getting into too much trouble so my brother said I should come and stay with him, which I did for eleven months before the police caught up with me. We got really close over that period, he became like a father to me, telling me off when I was wrong and basically looking out for me. He took me everywhere, to every club he went to.

There was even a reference to me at the time in the *Passengers* programme he made, where he says: 'PC Whatever-your-name-is, you're not going to get him, see you later!'

Eventually I got caught when I went home to see my mother, and was given a two-year sentence. When he dropped me off at the station before I was going to be locked up, we cried and cried, but while I was there he visited me all the time until he had an argument with one of the screws, chucking a fifty-pound note at him, saying: 'Here, cop hold of that, you fucking need it.' I thought it was really funny, but they took him off the visit.

When I had home leave he organised for a limo to meet me at the gates, and all the time I was inside he organised for me to get fifty pounds every two weeks, which is far more than you need. Inside you can live really comfortably on seven pounds a week so I had everything in my cell – food, everything. He really looked after me.

I guess that of all my brothers I'm closest to Stuart, probably because we hung out so much over that period. My relationship with him is different from that with my other brothers: things are no longer good between me and Melvin – we don't see eye to eye and I can't get on with his lack of morals. I can't stand him, and he overstepped the mark one too many times, and even though he's my only blood brother, I don't think that's how brothers should behave. It's like letting down the team and scoring own goals all the time. He never learns from his past mistakes and never will as far as I can see. It's different again with Jo-Jo, who's sixteen years younger than me. He's a cool guy, always the quiet one in the family, very like his father Pusey, resilient and strong. If all the brothers are together we all start mixing it with each other, which can be really funny. But I've always looked out for Stuart most, and he went through a lot when he ended up in prison, which is why I wrote 'I'll Be There For You'.

That song was just one example of my new approach on *Saturnz Return*, because it was so deeply personal to me. I stopped taking other people's breaks and started creating my own, whether it be a guy playing drums in Spain or my voice recorded backwards. I built up a library of sounds which became a wine rack; I'd leave them to ferment and then break them open. And I realised that I had to use my own voice on certain tracks. No one could sing about my own misfortunes more than myself, and that really came through on 'Mother', the sixty-minute track which took up an entire CD of the album. I didn't speak to my mum for years, but I had become conscious that, using my life as my book, I had better check my relationship with her for what it really was. I had to look at what the primal wound was and try to explain beyond my temper tantrums, look at what motivated me.

Pete Tong: He told me about 'Mother' from the beginning of the project, and my view was: 'Do we have to do this?' I actually think 'Mother' is good, to be honest, but I think he got in a mess because he was in a mess. Nevertheless, 'Mother' is a very bold piece of music, but unfortunately there weren't many people with the attention span to deal with it. And when you're doing all these other things which erode your reputation in other people's eyes – being in the papers and partying all the time – they aren't going to take you seriously enough to sit down and listen to something for more than an hour. Therefore the critic at the

Observer and *Q* magazine reviewing it that month didn't review it well.

Like 'Timeless', 'Mother' was based on this two-chord sound, almost a disharmony: 'MO-OTHER!' It was a primal scream at the centre, and I built this huge soundscape around it. The interesting thing about 'Mother' was that it challenged people like John Altman, the inspired arranger on *Saturnz Return* who has collaborated with absolutely everybody. He was blown over and really put a lot of his mad orchestration and arranging skills into it. Before I went into the studio to record 'Mother' I had it all planned out, the whole thing. I drew the plan out on the wall – the shape of the beats, the vocals, all of it in a diagram which looked like a fish! That track was totally designed, from the sound of butane burning at the beginning to the way we used and abused the equipment. We had the two software packages Cubase and Logic locked together, which hadn't been done before, it was breaking the rules. Digitally I was using everything available to me at the time; for 'Mother' I had 48 tracks on tape and 109 chan- nels, which means that when you listen to it, it's a journey in sound.

When we worked on 'Letter Of Fate' during *Saturnz Return* this strange thing happened. I'd whispered in the background to the song: 'Nobody . . . ever . . . said . . . that . . . living . . . would . . . be . . . easier . . . than . . . being . . . alone.' We turned the tape over to get the reverse effect, to play it back- wards. As I nipped out to the toilet and was walking down the hall I heard this haunting sound, which was my vocals backwards. We listened to it through and it sounded like some kind of Gregorian chant, something fourteenth-century monks would sing. And it worked totally backwards, the chord progression, everything.

So we decided to make it a new track on its own. Me,

Mark and engineer Will O'Donovan set the grand piano up. Will suggested putting instruments on the piano wires so that when you played the keys it made this strange noise against my backward vocals and muted chords. At the very beginning of one take I ripped a piece of paper up right next to the mic, as a way of saying goodbye to the suicide note which had been the origin of 'Letter Of Fate'. We went through three edits: reversed that cymbal, reversed that conga, all these mad things on it. And we got the best bits and laid them over each other and it became this unbelievable Gothic-sounding piece which we made the hidden track at the end of *Saturnz Return*.

To me that secret track after the last one, 'Demonz', represents a past life of mine, I don't care what anybody says. I still believe it was the sound of me back then.

In a way I was also trying to deal with minimalist people like Philip Glass. *South Park* used to make me crack up with their: 'Look, it's Philip Glass!' and him playing this three-chord wonder. And I remember hearing his soundtrack to the film *Kundun* when I went to see it in New York with Val Kilmer and Josh Evans and just thinking: This is Philip Glass? Fuck this cat!

What was great about *Saturnz Return* was that it meant I got to work with some of my musical heroes, and they were all very different: David Bowie's a complete British icon who I connected with so much, Noel Gallagher was a mate who brought real punk rock racket to the mix, and to me KRS-1 is the fucking blueprint, man. That nigga was the best, the block, a hip-hop hero.

David Bowie: I really liked his music and thought his first album was fantastic, but it was meeting him which made me care more about him than his music. I just thought, this guy's a very nice guy, he's very cool. The music didn't matter as much after that.

It was him. I was at school with blokes like Goldie. He's completely irresponsible, lovely, a real terror.

Bowie had always been a secret hero of mine. He is an ancient soul, very serious. Get on the wrong side of him and you know it. He has rage inside him and passion which he has managed to deal with, and I knew that this song I had, 'Truth', would be perfect for him:

> Truth.
> Would you lie to me lately?
> Truth.
> Would you die for me maybe?
> Truth.

Up until this point I don't think I'd really expressed the poetic side of me. I'd always read and written poetry, and now that softer, Pat Metheny side of me was screaming to be let out, especially since the beast had been living alone with his thoughts.

So this lyrical aspect was really coming to the fore and I'd finally cracked it in terms of writing lyrics and songs, rather than just poems. Björk had shown me the way.

Immediately I wrote 'Truth' I heard David's voice. He had already approached me because he was entering his own drum'n'bass phase which I thought was great, but I'm a real purist, you know? What was good was that it showed that you cannot stop anybody – David Bowie even – being influenced by this music.

But Bowie is special, like John Altman. With someone like Bowie you can come into their lives in the blink of an eye, and leave it with a blink and a smile, do you know what I mean? He was very important in letting me know the true meaning of reinvention.

David Bowie: He had a musical sketch of the piece that he wanted me to sing on and once I'd got into the vocal booth he sort of described line by line what it should do. Not musically, you understand, but what the line should indicate emotionally. I'm used to working with quite odd methods so I got into it quite quickly.

So I read the lyrics to him and he picked up on the line: 'Sorrows hide in sculpture,' telling me in his Michael Caine voice: 'Did you know that Michelangelo said that sculpture already exists in stone, you just have to brush away the dust?'

Well, I didn't, but I've always thought that sculptures look so sorrowful, as if artists pour their hearts and souls into them. That's why I wrote it. So when he told me that, it rang true, it hit home for me.

And that night he came to the studio, stood on the plate and said: 'Look, man, let me work this.' So we worked and reworked the track, moving the verses around and arranging it. Of course, there was a problem when I gave him a credit on the songwriting. Trenton just said: 'But you wrote this,' which was ridiculous because Bowie put so much of himself and his talent into it. Even though I wrote the words he made the song. It was as though I was speaking through him; what he did I wanted to hear. I saw David outside Black Market Records and he said: 'Goldie, when you're writing with somebody else just give them something, because it shows the difference between you and them.' There are people who rubbed him many years ago who are nobodies now, so Bowie knows.

With 'Temper Temper' I wanted to tap into the stuff I was into way back when I was in the Lew Joseph Children's Home; Public Image, the Clash, the Stranglers, the stuff with post-punk edge. And Noel was perfect for it.

Noel Gallagher: He brought round this track and said he wanted some really heavy guitars on it. At that time it was called 'Seven Eight' because the drums were in 7/8 time. I listened to it in this studio I had at the top of my house – and that I subsequently gave him, and he did nothing with, the lazy cunt – and I couldn't make out a rhythmic pattern in it, it was so off the wall. Then I listened to it drunk; still nothing. Then I got out of it and it started to make more sense.

He kept on asking me what I thought and after a while I said: 'Of course I'll do it but I don't know what you want.' All he said was he wanted it to be 'dark', so I thought I'd just get in the studio and busk it.

On the day of the session I'd just bought this BMW 850. Like a silly cunt I got on the M25 – because I'd also just moved into my house in Hertfordshire and didn't really know the way then – and got lost, taking the wrong turning. So I turn around and I'm haring down the M1 at 120 mph and I'm pulled over by the cops and given a ticket.

I finally got to the studio and Noel, while he was waiting, had sorted his intelligence out.

He just went straight into this unbelievable riff but Rob Playford didn't get it on the first take, which didn't help prop up the deteriorating relationship between us. The fact that Rob didn't get the first take didn't make any difference in the end. Straight away, once everything was set up properly, Noel delivered an equally great riff to match the anger and rage in that song.

Noel Gallagher: I got them to turn the drums up so I could get into the pace of the song and then thought I'd better check what key it was in. So I asked him and he looked at me and said: 'What's a key?' I explained that it was the musical note that the song was in, so we had to play the track and hold a guitar tuner to the speakers to find out it was in G flat. He explained it was thirty-six bars and said: 'Do what you do.' I don't know why, because I've never done it before, and would usually play some Jimmy Page-like solo, but I played that riff and it just fitted perfectly. He was jumping round the room shouting: 'Darker, darker, darker!' And I was thinking: I'm not really a dark person, I'm quite happy really, but we carried on and I think it's fucking brilliant, one of the best things I've ever done. I think the video's shit, though!

The video was great and got me banned when the BBC, ITV *and* MTV objected to the 'excessive violence', which was actually just me taking a chainsaw to everything and smashing a china shop up with a baseball bat, going absolutely nuts while Noel stood there cool as ice bashing out his riff. Noel's a geezer who made it out of Manchester and has done everything you expect a rock star to do. Supernova Heights was amazing, man. I went round there once and he called me up to the top of the house and there was this bath in this room with a great big Mod target set into it. But when you're blown into being one of the biggest rock stars in the world, people flip out. Liam's a Virgo, so of course he's going to be crazy, he's a young Virgo.

From an outsider's point of view, Noel's God, he's larger than life but he's also the most down-to-earth geezer that ever walked the fucking planet. Noel does what he does and he does it damn well. I don't expect Noel to change what he does because that's what he stands for. He can be what he wants to be and no one can take that away from him. He's out there living it. Things like the Beatles were what we grew up on. Noel's making tunes that kids of nine or ten will remember in the same way.

But to this day Noel will never let me forget that, although his name appears on the credits of *Saturnz Return*, he didn't appear among my shout-outs.

Noel Gallagher: You know what these fucking hip-hop guys are like with the credits printed really small with no spaces, and it took me three weeks sitting down with the sleeve poring over it, with a magnifying glass, off me head, going: 'It's got to be here somewhere,' just to find out that every person in England is thanked on that album apart from me!

I emphasised to people that it had to be there, but it was missing. Maybe that was one of the things which made me think I was losing my grip. I was always very fussy about artwork and detail, and for that important one to be missing enraged me.

Although it was a great experience, there were a lot of problems surrounding the making of *Saturnz Return*.

From the start I had a big problem with Rob Playford in that I couldn't get through to him.

Pete Tong: *Timeless* really put Goldie on the map, but there was a lot of jealousy and rage surrounding the success of the album. Some of the most difficult relationships in rock'n'roll history produce greatness; it's the angst and the battling which often produce the best stuff. It would have been good if he'd stuck with Rob particularly, but it wasn't to be.

What made things worse was that he started seeing Lorna Harris, who had been a girlfriend of mine before we fell out over her religious views. I saw that Rob was getting close to her and I warned him to stay away because I could see it would end in tears. I warned him that having a relationship with her would fuck his head up. But I knew he had been sucked in. He's a white guy, he'd probably never been with a black girl, and this one was into martial arts and could do the splits and turn you inside out, all the while making the sign of the cross. I ended up throwing a chair at him when I found out because he just wouldn't talk about it or communicate like a grown man. Rob could be very uncommunicative and it was this which enraged me; I didn't feel proprietorial about her but frustrated because I couldn't get through to him and warn him about the dangers of the situation. So the only thing was to smash the chair up.

The main engineer in the end on *Saturnz Return* was Mark Sayfritz, who played a fundamental part when Rob fell out of the project about halfway through when our working relationship completely collapsed. The final straw was a small incident but it showed how bad things had got. I was EQ-ing 'Dragonfly' and turned around to see him with hands clamped over his ears, wincing. It was kind of: 'Well, if you've got a problem, talk about it, don't go behind my back!' But Rob's uncommunicative nature stopped him from opening up and we just fell out irrevocably.

David Bowie: When I worked with him on *Saturnz Return*, he was still collaborating with Rob Playford. Things were somewhat odd in the studio as I think there may have been a bit of falling out going down so it was kind of uncomfortable.

So I had to find someone new to help me complete the project. Although Mark comes from Wolverhampton and I knew about him on the scene, we'd never really had dealings before, but he came through when I went to see him with all of the material that was left after Rob walked.

Mark is a producer in his own right but he's an absolute all-rounder in that he's an unbelievable programmer, engineer and musician. Mark had to fish through all the disks and software with music in various stages of completion and put it all together again. He pieced it all together and worked out what planet we were on.

I also brought in Optical to engineer and provide beats. I'd known him for a really long time, he was always Grooverider's boy. He's very open-minded and has got great technical skills which he showed when we worked on making 'Mother' a dance-floor track, 'Mother The VIP', for the *Ring Of Saturn* mini-album of remixes, which was when it became a big four-on-the-floor tune. I still got heat from people on the scene, as small as it was, but my response was: If you want those tunes, go to the centre of 'Mother' and there they are. But this was outside of the loop and it was breaking barriers, the *Starship Enterprise* at warp speed.

The other big problem was money.

I had wanted to make *Saturnz Return* my most ambitious project, and we moved between studios racking up huge costs over many months. We were at the large Ridge Farm and some of the stuff was recorded at Rob Playford's Manic One, which he moved from Stevenage to take over Trident Studios in Soho, the place that Bowie used a lot in the seventies. One track was done at the Hit Factory in New York, and there was recording, mixing and engineering all over the joint: Angel Studios, Jacob's in Surrey. There was a complete squad there – orchestras, arrangers, conductor John Altman, for whom I have the greatest respect, and people like Cleveland Watkiss; even Diane Charlemagne made a comeback on a couple of tracks.

'Mother' alone was recorded at three different studios. My attitude was that, if you're going to rob a big bank, you need a fast getaway car, the best. So when it came to addressing the spiritual journey of my relationship with my mother, I had to use the biggest and the best. Once again we were joyriding the technology.

At one of those studios, Ridge Farm, there was this terrible incident when, after weeks of working on it, we lost all fifty-seven minutes that had been recorded because the desk crashed, which rarely happens. That was remarkable. We managed to get it back but the operator was really sweating!

For the whole album we used 9,000 audio files, 48 tracks of tape, 40 tracks of ProTools, 109 full channels on a JP-9000 desk and 32 tracks of DR-88 running at the same time.

From the record company I got constant pressure about

Saturnz Return being a double album, because they are more difficult to sell. The usual. At one stage a lot of money had gone into it and I needed more to complete and Pete really came through, which meant that Mark and I could realise my vision.

Pete Tong: Where our record deal with him stopped being good business was when we tore up the contract and indulged him on the second album, which was made across a lot of studios and took for ever. He's one of the brightest people I've ever met but sometimes he doesn't think things through. Add to that the fact that there are two or three Goldies in his head and it all depends on which one gets up that day . . . It was a fantastic day making the video for 'Temper Temper', all these people like Naomi Campbell arriving in limousines with Noel and Goldie at the centre of it all. A lot of madness. But to be honest we knew we were going into the *Saturnz Return* campaign without an obvious single. Regarding my own battles here, the record company bottled it a bit becaue I would have rather made a fantastic video of 'Digital', the track he did with KRS-1, than 'Temper Temper'.

It was great working with KRS, really funny, because we talked for about four hours then did the track in twenty minutes. So we released 'Digital' as the first single but London decided that a video shouldn't be made for that – instead the money was spent on promoting 'Temper Temper'.

Pete Tong: The issue was: How can it be a Goldie video with KRS-1 rapping all the way through it? We ended up spending a fortune on 'Temper Temper', making a great video for what was basically a not very good record. The remixes were good, though, and, as I say, the video was amazing. And although it got to number seven in the chart it didn't mean very much because of the state of our charts here. It doesn't take much – a bunch of committed people with advertising and hype basically – to get a hit for one week. I'm sure 'Temper Temper' slid quickly. 'Digital' was a far better record and that's probably where we had a bit of a clash. For a long time he thought that *Saturnz Return* didn't take off because I couldn't convince the record company to release 'Digital' as a single to break it.

There was always this problem with the record company's perception of how to sell me in America. Now I know America – I've lived there, worked there, and had made a name for myself with *Timeless*, made headway, you know what I'm saying? My idea was that a great video of KRS-1 and me would have broken MTV there using the best breakers in the world at that time: Storm from Germany, a couple of guys from Paris and the UK, B-Boys who had taken that stuff to another level, guys breaking up the side of buildings on 52nd Street, guys breaking on glass. But they wouldn't have it.

Pete Tong: I just think he gave himself too big a challenge and his eye wasn't on the ball musically. He wasn't as down with the street or as popular with his own people as he thought he was, although a lot of them were too scared to tell him. He also took a major leap by unhinging himself from Rob and diving into new musical relationships. The pack of cards came tumbling down. *Saturnz Return* cost around £250,000–£300,000, but the contract probably said he was due to deliver an album for £100,000. What happened was that his first period sales exceeded their targets, so there was more money in the pot, so he thought he had done a fantastic job and had access to more money. But a lot was spent touring – he probably came out of that first album without earning anything but was in this position where he was a great success and could command a higher budget. So we refinanced his deal.

Also I got a lot of shit from one of the guys at London Records in the US, although I have to say I gave a lot back.

And that's where we started to fall out seriously. One night we had a party at the Roxy in New York and it was a shambles. Record decks on top of bass bins so that every second the needle would jump, that kind of unprofessional crap. It was a disaster. They hadn't thought it through, and I was prepared to go to this guy at London US and fuck him up. He tried to explain to me: 'But G, but but but . . .' and I was like: 'G but fucking nothing. I'll cane your cranium if you make me look like a cunt again!'

Pete Tong: So, with *Saturnz Return*, the album was bloody long again with 'Mother' being an epic. It was basically too much information and very difficult to promote without a solid hit, so was a massive disappointment in sales terms; maybe seventy thousand in this country. In America it did much better, because the fans there tend to be more loyal. The stupid thing about that album is if sixty minutes had been hacked out of it and 'Mother' had been, say, twenty minutes long, there's a very good album hidden in there. But there was no telling him at the time, especially since it involved his mother!

I like Pete; not only did he show vision in his job but he also showed me a lot of respect. But I think he listened to too many of the voices from executives above him, particularly the A&R people in America. But he did support me.

Around that time, and to make matters worse, my private life became a mess again. I had become a face on the celebrity circuit and I was doing a lot of drugs. The break with Björk had been ugly but clean, so I decided to make a go of it again with Tracy. I kind of moved in with her in her little flat in Northwood and she became the most significant woman in my life at that time – I dedicated *Saturnz Return* to her.

The problem with Tracy was I had always been a womaniser and it made it very difficult to prove that I was trying to be true. She was suspicious of me in every way and I have to face it, I couldn't fully commit. When Tracy said to me: 'You'll never love anyone,' the words rang true. Sometimes I'd see Anoushka, an actress, and she was more like a friend, a soulmate who I could talk to about women and Tracy in particular. But Tracy just thought that I was fucking every woman I spoke to. Which was sometimes true, certainly in the case of Naomi Campbell.

I first met Naomi at Donatella Versace's show in Paris when I went over on the Eurostar with Fran (Cutler) and Meg (Matthews). I used to chaperone Meg for Noel, make no mistake. There was never any danger of us getting together, which makes those rumours about their kid being mine really stupid. Anyway, that first time at Donatella's I saw Naomi have this colossal row with that dancer, Joaquin Cortes, who was trying to get her to open the door after she'd locked herself inside a room to get away.

Incidentally, that very same night was also the first time I met The Fish. We were all in this house in Paris with this massive row going on and this geezer walks in dressed head to foot in Indian garb, a long dress, the works. He starts talking freestyle and I'm off my tits, having had a bit of a sniff. He talked incessantly for fifteen minutes non-stop. I went to him: 'Where the fuck did you get that from?' And he told me he had been quoting from this book of prison poetry (which he later sent me). It was of course Laurence Fishburne, an incredible person. He's also friends with my friend Ozwald Boateng, so I got to know him really well. An incredible cat, the only American actor who can do all types of English accents, Geordie, whatever, convincingly.

But back to Naomi. A few weeks later I went to the launch party of the London Fashion Café with Fran and this time Naomi came with us. I've known Fran for ever – well, since 1990 at least. She was part of the Michiko Koshino / Crash Crew posse who went on the Iceland trip that year, and I

always called her my London sister. That night in the limo on the way to the launch Fran was whispering: 'Naomi really likes you,' and I could tell that was true, because Naomi had slipped her hand behind me and was surreptitiously stroking my back.

We went to this thing and then back to the Met Bar for a drink and then I went up to Naomi's room. And that was it. Kiss: BAM! Touch: BAM!!

Afterwards I remember going into the bathroom and thinking about her conquests. I looked in the mirror and went: De Niro, Tyson and now Goldie from Wolverhampton. Yes!

As soon as we got together she started calling me twenty-five times a day. Compulsive doesn't start to describe her, or me for that matter, because I was soon calling her as much. We were at it, mate. Soon I had to go on a tour of the US and saw her in New York before she went off on some mod-elling job. One night I played this club in Philly and looked up and there on the dance-floor getting into it was Val Kilmer, who I got to know really well, meeting up with him in LA later on. Val hooked me up with Josh Evans. Josh is another amazing person, the son of the legendary producer Robert Evans and a great director in his own right. He's been such a pal and we've had some high old times.

Josh Evans: I was working on this film project with Val Kilmer and mentioned that it would be great to have the music done by Goldie. He said: 'Are you kidding? He's one of my favourite artists.' So Val introduced us. Goldie and I come from very dif-ferent backgrounds but I've been there for him and he's been there for me. When we get together we don't talk about the past that much, it's much more about the future. And if it wasn't for him I wouldn't be with the girl that I'm with today. Goldie has that kind of effect on your life.

The same night I met Val I got a call from Naomi saying that she wanted to see me in New York NOW! So the tour manager, Cliff White – or the Bull, as I call him – organised a car and we drove the two hours to NYC. It was getting later and later and she was on the phone shouting: 'If you don't get here soon that's it!' And when I got to Naomi's place, because it had taken longer than she wanted, she refused to answer the door. So I'm straight into nigga-black mentality, hammering on the door, shouting: 'If you don't open the door I'm kicking it in, understand? Simple! End of story!' Finally she let me in but it showed what our relationship was about. She was very demanding but I wouldn't stand for any of her shit. I was bang into gear at that time but I wasn't having it, I wouldn't let her destroy me. There is a great woman inside her who needs looking after. I'm a ghetto youth who appreciates where he has come from, and my thing with her was: 'Can you still remember Naomi? You're from Streatham and don't forget it. I don't care how much paper you've got.'

Naomi's a cool person but she needs to be herself. It was the same with me around that time; I wasn't even me. I was drug-fuelled and crazy as fuck. I was doing far more gear than she was.

Pete Tong: As his celebrity rose and rose and rose, Goldie got more and more carried away with who he'd become, and his new friends.

I did start to spin out there but for someone like me – the kid with the suitcase packed and ready to go, remember? – all of that whirl became difficult to turn down, particularly when it meant I was getting paid.

I did everything; helped Donna Karan launch her Old Bond Street store, appeared in fashion shoots from *Vogue* to *FHM*, appeared in ads and on catwalks for everyone from Levi's and Evisu to Versace, Alexander McQueen and Stella McCartney, was given membership to every club, and, all the while, every hotel was bending over backwards to have me use them for location shoots because they knew that people would pay attention when they saw me mentioned. I mean, it still goes on today, and that's part of being a celebrity, but now I've got a grip. Then it was out of control. Award shows, premières, club launches, parties, night after night. And who wouldn't go? Would you back off, saying: 'Oh, I'm washing my hair tonight'? I doubt it. Also, for me it was giving the finger to everyone from my past, everyone who had doubted me.

Pete Tong: There were two levels of resentment, the really dangerous one building from the people who had put him there in the first place.

After I finally finished *Saturnz Return* I sorted out some of the things in my private life. I made the calls and arrangements and reunited my mother and father after twenty-five years – my dad was over to see his brother, my Uncle Melsy, who was ill at the time. I put them in a room and took a picture. I had one of my sons, Jamie, there, so I could say: 'Hey, that's your granddad.' It was physically hard to face that. But once that was over I could finish the album and take another breath. That was the last page, the epilogue.

So the album finally came out in the spring of 1998 and I did take a beating.

Josh Evans: He took an emotional beating over *Saturnz Return* which I think was so unfair. Fuck, man, the record was incredible! No one can deny that 'Mother' was a great song. I remember sitting with him in the penthouse of the Royalton and he played it for me at three in the morning. That was a powerful experience.

Bowie was the only one who had told me that would happen. He forewarned me when we worked together that I was going to get a lot of stick for it, but it was important for me to swim upstream, against people's preconceptions.

Noel Gallagher: English people, and especially spotty students in the English press, don't like people from council estates like him and me going out with Naomi Campbell or selling twenty million albums. That's wrong, particularly because we're not shy, introverted student types. We're from council estates, we don't give a fuck!

One night I was out with him and he had the editor of the *Melody Maker* up against a wall in the Met Bar. He called me over and he was telling this guy: 'Go on, fucking say it to his face!' about some slagging they'd given us. I was on a peace and love one that night, so I wasn't looking for trouble, but the guy was stuttering: 'Er, well, I just didn't like the album . . .' Goldie didn't lamp him or anything but he scared the living daylights out of him, which is good because he deserved it.

When we went out on the road again Mark Sayfritz became important because he's the kind of guy who's a total professional but he's a right laugh, so we were blowing thousands on the roulette tables in Vegas, shagging the dancers on the tour bus in Rio, São Paulo, throwing blow-up dolls on stage while Perry Farrell was performing, having a laugh in the hot tub in LA. Mark's hardcore, but he was really important in making shows like the one we did at Heaven work. That was very important for me because I was returning to the place where I had first encountered the music, during the days of Rage, and what made it even better was that Noel joined us on stage.

Noel Gallagher: That was an extremely mad night, man. I knew it was important to him because he kept on going on about it when they had Rage there, but it really brought home to me how many people the geezer knows. At the after-show I must have made a thousand friends. He kept on coming up to me and introducing me to people: 'This is Fabio, and this is Grooverider, and this is . . .' I was worn out from all the handshaking.

Overall, the critics didn't like *Saturnz Return*, and once it was done I was exhausted. I did the 'Mother The VIP' mix for *Ring Of Saturn*, which included my only cover, 'What You Won't Do For Love'. Then I decided to carry on with a third album, but it just wouldn't come together. And you know why? I hadn't taken on board that by recording 'Mother' I'd carried out an autopsy on myself, but I forgot to sew myself back together. The tray wasn't quite within reach and the scalpel had dropped to the floor. It felt like: 'Oh, fuck, there go my insides again!' I had to inch my own way towards that tray and sew myself back together again; it could only be me who could do that.

Storm: You could tell Goldie wasn't happy during that period. I always say about *Saturnz Return* that there's an album in there, you can almost hear it, but it's buried. And what was weird was that when he came back from the *Saturnz Return* tour he literally looked five inches shorter. Flogging himself to death promoting the album had really taken it out of him. The spark wasn't in his eye and Kemi and I said to him: 'What's happened? You look terrible!'

Saturnz Return sold more than a hundred thousand copies, but I did feel a bit let down that people hadn't shown enough understanding. But it was a very tough album where I wanted to explore and confront a lot of tough things in my life. On the lighter side Chance had come into my life, although my relationship with Tracy wasn't helped by the fact that I was out there a lot, and out of my head a lot too.

One other good thing was that I had realised while making the album that I had to get out of town, away from the temptations and the pressure, if I was to survive. I decided to move into a large house in a quiet lane in a sleepy village just north of London. Another reason was that I had all these aerosol cans and canisters of butane for my work, and the neighbours were really worried that if something set them off there would be an explosion which would take out the top four floors of Dorney!

Gus Coral: After about ten years of basing himself at my place it was time to move on, and I persuaded him to buy somewhere. I just told him: 'Before all the fucking money runs out, go and get yourself a house.'

It was time to leave. My Mercedes was always being broken into, but there was something else; I'd kind of finished my degree at the art college Gus had set up for me. So I was set up in this great place surrounded by countryside. For the little boy with nothing but a few singles and some pens and paper in his locker, it was a big move.

Pete Tong: Part of refinancing the deal was so that we could put more money in so he could move out of town. We started to plough on and do the third album, refinanced the deal again, and bought the studio in his house because a lot of the money wasted on *Saturnz Return* went to the big residential studios he used. A very strict deal was organised so Goldie had to come in and see the head of business affairs here and the idea was to look him in the eye and say: 'We go once round here. You fuck up and that's it.' There was enough money in the deal and we hired two people to work with him, including a classically trained pianist. He did make a really promising track for the movie *The Beach* which became 'Beachdrifta', which he released himself.

One thing which had emerged during the process of making *Saturnz Return* was my will to make a film not only about my life but also encapsulating all of my philosophies. Now called *Sine Tempus*, it's taken me three and a half years to get it fully developed, but with hindsight I can see this is why the third album did not come together at that time. I wasn't ready, as the film project took hold of my imagination. When something isn't sitting right with me, I have to say it. The record company had been badgering me for more commercial material so I kind of went: 'You know what? The album is not ready!' The proof's in the pudding – if I had been ready to make *Timeless 2* at that time, I would have taken it to Polygram or whoever and I'd be on the road again, away from Chance. After we didn't really get anywhere with recording the third album I put a break on making music. I'd gone from hardcore club sounds to contemporary classical in a few short years.

Also, this was the time when I really started doing a lot of drugs, and I felt very powerful, which scared me. That was when the increasing darkness that had entered my life really took over. I'd been bang into gear for years on end, having been introduced to cocaine through a big player in London in the eighties. I asked him what it was like and he said: 'Imagine that you're a super lawyer and you know everything. That's what cocaine is like.' So I took a couple of lines and really got into it. When I went back to New York and hung with Brim, I did a few bits of blow and then, as you know, when I was in Miami most of my friends were big-time dealers, moving keys of the stuff. So it had always been around me, but during the nineties it really began to get a grip. I developed a love for it.

Pete Tong: He would talk about coke, and go up and down on it. But the problem with any addict is that however much you tell them, ultimately they can only handle it themselves.

The fame thing had kicked in with *Timeless* but during the making of *Saturnz Return* I was still really angry, and couldn't work out my relationship with my father and mother. I'd been through the ecstasy culture and rejected that because I didn't want to be happy. I wanted to be a womaniser, on the edge, doing more coke than anyone else. I was out there.

Gus Coral: I was slightly aware of his drug-taking. I thought that he did it much less than he actually did. I've got one or two interviews which I'd taped, when he wanted to talk about something, and he's obviously quite away there. But I never saw any behavioural problems. He was always ace number-one gentleman with me.

Coke put me on an edge which was familiar to my upbringing, all that angst. I always did coke on my own, never did it socially very much. And whenever I did it, I'd write things, pieces of prose and poems with titles like 'I Die Just Every Night' or 'I Cry Therefore I Am'. Soon I was doing an eighth of gear a night. I'd sell it and hustle it, but I didn't freebase or do crack. I just loved cocaine, pure and simple.

Wendy Mandy: Cocaine puts Goldie in the familiar state of the absolute loneliness, paranoia and anxiety of his childhood. But he is also drawn to it from a positive angle; it enables him to see the potential that his parents never saw in him. So he has the high of feeling that he can do anything but at the same time it puts him in the state of not feeling wanted, not because it is nice but because it is familiar.

When it got to an eight-ball a night, everything else came with it: sleazy people, bullshit talked for days. I was also playing heavy mind games, a game of chess with everyone. That peaked with the Latin sleeve notes for *Saturnz Return*. You translate them and they're about playing a game of chess. How fucked up is that?

Noel Gallagher: The coke definitely kept us awake longer so we definitely got to know each other well because we'd be yakking for twenty out of twenty-four hours. In a way it did help cement our relationship, but it brought out the crazy side of our natures. I had a couple of hairy moments with him when he got in a bit of a bad way over his kids. I come from a similar background – my parents were always rowing and they split up – and we talked about his a bit. With all the drugs we were taking we must have talked about it, because we talked about everything else – the pyramids, aliens and the existence of God.

I realised that maybe I should keep my distance from Noel a little bit. I'm too much for most people and he had to clean up his act, so I thought maybe it was time to leave him to it. The last time I saw him was at a première for *Snatch*, when it had gone pear-shaped with Meg, and we've kind of gone our separate ways, but we can still have a great laugh together.

At the height of my addiction I felt so disgusted with myself I'd bathe three times a night, obsessively cleaning myself. It wasn't difficult to see that it was all about self-loathing. Coke is like an emotion. You try to replace what you don't have with cocaine, but of course it doesn't work.

When I was really down there were just a few people there for me, including this Camden Town geezer called Dave, but I call him Flat Eric, because he's got a boxer's mug and whenever he's had a few he looks like he's going to fall over flat. So when that tune Flat Eric came out a few years back I christened him with his new moniker.

We'd knocked around the same haunts in Camden, places like Nicky & George's Golden Grill in Parkway where everyone used to go – Nellee, Howie, everyone – and I got to know Eric a little bit. The important thing is that he supported me when I was doing a lot of gear and had been let down badly by somebody close to me, so needed some dough to tide me over. Eric sorted me out because he's the kind of guy that, if he had £100, he'd give you £50. When you're Goldie and somebody has fucked you over for cash, it's difficult to go anywhere for help because of pride. But I could let my guard down with Eric, and I'll for ever be in his debt for that, because he was in my corner when a lot of other people were glad to see me down.

Obviously one of the reasons I got so into coke was that it numbed me, particularly about my non-existent relationship with my dad. So, as part of the healing I took a documentary crew over to Miami and confronted my father about what had happened. It was the most gut-wrenching experience and I'm still trying to get my head round it. He's still going on about what happened the night I was supposed to have seen my mother with Pusey, but what I wanted to find out was why I became the victim.

Clement Price: When I met your mother and she got pregnant I did all the work. And one day I got back and you said you had bellyache. So I asked your mother to get you some tea, and when she went you said to me: 'Daddy, Daddy, I'm not sick. I wanted to tell you I saw Mummy in bed with a man.' And that was Pusey, my best friend. And I thought: Oh Lord, not again. So I came back to take you away and they told me that you had been given to the social services.

I feel numb about my father. In a way I feel more hurt about the fact that my father wasn't there at all – at least I was reunited with my mother, but I had to track him down in Miami, and even then he couldn't come up with a decent explanation for his behaviour. OK, they had had their problems, but that still doesn't explain why I had to be given away. It's a mystery I don't think I'll ever fathom.

My dad said he had left to try and fulfil his ambition to be a minister, which meant that he couldn't be around us.

And then I found out he had another kid by a marriage in Jamaica, and called him Clifford Joseph Price, the same name as mine. I asked him why and he said that he'd done that in case one of us didn't live. How am I supposed to feel about that?

Wendy Mandy: In Goldie's mind it is very much his father's fault that his mother had to give him away; he's bought that story. His father was only acting as men from the Caribbean do. I think he has to process much more information on his dad. I think he is less angry about him than he realises. Probably because his father didn't do anything particularly destructive as far as he can see; he just wasn't there. But the tradition in the Caribbean is that it's much more about the mother, and the fathers come and go, the village looks after the children. Here we still have that Western nuclear family ideal. It's a different deal. But then Goldie did the same sort of thing, which is absolutely textbook.

I have no respect for him. I realise with him that I'm chasing a rainbow and there's nothing at the end of it. With Gus it was different. He didn't need to take me in and look after me but he did, and that's why he's always going to be Pops to me.

At the same time I was always asking the question: Do all women want to abandon men? Abandonment by women has been the story of my life. My mother left me, social workers who promised me everything would move on and never be seen again and my foster-sister Rowena abused me.

The worst thing was that Christine turned on me and cursed my life. I never got over the pain of Christine from all those years before. The only way seemed to be to womanise as much as possible. I was out birding it up all the time, down the Wag, getting fucked. I see girls now and think: 'Did I or didn't I?' I could go up to the Blue Note or later, when we moved Metalheadz, to the Leisure Lounge and get fucked.

Everyone did. I was blazing birds upstairs or even in the bogs. They were on tap. I had become this playa, out there every night cocked and blazing. But here's the news: it got me nowhere.

Gus Coral: Goldie's had a complicated relationship with women, but there again so have we all. Over the years we didn't really get into it much apart from a couple of occasions where I interfered. There was one incident, which I think sheds some light on one part of his personality. He cheated on this girl he was very close to, Rachel, and I told her when she asked. He was upset, but not unduly. He took it like a man. You wouldn't quite expect that reaction, but a stronger one. But he took it on the chin.

I met Rachel on the scene. She was very possessive and I didn't really give a fuck, to be honest. She knew I was going places and became quite dependent on me, and when that happens that's when I say: 'See you later.' I still think Gus had no right grassing me up, though; we were both banging girls, like two geezers do when they share a flat. I didn't think it was his place to go ratting me out, but maybe he was too much of a father figure.

Wendy Mandy: What happened with Goldie was that he worked out his relationship with women on a creative level, which is what artists do. But, as so often, they haven't worked it out in their own lives. So he may have been creating all this art about his life but he was basically dumping what had been done to him on all these people, exactly the same thing, abandoning them. He was hurtling about.

Just when I thought things couldn't get any worse, in April 1999 we all received a devastating blow when Kemi was killed in a freak accident. She and Storm had begun to peak as DJs, really making a name for themselves as a duo. They had just come back from an American tour and they were travelling in a car back from a gig in Southampton, a gig they didn't really need to do. That night the car in front of theirs dislodged a cat's eye, which flew through their windscreen and plunged into Kemi's head, killing her outright.

Storm: Kemi's death reunited me and Goldie. I had to be with someone who had really loved Kemi, which is why I called him first.

I heard about Kemi's death sitting on a mountain in Alaska, where I'd gone on a snowboarding trip with Damon Way of DC Shoes. We'd been heli-boarding, dropped out of 'copters on to a mountain in this surreal place, surrounded by mountains covered in snow. I went back to the chalet and I got a phone call from my brother Stuart just saying: 'She's gone.' I sat with Damon, screaming and crying. We made arrangements to get a private Cessna back to the mainland the next day, so while we were waiting I went up to ride the mountain. Zooming through the snow, I looked up and saw a cloud. It was in the shape of Kemi's head, with her familiar locks and a spliff. Somehow it made me feel good.

Damon told me later that he saw my aura that day, that I was surrounded by my violet aura in this pure environment. We flew back across the mountains and I sat in the plane with my head pressed against the cold window, playing the fourth track on a Sam Prekop Latin jazz CD, *The Sea & Cake*, time and time and time again.

I had reached rock bottom.

The thing was that the three of us – me, Kemi and Storm, who lived in what we called 'the triangle' around Alexandra Palace – always thought that I would go first, mainly because of this incident years before in Crouch End. One night I walked into the bedroom and there was this blackness there, a really weird feeling. I looked across at the wall, and it was as if a shade had been there, a trace of something bad. Kemi was lying face down on the floor with a look of absolute terror on her face. It was like some kind of fit. I put water on her face and she came round, saying that something black and evil was in the corner and it was pressing down on her. Honestly, we hadn't done any gear, this really happened.

About a week later I was in the bedroom with her and I felt something black and heavy moving towards me and I just couldn't move or speak. All I felt was extreme fear. Kemi reckoned it was death coming for me via her. But she was wrong; it claimed Kemi first. And what registered really hard with me was that Christine was responsible – this was dark magic at work again, man.

Storm: We always thought that he would die first, and even talked about it during that last tour we did in America for our album, which had this really dark atmosphere to it; things kept on going wrong and I felt really ill, getting angry at people for no reason. Something definitely didn't feel right. We had this talk in this hotel in Tampa, Florida, about how Goldie had kept on inviting us to the house but we hadn't made it and Kemi said that his life had become so mad that she really felt he would die in a plane crash. She said: 'As soon as we get back we'd better go to Goldie.' Our plan was to go and see him on the Sunday night, and she died on the Saturday.

At her cremation I read a poem I wrote for her and we all cried so hard. It's still difficult to believe that she has gone. Kemi's death came as a blow to us all and hit me particularly hard.

Storm: He was in pieces at the funeral, which was very difficult for him. Maybe there was some guilt there over their break-up, because he really did love her. I think he was thinking: And what if . . . and what if . . . ?

We all played a memorial night for Kemi a couple of months after she went at, appropriately enough, Heaven, the very place where she introduced me to music. Along with Storm, Grooverider, Jumping Jack Frost and 4Hero, I played my heart out for her. Even though we had split many years before, we had always been in touch. She was in many ways my Angel.

AND SO TO THE RELATIVITY OF TIME... DISTANCE SPACE NOT SO MUCH IN ITS
ACTION AS WE KNOW BUT FOR WHERE WE, THE INDIVIDUAL SOUL LIES, AND
ONE'S OWN CONCIOUS, THUS CONCEPTUAL. ABYSSICAL CHORD OF LIFE.

I LOOK THROUGH MY PRISM TO TRY TO FOCUS ON PURE LIVING WISDOM... AND
THINK HOW FRAGILE WE REALLY ARE, YET THE INTERNAL POWER AND POSITION,
MAN HAS OFTEN, THROUGH TRUTH AND WAR..... ARISED ON..

I SEE THE ANT 30FT AWAY, DO I CONCIOUSLY GO TOWARDS ITS FORM AND
CRUSH IT?, OR UNCONCIOUSLY THROUGH ITS OWN CYCLE, END ITS LIFE??

I PONDER FOR THOSE MAN MADE SECONDS... TO THE ANT, IT WAS 300 YEARS,
OR 30 YEARS? TO ITS END... IN RELATIVITY TO MY FORM IT WAS ONLY
30 SECONDS TO ITS FATE.... SO I PONDER AGAIN... AND LOOK AT THE STARS
THE EXPLODING STARS... THE FIRES THAT HAVE BURNT, BURNING, BURNING
OUT... 'BEGINNING'... ENDING? THE SLOW PHOTOGRAPH OF THE UNIVERSE...
THROUGH THEIR DISTANCE, LIKE THAT OF THE ANT, 3 MILLION LIGHT YEARS AWAY
3000 YEARS AWAY - THE RELATIVITY IS SOMEWHAT THE SAME. THEY ARE
ALREADY THE PAST. SO, I LOOK THROUGH THE PRISM OF MY OWN CONCIOUSNESS
AND CONCLUDE, WE ARE YET SIGNIFICANT IN OUR OWN INTEREST. BUT IN
RELATIVITY TO THE EVER CONCIOUS UNIVERSE, A SPEC OF DUST.

I CONCLUDE YET MORE TO POSITIVELY SATISFY MY OWN FORM, WHETHER I JUST
BEGIN THE SLOW BURN, WHETHER I BURN AT MY HOTTEST POINT, OR FADING
OUT, LIKE THE STARS, OR ARRIVING AT THE COMPLETE WHITE GLOW OF ENERGY,
WE ARE JUST "BURNING" AND THAT IS ALL TO ENSURE WE CAN PHYSICALLY, AND
POSITIVELY COMBUST LIFES SOURCE AND DECIFER FROM ALL FORM, AFTERWARD
POSITIVE SHIFTING ENTIRELY, IN WHAT WE SOMETIMES CALL 'SOUL' THE CONCIOUS
SOUL THAT IS... THE GEARBOX OF THE UNIVERSE, THAT MAY BE
ONE DAY I WILL BE ABLE TO DRIVE AND SHIFT,, INFINITIES REALMS....
ONE DAY IN TIME HOPEFULLY I WILL MASTER MINE

WHAM!! JUNE 98..

Ⓡ

Colder . MRDKUS

9: Aurum Metallicum

Goldie comes to terms with his demons and his past by successfully seeking help for drug addiction. Respite from a hectic schedule of DJ and acting commitments, including EastEnders, is found in his country mansion with his partner, Sonjia Ashby. He also works on a range of projects including a new album and an autobiographical film.

THE PHARAOH EXISTS,, A DARK FORCE, MANIFESTS THIS PURELY....
THE INSTRUMENT, FOR THIS FORCE CAN DWELL, IT CANNOT
REACT IN ITS VOID, ITS TRUE EVIL CAN ONLY BE SEEN IN ITS
EMBODIMENT OF THE FLESH... TO LIVE ...ITS DESIRE~ IN FORM ,,
THE PURE FORM OF ENERGY THAT EXISTS IN OUR TRAIT
TO SURVIVE... OUR INSTINCT.. FOR TRUTH, AND CONCIOUSNESS..
GROWS WITHIN US ,,~ THE PHARAOH, HOWEVER MUST TO LONGIVITATE
ITS CYCLE FROM BEGINNING,, TO DECEIVE, CONFUSE,, TO WAR THE FLESH..
CONDITION OUR EXISTANCE .. DISSOLVE OUR BELIEF .. OUR FAITH,
MANIFEST~BETRAYAL, OUR SELF DENIEL. ITS OWN PURE EVIL
CANNOT REACH ,, "THE BEYOND".. THE PURE SPIRITUAL ENERGY
OF INFINITY ~ AFTER DEATH,, IN ONLY THE "FRACTAL" OF LIFE~
THIS BREED CAN LIVE.. THE NECESSITY TO SURVIVE, CONTRADICT,
CONFUSE ..CONCIEVE.. THERE IS NO NEED FOR THIS TO BE WHERE
IT CANNOT BELONG. FOR IN ITS OWN SELF DENIEL THE INTERNAL
ENEMY IS BUT ITSELF.. ~ ITS SPIRIT IS VOID .. VACUUMED,, CRUSHED
IN THE EXPLODING REALM OF AN EXPANDING UNIVERSE OF
POSITIVE MATTER,, AND SPIRIT OF ENERGY.

THE VOID IN ITSELF MUST LIVE, FEEL AND JUSTIFY~THROUGH,, THE EYES
OF PHAROAHS ~ UNBEKNOWN TO THE FLESH THAT KILLS TO SURVIVE....
LIES THE MAN... UNCONCIOUS ..INCEPTING.. THUS~ IS THE DOORWAY FOR
WHERE THIS PURE EVIL CAN DWELL..
IN THIS THE GREED WILL BREED ~ THIS TIME AND SAND IS RUNNING
OUT FOR BOTH FORCES..
FOR PURE CONCIOUSNESS, TO GAIN FROM THIS TIME, IN ONE MAN'S MIND..
THE FREEDOM TO DEFINE IN SHAPE AND SOUND.
FOR THE VOID ~ TO GAIN IN THIS TIME ...
TO FORCE THE HAND OF MAN IN SCIENCE...ITS FEAR TO GO BEYOND,
TO CREATE THE ARTIFICIAL WOMB, TO CONFOUND FAITH, AND BELIEF OF
THE MIND, AND MANIFEST IN THE FLESH, THAT MAN BE BAT MAN...
AND THIS IS ALL I AM,
THERE WAS ENERGY BEFORE MAN....
THERE WAS A VOID BEFORE MAN ~..

I KNOW WHERE MY SOUL STANDS.

'll admit it: I am confused, I am intense, angry, poetic, I'm all of those things. I'm a man of extremes, so there's no grey area with me. If I go on a bender, I GO on a bender, but if I straighten myself out, I STRAIGHTEN myself out, and now that the healing has started, it's given me balance. A lot of kids out there look up to you and you think: If I can't help them, what can I do? So I want to at least give them some hope or show them a way.

Stuart Meade: He is like a father figure to me, even though he's my brother and is eleven years older. On my birthday recently he bought me about a grand's worth of clothes and gave me cash, and he's always giving me things because he is a really caring person. But at the same time I've had the best laughs with him, only the ones you can have with your brother, do you know what I mean? Playing computer games for hours, going on a bike ride, just getting up to loads of things.

After *Saturnz Return* and Kemi's death, I knew that I had to rebuild myself, and that the only way was to face the reality that I was a coke fiend and then handle it, stare it down. I realised that I didn't need to be on the edge that cocaine brought me any more, and that I had to build myself up in healthier ways. But I didn't want to go through rehab – that's for losers, like getting a badge from teacher. I was hanging with a friend of mine, Steve Brookes, at his hairdresser's, Cuts, and maybe one too many times I'd turned up looking a bit the worse for wear after the night before. So I said to him: 'I can't do this any more.' I'll always be grateful to Steve that he turned me on to Wendy, a specialist in Chinese medicine who really changed my life. That's why I call her my spiritual mother.

Wendy Mandy: I do treat celebrity types but I try and avoid that sort of thing because they behave badly. They don't turn up, they always want you to deal with their PR company or their PA. It's actually very depressing because they're all over the place. But Goldie's different. It was a nice street-level introduction, very much from a friend who he trusted. My client Steve told me his friend wanted to see me, and didn't give me any background, so when he came in I didn't even clock that he was the person who made *Timeless*. But I did think: This guy's great, I want to work with him. I thought that I had to take him on and be there for him, even though he would mess me about and shout at me. People come to me when they want to integrate their body, mind, emotions and spirit, and he no longer wants to be split between Goldie that takes coke, that plays music, that DJs, boyfriend of Sonjia, father of Chance. He's like the others who come to me when they want to be self-sufficient and responsible for themselves. To a certain extent, for Goldie I'm a safe haven. He can throw bricks at me, fuck me around and I will stay in the same place.

The first few times I went to see her I'd say to Steve that nothing seemed to be happening. She'd apply acupuncture to the points which were supposed to allow my mind to flow. Chinese medicine and healing is all about working on those points of your body which reflect what's going on with you spiritually. I guess maybe I expected a more immediate re-action. Probably I wind myself up all day, and a lot of what I go through with Wendy is the opposite; it's about releasing. Steve was great because he explained to me that I couldn't expect an instantaneous result. He told me: 'Wendy's like a shaman. She can guide you but you have to find out for yourself.' I'd spent so much time feeling fucked up at the expense of others and now I was in this place where I felt I had to prove to myself that I could gain that complete balance.

So I stuck with it and gradually we began to talk about all the aspects of my life and she started to prescribe me homoeopathic remedies.

While I was establishing my relationship with Wendy I began to wake up to the fact that many areas of my business needed addressing. The final straw was when the tax people turned up and said that they wanted to repossess my house because I owed them £290,000. It was unbelievable to me, and I realised I had to get out of my situation regarding management, the label and the club. I also realised that I had played my part in fucking things up, whether it was relationships or the label. So I had to deal with it.

I had put making music behind me, mainly because the *Saturnz Return* experience was so draining. I'd kept on DJing, largely, on the back of Blue Note and the Metalheadz nights, and found fans from New Zealand to Bulgaria, from Detroit to Tokyo, wanting to hear me spin. But Metalheadz was beginning to come apart. There was a lot of infighting and, to be frank, I wasn't around enough. For a long time when things were going wrong at the label I was on the road in the US supporting Perry Farrell, out of my mind every night and not wanting to get involved in the bickering going on back home.

Storm: The main thing he gave to Metalheadz was making it an extended family. He's great at nurturing people; he really wants to be the father of it all. Everybody wants to work with Goldie; you're going to see the good, the bad and the ugly, possibly all in one day, or maybe in the same hour if you're that lucky!

But when he wasn't around things started to go seriously

wrong. A lot of the people originally involved, like Doc Scott, were pushed out of the picture while certain artists were discouraged from contacting him directly, especially if they were going to whinge about money.

Eventually I left because it was turning really sour and my relationship with Goldie had fallen to bits. I spent my time trying to get hold of him to talk to him about label and club business, and when I did, I was going through all these things which had gone wrong. He just thought I was getting on his case, so what would happen is that we would row. Eventually, something happened in the office one day and I just walked.

As things were getting out of control at the label, my relationship with my manager Trenton also crumbled. He could manage Goldie the producer, but he couldn't manage Goldie the artist, who wanted to do so much more.

Pete Tong: Although I saw Goldie's dark side I always had a great relationship with him, maybe because I never went into the difficult areas too much. Trenton had to confront all the issues, and maybe that's what caused the end of their relationship. And maybe there were problems with tax or whatever, but Goldie knows what he got up to, and knows he can be a liability! Unfortunately what was going on in his private life started to have an effect. We'd have a great meeting and everyone was hyped up and then . . . nothing would happen. That's the sign of somebody who is caning it too much and has got his life upside down. What used to hurt was people slagging him off to me, people who used to love him so dearly. He even fell out with Grooverider for a long time, and Kemi's death really knocked him, because by that time Metalheadz was coming undone. What didn't help was that the whole drum'n'bass scene fell down around him. He was probably one of the only people who could hold it together, so with him removed for a time, and being so crucial, it was bound to suffer.

Metalheadz basically came to a stop and then I finally dealt with Trenton. There had been this plan for me to be managed in the States by Ice T's manager, who had got Ice into a mini-series on television, and I was hooking up with people like Billy Zane, Val Kilmer and Josh Evans and had contributed to soundtracks such as *The Jackal* in collaboration with J. Majik and *Spawn* with Henry Rollins, so the film possibilities were opening up, but Trenton wasn't up for being a film agent or working with an American manager. Add to that the fact that I was beginning to see the light as I got a grip on the drugs. So one day I caught up with Trenton in a park in Knightsbridge and said: 'That's it. It's over.' I felt let down. Trenton didn't have any experience of drugs but I still felt that as a manager he could have tried to help me stop. He was very much a father figure to me but I felt that he'd failed me by not carrying me somewhere for help.

The interesting thing about the power that comes with fame is that people become fascinated by you, in awe of you, and it's not good, especially for somebody like me. I find it stifling, and then the kid in the home comes out. I put the catches back on the suitcase and I fuck off out of there. And I'd just done it again.

Pete Tong: Eventually we parted in 2001. The last six months of our relationship were after he had split from Trenton, which was a blow to me as well. It just petered out. When we did finally call it a day we had a really good long talk and I was happy that he was getting into acting. He is an artist. Music is just one element of his abilities. I don't know whether he has the patience to do the dog-and-pony show which comes with selling a record. He should be proud of *Timeless* and 'Inner City Life' in particular because it was so ahead of its time. The Radio One of today would consider that to be a 'recurrent record', one that is such a classic it is programmed into the computer and played again and again.

My treatment with Wendy must have been working, because I took control of my career completely. After Trenton and I split I started managing myself and then was introduced to the person who now handles the business side of things in my life, Colin Young.

I met Colin through this character Dermot Smythe, who I go way back with. Dermot's another switchboard operator, plugging people into one another, and always trying. God loves a trier and I have enormous respect for Dermot, because he thinks on his feet. I was in LA one time doing a show and Dermot appeared out of nowhere and said: 'G – look what I got you,' and presented me with a *Star Trek* stun gun, an original from the series! We'd never talked about it, but he just knew I'd be knocked out by that.

So when Dermot found out my bacon needed saving over Metalheadz falling to bits, he plugged me into Colin, who is pretty square, in a tie and a suit, but you need that from someone in a business role, not a cat with locks falling out of his head, wearing DC trainers and trying to be down like some old-skool Aswad geezer.

So Colin may look like a super-geek during the week but catch him on the weekend when he's out on the open road on one of his motorbikes and you're fucked. The super-geek becomes super-freak. He's a real playa, very level-headed, and respects me for what I am.

Another major part of the team is my assistant Jessica, who is the missus of one of my closest friends, Moose. Jess is like a big sister, she's got a good vibe because she's a Scorpio and has balance, and she's very strong. What's important for me is that she is a woman I respect. So Colin handles the business, I handle the grit and Jess, bless her heart, carries the burden. And Moose himself has been one of the most important people to me in the last three years. When I was really down on my luck and holed up at my house in

Hertfordshire, Moose was there for me and made me realise that a lot of the people around me weren't good. Moose simply said: 'You've got to decide, bruv, it's either you or drugs. What do you want to do with your life?'

Moose once dropped me off at Wendy's and she spotted him from forty feet away through the window. 'That guy's Moose, isn't he?' she asked. 'He's a good guy, he's good for you.'

And Moose got me training three days a week, turning up at my house and taking me to the gym. At the time I hated it, but now I go on my own and train with my pal Rhino. Moose is a lifer and a gentleman and he's the only person I'll move with, he's true to the game. I don't like hanging with people so much any more, and, in fact, if you check out my history, I've always been a bit of a loner. I may have always had a crew, a team and a family around me, but I always felt alone, and now I'm facing up to that a bit more. I'm not the kind of person who's always inviting people back to my place for a party.

All of which is a long way from my reputation for only hanging out with other celebrities and going to parties all the time. It makes me laugh, because it's so blown out of proportion. There have been loads of stories that came out of nowhere, linking me with girls such as Mel B, Natalie Imbruglia and Stella Tennant. Nine times out of ten it would be because we were photographed at some party, but with Stella it was slightly different. Not that we had a fling or anything, but we made a good team visually for fashion shoots, and I've got a lot of time for her. We were among the first of those models from opposite walks of life who'd be shot together. It worked really well, and we were photographed by great people.

But I haven't been to the Met Bar for fucking years and I never shagged Kate Moss, we're just good friends. But we were part of the crazy gang – those were mad days.

One of the experiences which helped me along the way to recovery was the making of *When Saturn Returnz*, the Channel 4 documentary I have mentioned a few times in this book. I had put myself through it the first time orally, by making the album. Then I put myself through it visually, making the documentary and confronting my parents on camera about what they had done.

There are thousands of people who have been through similar experiences to mine, but given the opportunity to investigate them, they would leave it alone. The documentary was unbelievably hard to make. I got through it and, yes, maybe you can say it was brave of me, but it was very painful.

The documentary was great in many respects; meeting up with Birdy, watching Gus talk about my graffiti and the experience of making *Bombin'* all those years ago, having Bowie and Noel take the piss. It was also very important to see Brim again in New York. That and meeting his son all grown up was an affirmation for me, showing that someone with B-Boy instincts can continue to inspire me.

When Saturn Returnz did put many things in my life into perspective. Going back to Croxdene Children's Home only to find that the building had been knocked down was like going back to school and finding the bully ain't so big and tough as you thought. It showed me that not only had I survived it, I had outlived it. There was a maths teacher at Frank F. Harrison school who I absolutely hated and who had persecuted me, and when I went back to the school to film there I found out that he was long gone. It was like it was over and I was free of my past finally.

But with hindsight I can see that, even though I was working through this stuff at an intellectual level, I didn't deal with it at the primal level. I have this phrase I've made up: 'the abyssikl chord', which is the thing which is within all of us, connecting us to life. I thought I was addressing that 'abyssikl' chord and dealing with the primal wound, but I didn't realise how deep that wound cut. It doesn't matter how much I intellectualised things by working on my relationships with my parents on *Saturnz Return* and in the documentary, I have only in the last couple of months been able to forgive my mother for what she did.

I thought I could make an album about my family at a distance, baring my soul to all, and then wrap it up, listen to it, and that would be it. Then I thought I could top that by making a documentary about it all. But when I put my parents on camera I was denied the answers. During the film my father came up with excuses. But he never answered the question: 'C'mon, Dad, what did you do to make her do that?'

My dad wouldn't tell me about what happened, and even the crew started asking him to be truthful. I felt that his ignorance had allowed him to bury his past, and I don't ever want to be like that.

And now I'm going through the process for real. One of the things I've learnt from Wendy is that you have to go through it. If you try to advance the process – like maybe what I felt after recording 'Mother': 'OK, I've done that, so everything's fine' – you're still not actually addressing the root of the problem. By making the album and then the documentary I had tried to force the process, and it's only now that I realise that something as important as that can only be achieved at its own pace.

The only way I can be successful in my life is by going through the Saturn's Return myself. Saturn's Return is a bit like going through a car crash: you're in a car and you know it's going to crash. The car leaves the road and loses traction, the point where you're balanced in life. You have to take the guy out of the driver's seat so that you can take the full impact, crash the car and then get out and survey the wreckage. So making the documentary was reaching over for the driver's seat belt and releasing him, and putting myself at the place of full impact. And, in a way, once I was in the driving seat I could say to people like Björk: 'Look, you'd better get out because this is going to crash.' I didn't want to take anyone down with me and make them the victims of my process. It was no longer any use turning to the passengers in my life and saying: 'I'm sorry I put you through the windscreen.' And that had happened to a lot of people who had got on board with me. With Tracy, for example, I kept on pushing that situation by being a womaniser, which wasn't right. I had to face up and say: 'Look, this has to end. I don't want to put you through this stuff.'

Wendy Mandy: Like all stars Goldie's driven from a place of imbalance. In most A-types who are ambitious and want to succeed, there's a screw-up somewhere. What I like about him is that he's so bright that he gets things immediately. Like when he asked about Narcotics Anonymous and Alcoholics Anonymous, I explained, and instantly he said: 'Well, that's not for me, is it?' He totally processes therapy-speak. He is also very comfortable with fame and celebrity, which is the sign of somebody innately confident of their talent.

There's obviously a difference between fame and respect. But I think I have a different kind of fame from a lot of other people because hopefully I've shown that in some areas I've gained respect, whether it's through music, DJing, graffiti-writing, art or acting. You do get haters, but envy is a hell of a compliment, so that doesn't bother me. The funny thing about fame is that the penny never really drops. We walked into a film première the other day and there were cameras going off everywhere, people screaming 'Goldie! This way! This way!' and I muttered to the missus: 'It's fucking ridiculous, isn't it? This is just silly.'

Stuart Meade: Fame did change him, but only in the way that he recognised who was there for him now, and who had been affected by his fame. There were a lot of people who came out of the woodwork when he started getting his name in the papers. There was a lot of pressure on him, everyone calling at once.

Celebrity is brilliant. But there's so much more I want to do. I was cursed, but now I feel I've been blessed. Maybe I can give voice to those people like me, who had to sit in the TV room at Lew Joseph Children's Home, suppressed, silent, waiting for an opportunity.

Gus Coral: It's nice when you see him on the telly, on things like the *Jerry Springer Show*. It makes you feel proud.

It's weird because I became more famous when I spent a year doing nothing. I had this large amount of work behind me and I just said to myself: 'Stop.' But then suddenly there was this new level of fame. I'm more famous for being Goldie than for that work now, which freaks me out a bit. If I wanted to be silly famous I'd have gone to live in LA years ago.

Another big move was that I realised that what I really wanted next was to prove myself as an actor. So I got my agent and put the word out among friends, and soon things started to happen. The guy that made me think seriously about acting was Josh; he made me realise that I could do it. I'd been on that side of the camera as a subject in documentaries and I wasn't shy about it.

Josh Evans: He appeared in my movie *The Price of Air* and he was incredible. He also scored the music for it, which I took as a real tribute. The thing about him as an actor, as in everything else, is that he is tough on himself. He's so hard on himself he makes it work.

As I always say, all my life I've been acting as someone who always wanted to escape. People ask me: 'So how long have you been acting?' And I say: 'Thirty-six years.'

Acting in other people's movies allowed me to breathe again, and gave me a fresh start and a new perspective on my life. And what better way to start than as a gangster in a James Bond movie? My part in *The World Is Not Enough* came about because the casting director saw me in the little movie I made with Bowie called *Everybody Loves Sunshine*. It came to me in the weirdest way, through a guy I knew called Danny Price, who was a breaker from Breaking Glass back in the day. He told me his mate had a script which I checked out and went for and then swung it by Bowie.

Gus Coral: It didn't surprise me when he broke into acting. We worked on the *Timeless* script for a long time, remember. But he's going to hate me for this: I don't think his acting is as good as it should be. In life he's a natural actor, but on film it's not as convincing as I thought it would be. But he certainly has screen presence.

The director of *Everybody Loves Sunshine*, Andrew Goth (who also acted in it), got me to play the anti-hero, a villain called Terry Marsh, an ex-jailbird gangsta who kidnapped his cousin's bird, turned schizophrenic and started a war with the Triads. Quite a role, and all the time I was playing the part I thought about the people I've met in my life. That has happened a lot; when I act I'm just taking from one page in my life. If I want to play the gangster from America then I think about Tracy in Miami, or if it's a street cat then I go for the Yardie diamond-setter I worked with. I chameleonise.

What I liked about it was that it was a very British movie, not trying to ape American gangster films, but unfortunately it didn't quite hang together or find an audience. But it was a valuable experience for me, getting established in another arena and, of course, going head to head with Bowie, who played a rival villain, Bernie.

David Bowie: He's a damn fine actor with alarming presence, so filming *Everybody Loves Sunshine* was a hoot, although unbelievably freezing most of the time. We were stuck on the Isle of Man or someplace and it was bitterly cold.

Everybody Loves Sunshine was an OK movie, which maybe suffered from the fact that the director also wanted to be the star. But it gave me a break. I got a phone call from the casting director of the new Bond movie and arranged an audition, but read in the papers afterwards that Vinnie (Jones) had got the part. I thought: 'Fair enough, he deserves it.' Then I got a summons from the director, Michael Apted, and that was exciting in itself because I love his *Seven Up* documentary series, and there was a connection because he'd been at film school with Dick Fontaine, one of the guys who produced *Bombin'* all those years back.

I was only with him for about two minutes, but I got a call saying he liked me, but could I speak with a slight Russian accent? Of course I could! I was like: 'I'll speak fluent Guyanese if it means I get to be in a Bond film!' So they gave me the part of Bull, full name Bullion. I was the chauffeur to Robbie Coltrane's character Valentin Zurkovsky and it was great.

Working on the Bond movie was fun, not least because my teeth made sure that everyone made the connection with the Jaws character from the seventies, including Pierce Brosnan, who said about me: 'I wouldn't want to meet him in a dark alley – he'd probably bite me!'

And as I kept on saying at the time, the thing about appearing in the movie is that my kids and grandchildren will get to see me on TV every Christmas and New Year!

Working on Guy Ritchie's movie *Snatch* was a laugh as

well. One day during the development phase of the movie Guy called me and my pal Addie into his office to test-read for the two lead roles. Obviously we didn't get those parts but he did give us a slice of the action, with me playing the jeweller Bad Boy Lincoln.

Guy's really cool, even though we were having a laugh tussling on set one day and he started putting some judo moves on me, and I think he fell, so I chipped.

That was as close as I got to fisticuffs on the set, even though Vinnie Jones was reported as saying that he had had to slap me down for being cheeky. He's since denied it, which is a good thing because it never happened. I see Vinnie around because he doesn't live that far from my place and there's never been a problem between us, we're both cool with each other.

A lot of people knock Guy because they say that he's trying to be something he's not, because of his background. But I respect him, he's a Virgo, which means that he's a sponge, absorbing everything. He doesn't claim to come from the street but he is intrigued by it and I can see that because it is a very fascinating subject. I found that my fascination for it increased when I presented the *Gangs of War* series for Bravo this year.

While I was shooting *Snatch* I stayed at the Sanderson and occasionally he used to come back for a drink when the day was done. Through him I obviously met Madonna a few times; we'd go to a nice pub in town and she'd come along for drinks. I had already encountered her a couple of years earlier, when I was right in the thick of things recording 'Mother'. She had rung me to talk about producing songs for what eventually became the *Ray Of Light* album, which was of course largely produced by William Orbit, who goes way back in my story because it was at William's Cargo Studios that I had made some of my really early Rufige Kru tracks. We talked for a while and she said that she wanted me to fly to LA within the next two weeks, which was impossible, because all of my focus was on finishing 'Mother'. As much as I loved her music and admired her as an artist I couldn't go, because I was dedicated to making 'Mother' as strong and complete as possible.

And later on it was a pleasure to DJ for Madonna when she opened her Music tour with the live webcast from the Brixton Academy. She is really nice and I have a lot of respect for Guy. OK, I didn't get such a big role in *Snatch* but maybe my appearance in that helped in some way to land the part of Angel in *EastEnders*.

David Bowie: I've not seen him in *EastEnders* as here in the States we are about nineteen years behind on the series. I'll get to see him when we're both about seventy, I suppose!

EastEnders was different. I was attracted to it because my life is about extremes and *EastEnders* is about as far from James Bond as you can get. I think they needed a bit of an edge and I provided it. It's not exactly pushing my acting skills to the limit but it's a good laugh. My mum loves me in it and it just feels phenomenal to be part of it.

Margaret Pusey: The first time I saw him in *EastEnders* he seemed to be running around everywhere, which made me laugh, I don't know why, but good luck to him, he's done so well and I'm so proud of him.

I get recognised by old women in the street now and it's great when I drive around and hear people shouting: 'Oi, Goldie! *EastEnders!*' I think it works for me to be in it, but a few years ago, if someone had said I would be in Albert Square, I would have told them they were mad. Apparently the *EastEnders* casting guy liked me as a character and wanted to build something around me and it happened that easily and quickly.

John Yorke (ex-executive producer, *EastEnders*): I knew about Goldie because I had a copy of *Timeless* and I'd also clocked him in the Bond movie. At the time we were developing this gangster character, who was white originally, called Samuel, and the deadline was coming up to make a decision on who to cast. One morning the phone rang and it was his agent Lucy, who I've known for years, and she suggested Goldie for the part. I said: 'That's really weird. I was going to ring you today about maybe having him in the show!'

When they came up with the name Angel rather than Samuel I thought it was more appropriate – Angel was of course one of my early singles, if you cast your mind back a bit. And the criticism that I play up to a racial stereotype is bollocks. The way I play Angel is how it is. When I'm ready to play King Lear, I'll step up to it.

John Yorke: The nice thing about that was that it wasn't planned that way – Angel just seemed appropriate. We don't go about things in that tricksy post-modern way, so it's great that it came about through chance.

The most amazing thing about *EastEnders* is the set; it's so huge it almost has a character of its own. Now I've been on some big sets – the huge tank at Pinewood where they shot the underwater scenes for *The World Is Not Enough*, for example – but the experience of coming out of the station at Elstree and seeing the whole of Walford spread in front of you is quite overwhelming.

After you spend some time there, and then maybe drive into Borehamwood, you still think you're on the set, it's that difficult to know where real life starts and fantasy ends.

Almost every take I do in *EastEnders* I do first time. Two takes is the maximum it takes for me to get anything right. It's easy when the cast is so professional. They're the dog's bollocks. They're really, really, really, really wicked. The directors are shit-hot and Yorkie is really cool. He sets up this vibe so that everyone knows what their job is; he knows what he wants from the character and I know how to give it to him. I like that, because it gives me discipline.

John Yorke: Because we have a pretty tight-knit cast they do tend to be a bit wary of outsiders, but there was none of that with him. He was just Goldie from day one, and everyone accepted him immediately. The only thing that happened was that he once mistook a shoot time of 13.15 p.m. for 3.15 p.m. but I guess he's allowed to do that because he is timeless!

The welcome that I've received has been great, because, to be honest, I was a bit shy and hesitant about turning up there. But they're a nice bunch, particularly Steve McFadden, who plays Phil Mitchell, who's a really cool guy, a local Kentish Town guy. He used to go to Paradise with us back in the day and not long ago he and I took his Jaguar for a drive down the A1 in our lunch-hour. Actually, trying to jump the lunch queue is the hardest part of working on *EastEnders*!

John Yorke: Goldie has worked really hard on the part of Angel, and it shows in his performance. We were always a bit wary about casting a black person as a gangster but there were no problems. The audience really responded to him, not only because he's a good actor but also because he has this fantastic presence and he's so real. That's why we had him back on the show in the summer and will keep on featuring him, because Goldie made the part of Angel his own. You can't imagine anyone else doing it.

I'm going to keep on acting – I enjoy *EastEnders* and am looking at a major role in a film by a major director.

I also want to challenge the medium, from a technical

point of view. I've had my own film project, *Sine Tempus*, in my head for a long time now, and I wanted to get into acting to understand how you put characters together and what happens in front of the camera. I've been working on *Sine Tempus* for quite a while with my collaborator Nick Ciraldo.

Nick Ciraldo: I worked in LA as an art director for music videos and so forth and also worked for a couple of producers. I wrote a script for an independent production and then came over to London three years ago. I had a script which I was working on, and didn't really want to get involved in anything else. Then I met G in June 2001. He's probably the only guy in England that I would have put my own project aside for. I didn't know that much about his celebrity because I'm American, but I knew him from his music and artworks and I saw *Bombin'* years ago.

I haven't known Nick that long but we have a strong affinity – he was also a client of Wendy's, having been a hot-shot script editor in Hollywood, and she made the connection because I used to talk to her about the ideas I had for *Sine Tempus*. When we met we just fused because I had the vision, but I didn't know how to put it together.

Nick Ciraldo: What he already had was more akin to a philosophical thesis than a working treatment for the story he wanted to tell. I guess my role is as the ironist, challenging him and bringing out the human element to the story. That makes sense because one of the themes of the film is the irony of life. We have worked really hard on this project and it's going to be really special.

Sine Tempus is the story of a boy called Tru and his journey into manhood. His father Grant has been locked up, having been set up by his stepfather Blu, who starts selling heroin on the estate.

The central three characters are Tru, Grant and this old Rasta called Father, who Tru sits beside on a bench and learns from on his way to school. They are the three generations. Father may sit on his bench drinking his Tennents and garbling at people, but you play him at chess and he'll kill you. Grant tries to do the right thing by protecting his son and surviving by selling weed on the estate. Tru is the latest version of these men, learning how to be a playa from both generations, in the same way that I learnt from other people's mistakes and even from the sub-culture music I heard when I was growing.

There is also Tru's brother, an artist character based on me when I came back from Miami and saw England from a new perspective. The artist is challenged by the ghetto when Grant asks him to get Tru out of there. I was going to play the artist but now I've decided to direct I won't do that because it just wouldn't work. I know from my experience working on *Everybody Loves Sunshine* that the work suffers when the director wants to be a movie star as well.

Nick Ciraldo: As a white kid I grew up on the outskirts of New York while he grew up in the ghetto in England, so we work together by me asking questions from a point of innocence, which helps bring him to the truth of what he is trying to say. I'm constantly questioning him. One of Goldie's things is the complexity of the process and the ultimate achievement of sublime simplicity. He wants layers to *Sine Tempus*, and for it to work on many levels. The idea is that you watch it again and again and get more out of it. At times we think: Hang on, this is the complete gangster flick, and then it'll jump into something else and meld genres almost on a monthly basis as it grows. It feels immensely ambitious; I never would have attempted something like this without somebody like Goldie. The closest genre I can get to it is magic realism.

Sine Tempus shows betrayal, murder, love, anxiety, lust in a different way from how they have been presented in film. It is a reflection of my own story, in that Tru has an effect on the lives of people around him and I was the very curious kid that saw everything. Tru is never with his mother because she had a very complicated pregnancy – that's another way of showing how I had a very complicated start to my life. And when he is born, Tru's father picks him up and cradles him to his chest. That's the same as me having been fathered by the ghetto once I arrived back there.

Nick Ciraldo: *Sine Tempus* sums up Goldie's unique ability to enter chaos and emerge with the sublime. That's what our protagonist does. He comes from chaos and emerges with the sublime truth about life. The premise of the film can be taken as a family drama woven with a gang sub-plot. I have never tried to write a script like this before, but my trepidation mixed with his somewhat reckless courage is amounting to something pretty fantastic.

We've always likened it to giving birth; I'm the father coaching him and encouraging him, but for Goldie he has to go through it himself. And he wants to push the boundaries, conveying the message sometimes without dialogue but with corrupted and perverted sound and visuals. It will border on a music video art piece, mixed with a straightforward narrative.

Hopefully, the film works by making all these connections, and it has been, in a way, self-inflicted therapy. I've had to work out a lot about myself by creating it. And the aim is that it works in the same way that that film starring Tom Cruise, *Magnolia*, works, on coincidence and chance. My vision is to base the film on the environment of Heath Town but to do what I did with music. It is a very complicated movie, but in the same way that 'Mother' deserved classical music with urban breaks and beats, so *Sine Tempus* is going to be a new way of creating cinema. I want to blow the audience away and not make my own version of, say, a Spike Lee joint, do you know what I mean?

Nick Ciraldo: We have an extraordinary working relationship, mainly because he burns creative energy. It's remarkable what comes out of him. I present him with a scenario and set up the conflict and before I finish he's off and running with it, in character and freestyling. He will go fifteen minutes at a stretch in character, out of nowhere. Then he'll pop back out of it and go: 'Something like that, or should it be more like this?' And then he's right back in with more brilliant stuff.

I hope that *Sine Tempus* will do for film what *Timeless* did for music; it's going to make people go: 'Ohmigod! What happened there? OK, let's watch it again!' Me and Nick have ensured at the script-writing stage that every scene in this film is like a beautiful loop. In fact, we've honed it and honed it until every fucking scene is perfect. Every element is precise, even down to the numbers used and the timing of the sequences. Everything has to be counted and accounted for in *Sine Tempus*, because I aim to show you that time is irrelevant. What's important is the time you share with people and the energy you can exchange with them.

Nick Ciraldo: Goldie does have a lot of potential as an actor and he's really great to watch, but his real talent and his future lie behind the camera. It took me about six months to persuade him to the idea that he should direct as opposed to star in it. He also has concrete plans about who he wants as editor, as director of photography. There is obviously a benefit from his creative credibility because that means he can pull in a lot of very good people who want to work with him. He just has to make a phone call and they want to be involved because it's him.

In many ways I've been biding my time for the last three or four years, since I released my last album. I've been a wolf in sheep's clothing, working away on my acting but all the while imagining *Sine Tempus* into being. For me it is the single most important project of my life.

Nick Ciraldo: It's difficult to say how audiences will respond. Goldie's work is 'innocently didactic'. You always hear from people: 'I saw this thing he did and I never knew about that aspect of life.' Or: 'I've never seen the ghetto in that way.'

Apart from my work, the important thing for me now is that I am centred, grounded at my house. When I first moved into it I realised I was out of breath most of the time, because I had to go upstairs to get something! I'd never had an upstairs before. When I lived with Gus in Dorney Tower, it was in one bedroom and my dog learnt to shit on a ten-pence piece. Having space is probably more important to me than fame; that's why I knocked the walls through in the five bedrooms, because the confined space reminded me of my days in the home. I've got a beautiful indoor pool where I can swim and chill out, put classical music on. I can walk around here, breathe the fresh air.

I've always liked cars, ever since I got my first one, that Rover for £275 back in the day, and when Stuart was around we were always larging it in my BMW 850 Alpina which was just a beast, steroids with chrome, the works, which I get for all my cars.

These days I've got a pretty solid car collection: the Ferrari FI 355 Spider, a Porsche Boxster, a Mercedes ML and my Cosworth Mercedes, the car I bought with my first big advance. I have it completely sorted and it's in storage, but occasionally I'll bring it out for a run. The Ferrari is amazing because it's a full-on racing car, and you can have such fun in it. Once you get used to driving it, you realise that you don't have to go super-fast to get the best out of the Ferrari, because it's the coolest car for cruising.

I've also got the Monster 900 bike Ducatti gave me – it was the 100,000th they had made and they presented it to me a couple of years back when I went to Italy and did a couple of shows. Naturally it's painted gold and it's brilliant, a one-off. I've only recently taken my bike test, having ridden illegally for years, so I'm really putting it through its paces now.

Then there are my collections of clothes and trainers. The biggest part is my Stüssy wear; I must have thousands of Stüssy T-shirts, hats, shorts, jackets, everything. When Shawn started out, and when we all started wearing it back in the day, it was a weird hybrid of surfwear and B-Boy apparel and it just kept on evolving. I got my first Stüssy shirt in London from this guy Barnsley, who's really big on collectable clothing, and haven't stopped.

The interesting thing about Stüssy is that they're a fairly big company involved in producing large amounts of clothes, but individual items can be quite short runs, so there will always be a few bits and pieces that I haven't got. Stüssy pioneered the techniques picked up by Adidas and Nike and the rest of them, producing certain lines in certain territories, or putting out a few shirts here and a few hats there. It encourages you to go hunting. I have got some pretty collectable Stüssy: a waist jacket in a paisley design with the original tag, an orange T-shirt using their 'little kid' print, a rare fisherman's jacket with a swordfish on the back, a Stüssy 'sister' baseball cap which I keep for Chance, and a black short-sleeved T with the skull-and-crossbones motif printed all over it.

Even though Shawn has retired now, the guys who took over the company, Frank and Jim, always welcome me to their warehouse just outside LA, where I can pick and choose. As a result my loft is rammed full of clothes, and when I clear out the bedroom it takes me four days because there is so much clothing there!

Recently I was in a club in Miami when this guy appeared out of nowhere and handed me this pack of Stüssy cards, one of a limited run of only twenty. He said: 'Frank said I should search you out and give you these because he knew you'd like 'em,' and was gone. So my Stüssy stuff is growing all the time and I keep it all pristine, dry-cleaned and shrink-wrapped.

Much like my trainers. I try and wear a box-fresh pair as much as possible – if not every day, at least every time I go out – so I must have close to two thousand pairs now from all over the place, kept in their boxes and in fine condition. The real crème de la crème are these Adidas running shoes with Day-Glo strips on them. I think they must be a proto-type, because there's no Adidas logo on the inside. There is also this very rare pair of black leather and rubber water-proof Adidas Apparel trainers with a flap which covers the laces. I've never seen them anywhere else. Probably the ulti-mates are this pair of black Wilson high-top sneakers I got from DJ Milo when he and Nellee lived in Delancey Street, Camden Town. I bugged and bugged him and got them in the end. I just love collecting rare shit and now I have the space to keep all this gear because the house is nice and big.

Gus Coral: What is Goldie's talent exactly? It's very strange. He seems to have the ability to process things mentally while occupied doing other stuff. For example, he didn't do any graffiti for a year but when he started again, it wasn't from where he left off. He'd developed it in his mind during that period, and he'd actu-ally advanced without even doing it. I've seen that happen often. He zaps around and you wonder how he has had time to think about what he's going to do next, but while he's out there living it large, at the back of his mind is a computer processing away.

What happens with me is that I start at the point where I'm at, not where I've been. The only exception was when it came to drugs: my conceptual side outstripped my physical side. I became blocked and lost balance. I'd always had this jelly-fish thing going on, in that a jellyfish can be submerged at huge depths and still be electric, and I was the same. But with drugs I submerged myself for too long in the concep-tual side of things and when I surfaced I was exhausted and there was nobody on the shore to save me.

I'd drained myself on fucking loads of women and all it did was leave me feeling empty. One New Year's Eve I'd had my final blow-out with Tracy, and we realised it just couldn't go on. I was in the public eye a lot and there was a lot of pressure, and I think that got to Tracy, with me being out there all the time. It had all become too much between me and Tracy, and I can't blame her entirely because I was also an out-of-control womaniser. It's just that Tracy always picked on the women I hadn't fucked! She was always barking up the wrong tree! I wanted to go to her: 'Well, if you must know, it wasn't her and her, it was her over there and her there!'

Anyway, a few weeks later I saw Sonjia in a club and, I swear to God, it just flashed across my mind: 'This is the woman that I will marry and settle down with.'

Sonjia Ashby: I was living off the New King's Road, on a fashion course at Central St Martin's. I also had this little-girl group thing going with my friend Holly and some other girls, so I knew a bit about music, but, seriously, I had never heard of Goldie. One night me and a girlfriend went to Twice As Nice in Vauxhall and I saw Goldie looking at me with all his mates. We didn't speak – I mean, I didn't know who he was. And then this ex-boyfriend of mine turned up and I had to leave in a hurry, and, as we were in the car making a getaway, Goldie came running after us, shouting for us to stop like a maniac. We didn't. But then a few weeks later he came up to me in Emporium, again with all his mates around him. We got talking and he asked for my phone number. I gave it to him but told him he couldn't write it down, because if I was so special he would remember it anyway. He obviously did remember it because he called me the next day, but he had to go to Australia to take part in this tour.

It was fucking bad timing – I went straight off down under as part of the Big Day Out festival which goes all over Oz, but I couldn't get her out of my head. And this thing happened. I didn't want to shag around any more. I thought: Fuck this, there's this girl back at home I really like, what am I doing? I rang her every day, obsessively, compulsively. At first she was quite cold with me but gradually she started to thaw. When I got back from the tour she had to go to the Bahamas to see her family, but I got the number of her aunt's place and we just carried on our phone relationship. Then she returned to London and we went on our first date, *The Beach* première. I picked her up outside Harrods and for some reason I really prepared myself to impress this girl who didn't really know me. It wasn't the usual. I picked her up in the Porsche and she was wearing all white, looking gorgeous. I looked at her eyes and her freckles and I thought: Stay down in my light trousers!

Sonjia seemed so innocent but yet she had this wise quality. She'd been a dancer at Stringfellows but she just went there, worked and left, didn't get involved. I never saw her dance because she stopped when I started seeing her because she didn't enjoy it.

She was living with her friend Holly, who we arranged to meet up with on Valentine's Day. They were driving behind me on the way back to the house here and in Camden I pulled up at the lights and then there was an almighty crash. She'd gone straight into the back and the front of her MG was caved in. Her nose was pouring blood, so Moose and I got them into the Jeep and fucked off before the coppers arrived. We pulled over in a forecourt in Finchley Road and I took my shirt off to mop the blood off her. Then I went into the garage shop and bought her the biggest teddy bear I could find. She came back and stayed the night, and looked beautiful, even with bog-roll stuck up her nose and two black eyes the next morning!

Sonjia Ashby: So gradually we started seeing each other and I got to know how nice he is, how loving. After about a year I was spending so much time here, away from the flat, and we decided I should move in. And we've been living together ever since.

Sonjia is the love of my life and has taught me a lot. At the time we met things weren't right in my life, and in a way she was the passenger who stayed for the Saturn's Return car crash I talked about earlier. I realise that she braced herself for that ride and survived.

Sonjia not only saw me through that but she saved my life. It's that simple. She took the drugs off me and flushed them down the toilet and told me to sort my life out. She helped to heal me. And once I started seeing her I ironed out all my past relationships, girls I'd been seeing on and off, or in between times down the years. Girls like Sandra, who was originally from Derby, but I'd seen her on and off going back to when I was in the B-Boys.

With Sonjia it's something new to me: commitment. And no fucking about. I've even got rid of the black book. We had an Aztec wedding in Yucatan, a spiritual thing in preparation for the real event. A guide came across at one stage and pointed at Sonjia and said: 'She's a mystic, that woman.'

Sonjia and I want to spend the rest of our lives together. Although she's very young, she's a Scorpio and very mature. She showed that by withstanding what went on when I came off drugs. I was in a very bad way, walking around with a gun with murder and violence in my head, waiting for something to happen. She was strong with me, constantly challenging me, saying: 'Why are you doing this to yourself?'

Wendy Mandy: It doesn't matter who the patient is who's coming up the stairs as Goldie leaves my practice – if he flashes them a smile they'll have a good day. He's almost overwhelmed by his power, I think. That's why he runs around half the time, because he's drained by people. And he needs someone like Sonjia.

Sonjia will grow with me, it won't be that I will outgrow her. We're now married and celebrating our lives together after a fantastic ceremony – complete with three best men Moose, Whitey and Drax – which we planned for many months. I know that we will have two kids, and the first one will be a boy, called True.

I gave a copy of Górecki's Third Symphony to Nick Ciraldo and he played it to Wendy, as he sees her for acupuncture. When she heard it, she said: 'What is this? It sounds like *aurum*.'

Wendy Mandy: *Aurum* is, of course, the Latin for gold. In homoeopathic circles, the people whose constitutional remedy is *Aurum metallicum* are defined by characteristics which completely describe Goldie: the sensitive heart; isolation; relationship with a driven man; rage; the blackness; emphasis on physical appearance. In fact in the homoeopathic remedy book it says: 'Aurum people tend to have compact, muscular bodies.'

When I next went to see Wendy, she told me that by having my gold teeth I'd been prescribing myself my own remedy, self-medicating myself for all these years. 'You're a rare example of someone who has tried to heal themselves,' she said.

Wendy Mandy: He's also very phosphoric, which is another homoeopathic thing. Those people have short, sharp enthusiasms. He might meet someone and will get all worked up: 'Let's do this, that and the other.' And then he thinks about it and realises it was a mistake. He whips people up into this enthusiastic flurry. I gave him a lot of phosphorus and it has calmed him down, he's better, because he's spreading his energy while the *aurum* has gone very deep down to his rage – he's better now. And the acupuncture helps him to feel a 'natural' state akin to the one he feels on cocaine, which helps to wean him off that. When it comes to drug addiction, I feel that, although NA and AA are very good, people who go to them and successfully come off drugs are inclined to remove that addiction and put it somewhere else. So they give up coke, but then they smoke like a chimney, or are obsessive about vegetarian food, or physical training, or about their cars or having to have loads and loads of sex. But they haven't addressed their addictive nature. With Goldie we're aiming to really cure that nature, and he is now showing signs of taking responsibility for his life, particularly Chance.

I have an unbelievable relationship with my daughter Chance. She's four years old and a ball of energy, the most gorgeous thing in my life. I take pictures of her all the time. I want her to have everything I never had. My daughter comes up to me and pinches me, saying: 'Goldie,' and then runs off – she knows I'm going to chase her and tickle her because she knows she's not supposed to call me Goldie. I'm Father to her.

I have a box for Chance which I stuff with artefacts, because I never had anything from my own father, apart from one letter to my mother which I read years later, and a complete numbness when I met him. In Chance's box is the *Daily Mirror* from the day of the eclipse, which we watched together, and all kinds of other stuff: train tickets, plane tickets, pictures, postcards, letters telling her that I love her, a bedknob from a hotel room in New Orleans we stayed in.

Pete Tong: To be honest, I never got engrossed in his private life, although funnily enough he's one of the few artists I've had round at my house. He's funny, Goldie, because he is a very loyal, family-oriented person, very kind and loving. He's one of those people who always asks me how my wife and kids are.

Of my other children, Daniel, who's now seventeen, is a fan. Sadly we hadn't been able to have much contact over the years but he's very proud of me, and I painted a great big tag for him to show that I love him. Jamie's thirteen, a bit of a hood-rat, out in the street. I said to him the other day: 'I know I haven't been the greatest father to you, but I'm trying, I've broken the loop as much as I can. At least you don't have to travel across the world to come and find me at the age of twenty-one. I am here for you.' I understand that maybe if he gets into trouble he wants his father's attention, just the same as me when I was destructive as a child. I wanted them to acknowledge me. I also did a piece for him, I painted for him, and he and his mother Madge keep in contact.

About five or six years ago I found out that I had another child. Remember the girl called Reed who slept with all of us graffiti writers way back? Well, it turned out that she didn't have an abortion, and it further turned out that the boy was mine. I was in Wolverhampton in the mid-nineties and the word was going around that I had a son I knew nothing about. I contacted her brother, and he said: 'Yes, man, that boy is definitely yours.'

I met her soon after when she was visiting a friend in London. I took one look at the kid and just knew. He's called David and, sadly, he's autistic. I took one look at him and said: 'He's my son.' The kid has spent most of his life with his nan and I was infuriated because, if I'd found out earlier, I could have provided some help, sent him to specialists. But now at least I can provide maintenance and make sure he's looked after. In fact I try and make sure they are all OK. I give my children emotional support as well as financial.

Wendy Mandy: He's trying to focus now, get himself healthy. He's trying to stop being an addict and trying to sort out his emotional commitments. He's trying to sort out what kind of relationship he wants with Sonjia. He comes from a pretty working-class background which has injected into him that thing about just wanting to be a homebody with a wife and kids, but then there is the intellectual side which wants a partner who understands everything about him creatively.

But no matter what I've achieved materially – the cars, the house – fame to me is Arnie Schwarzenegger or Donald Trump or Tiger Woods. That's on a massive scale and that to me is fame. But I don't want that. I'm really getting back into making music again. Everyone has to take time out to re-invent themselves. Bowie is always telling me that, and if you think about it, he reinvented himself on the back of my music, the drum'n'bass scene. So I've been taking a breather to reassess and now I'm ready again, firing on all cylinders.

Noel Gallagher: I'm still cool with him and I expect to see him one day just on the street, him jumping out of the back of a van and putting me in a headlock. What was funny was that when I moved to Buckinghamshire, who, of all people, was living ten minutes away? My old mate Goldie! So it carried on. In fact, that's what you should have called this book: *Carry On Goldie*!

You know that nine was my significant number. Well it's also the number of completion, and, as I write this book, I'm thirty-six and three and six are nine, right? I do feel that I have completed a cycle in my life and my time adrift is over.

David Bowie: I think Goldie could make a go of almost anything he turns his hand to. He has got so much talent in a million different areas. Like so many artists who don't stay within the parameters of what they are first known for, Goldie gets really unfair criticism for working in so many different areas. He'll have the last laugh, though, as he's bloody good in most of them. And as the man said, they never erected a statue to a critic. Anyway, Goldie could sculpt his own.

Musically I'm back in the saddle with a new album called *Sonik Terrorism* which I'm making with Danny J, who used to work with J. Majik. Danny's the guy that I made 'Beachdrifta' with, and he's a genius musician. He can pick up anything and learn to play it, and he's become a really good producer and engineer as well. I've spent a year preparing this album, and he's been working with me at the studio at my house. He's helped me get my head down and seriously get back into music, because he's very patient as I deal with all the other stuff which is happening in my life. We finally have the studio mapped out, and I'm back doing what I want to do.

Sonik Terrorism is more down-to-earth and grass-roots than *Saturnz Return*, with songs like 'Ghetto Blue', 'India' and 'KMS' bringing out an open-minded musical approach, and I think that's because Danny is like a sponge in the best possible way – he'll absorb everything and he's prepared to try anything. I always need somebody to bounce off, and I've enjoyed that process with him. I kind of got an inkling that music was coming back into my life when I compiled the album *The INCredible Sound Of Drum'n'Bass* in late 1999, a fitting tribute to the last great musical genre of the last millennium which traced the trail we had blazed and pointed towards the future. Everyone was represented, not just me with 'Terminator' but also Doc Scott's pioneering 'Here Come The Drumz' and artists from Photek and Digital to Dillinja and 2 Bad Mice.

More recently Metalheadz has gotten back on track, with releases like the compilation *www.metalheadz.co.uk*. One of the reasons why we never really capitalised on the label or sold out is because I don't think the icon itself wanted it. I truly believe it is its own entity. Even when I wanted to capitalise on it something would go wrong. It wouldn't have it. The twelve-inches which we put out by people like Wax Doctor, Alex Reece, Hidden Agenda and Lemon D were just so strong. I had offers but I always listened to the echo of people like Russell Simmons at Def Jam and their ground rule number one: unless you own 52 per cent of your own label, don't bother. So 'Headz is still with us and it's survived, even stronger than before if that's possible.

Storm: People can't wait for him to come up with some new music, particularly on the drum'n'bass scene where things like 'Beachdrifta' showed that he's still got it. He and I talk a lot these days and we're over all the shouting that went down. It's just like Kemi always said: 'I'll be the thorn in your side for ever.' I get on well with Sonjia, she's really cool, but one time I told him: 'All the women in your life have left but I'm not going to, I'm going to be around for ever.'

On the musical side of things I'm finding a safe place where I have been able to work again, because I was lost for a long while. Every artist goes through it, and has to undergo reinvention. Now I'm inspired by people who are taking the scene forward, particularly guys like Total Science from Oxford, who've been in the game a long time with tracks like 'Oxford Hardcore', and Intalex, who I rate among the best for his DJ skills. There's also Future Cut, who I've also been working with on *Sonik Terrorism*. Future Cut are an interesting fusion of an African guy living in Manchester and another guy who's mixed-race with a Venezuelan father. When I first heard what they brought to my *Obsession* EP I just thought: This is me ten years ago. Future Cut brought a new B-Boy attitude to the game when musically it was slipping a bit. They've got a lot of sides to them, doing a laid-back, jazz-fusion, funk vibe, but can shift gear whenever they want. They are not just a drum'n'bass act. Added to that, Future Cut's production standards are excellent. They have also shown me a lot of respect, checking me for tracks I did years ago and giving me props.

It's people like Future Cut who show that the drum'n'bass scene is still really lively. Everyone thought it had died but it's stronger than it ever was: look at how artists like Shy FX broke into the charts early in 2002. The scene has sorted itself out, which we on the inside knew would happen. During the bad times we kept the faith. A lot of people gave up on it, not realising that there is a lot more there. The genre's only ten years old, compared with rock'n'roll's fifty years or eighty years of jazz.

Noel Gallagher: He should stick to music, man. He is a fucking rubbish actor. People say to me about *EastEnders*: 'That's your mate, isn't it?' And I say: 'No, that's some geezer playing a part, on a Marlon Brando trip.'

My mate is Goldie, one of the best DJs I ever heard.

My mate is one of the most genuinely talented people in the dance field.

My mate is the guy with the biggest heart in the south of England.

I suppose G is an urban artist. That's what I'd call him, and, remember, it was me that called him 'the sonic terrorist'. He's too cool just to be a musician in a way, because he wears too many cool clothes and has fast cars, and musicians are usually geeks like me who are only interested in collecting guitars.

He can paint, graffiti, make music, DJ, act, write. He's an all-rounder. I would absolutely make music with him again. In fact he owes me because I gave him that £60,000 studio and it's in his garage. So it's either that or get my studio back!

For me, the new album is about being in the present, as opposed to being too far ahead. It's not just a lesson learnt from *Saturnz Return*, it's a lesson learnt from life. People are ready for a Goldie album in sync with the times. But like all my other stuff, you can't call it drum'n'bass, it's Goldie music.

Music has come around again. Garage is the latest mutation of House and Old Skool is celebrated because it never really was before. The barriers are breaking down again.

At one stage I did think: Fuck it, I've done everything I wanted to do with music. But I've found the key again, and that was partly through creating the soundtrack for my film, *Sine Tempus*.

Putting *Nine Lives* together has been important to me because it represents one of the last parts of the jigsaw in achieving balance. My life was shattered when I was put into care. I, and my feelings, were suppressed during that entire period. It was the only way I could survive, by freezing my emotions and putting my life on hold.

That's why, when I went back to my family at the age of eighteen, I started to speed through life, doing and feeling as much as I could. I guess I was playing catch-up with myself.

I've always been hyperactive, speeding around quite naturally and taking loads of things and people on board. But now I realise I have to mend those shattered halves of my life and attain that balance.

What I've learnt is that science and faith are the most important things and the combination has changed our lives.

It has certainly changed mine, allowing me to joyride technology through graffiti, art and music. I always said that we are all Jesus, we all have that spiritual potential. There are a thousand Jesuses on every estate, and every fucker's going to get crucified.

Science has taught me so much but I have always kept my distance from it because I know it can engulf me, while there is a beauty to faith which balances technology. Using both of these, this generation has learnt to fold time. You only need to know that all the major developments have taken place in the last hundred years whereas fuck-all happened in the previous thousand. But we're at another level now, and we've moved even beyond the letter font replacing the Gainsborough portrait or the ploughed field as the central subject of art. The Apple Macintosh has helped turn what we're using from two dimensions into 3- and 4-D, in the same way that the camera replaced the easel and canvas.

And it's happening across all media. I got a digital sound and threw it into an analogue machine when I used the HF 3000 harmoniser on 'Terminator'. And that means that we can synthesise and create hybrids: blues/jazz, Detroit funk, shantytown reggae, drum'n'bass. All of these were created because of suppression, they were sub-cultures. And of course they became very strong because they withstood that suppression.

Technology is allowing us to open the page at any stage we want and select sounds, images, voices and create something new. You're never out of touch with your heroes these days – you can tap into it because now we have equipment which opens up the timelines. All that you need is the faith to match the science. I just had to believe to get into Miles Davis's head; look at the notes on *Bitches Brew* and then the sleeve notes I put on 'Internal Affairs'. No difference because I learnt from my predecessors, and learnt when to get on the train and then look out at the carriages which came before me.

Here's a case in point: I met Lee Quinnones in Miami recently, one of my heroes from right back before I was breaking, and he told me he listens to my music to help him paint. I want the kids today, the Thumb Generation, to realise that they may do something unconsciously one day which will reflect on them in later life. I feel like a Yoda figure to them in some ways.

It's got fuck-all to do with religion. I think religion sucks, but I do believe in an ultimate force. I feel connected to everything now, and believe that things happen for a reason, because I have lived a life in such adverse circumstances and been a sceptic for so long. When I was told what to do or how to behave or where I should go or what I should expect from life I'd go: 'Fuck off. You're having a fucking laugh.' Now, somewhere at the bottom of all this, I realise there is a reason for the things that have happened. That's where I find myself at. I have a belief system.

Tyrone Lewis: What's important to Goldie is trust. Once you cross him he will never trust you again. He's loyal as a friend because he expects that back. I don't think fame has changed him. I can go out with him sometimes and he says to me: 'Am I famous? What do you think?' He still thinks of himself as a normal person. We still do the same things as we did twenty years ago.

Whatever happens to me now, one thing is for certain – I'm no longer Clifford Joseph Price.

Very few people call me Clifford these days – just some of the guys up North, and that's OK because we go back. But Clifford Price was a really bad kid that had a bad upbringing and I've buried him now. Clifford was this scrawny kid who got beaten up and bullied, who was just a number. That name still has a police record. I left him a long time ago.

One day I took my brother out in my Ferrari and he said: 'How did you get this? I can't believe it!' And I said: 'I can't believe this either.' Sometimes I just can't get my head all the way around it.

But then I think about all those years, those cold nights, painting every night. I was crazy to be someone, to be recognised. And now I've arrived I've written about it, because, I hope you'll agree, it's been an incredible story so far.

Believe.

ANNUS VITAE.. SATURNUS REVENIT:

"... CUM MEMINI ME DISCERE ME SCACCOS SPECTARE LUDEBAM ET LAETE MOVEBAM PAPILIONEM INTRA ME. METUS TIMORQUE; ERAT SENSUS ILLE SENSUS QUI NUNC UT SUO, LIBERTAS ERAT ME MOVERE INTUS. NON PRO CERTO HABUI UBI VITAE PER QUA DIRATA ME DUCEANT; CIRCUMIBAM. CAUTAM MEAM PERSEQUENS, ANGULI MARGO QUEM CIRCUMIRE GESTIO... NUMQUAM VICTOR ERAM. LATRUNCULI CADEBANT DEVICTO ME VIDUS. PRINCEPS LANIATUS EST DUM REGES. ROBINAE, CORVI EQUITES SICUT FAMILIA. SOLVUNTUR CURSUS PRIMUS EST ARCERE SECUNDUS QUIDEM UT LACESSOR... ARS MOVENDI EST NOVUS MIHI AMOR. UESTIGIA RETRO SEQUOR ETUAS NUNC UACAS SPECIO APERTUS EGO AD MOTUS RAPTUSQUE UITAE DISCRIMINA. APPETITIO ME AD REPUGNANDUM PELLIT. PUERUM INDUCTAE AMOR ARTIS SUOS QUEM INUENI. PROUIDUS HAUD EST. ARS DISCENDI. VISUS AD OBSERVANDUM UT CONSPECTUM PETAT; VIA LONGA PATESCIT. OMNES, PROPTER QUOS SUM, ICTUS, CORDI VULNERAT MAGNA REPENDUNT ME DOCUERUNT UITAM FICMARE; IN UITA VERSAS; ET CAVEREL SEMPER EXSISTEBAT - MIHI EST MORTIS REGEM NECARE; EIUS RATIONEM NOSCERE SIGNUM EIUS PALLIDAM FACIEM. AMO VOLUTATIS LUDUM LUUM PERCIPERE ME DEDEBAM UT PERITUS ESSEM ET FIUS; IN OMNI QUA CALIGINE VITA EST COMIS IN ME QUAM OPORTET. ILLO DIE SI POTERAM DELERE RES NUNC DE NIHILO HIC VIVO HOC LOCO, SATURNI TRANSITUS FINIS POSTREMO RUINAE. ILLA NOCTE CANDENS SATURNUS ERAT A SINISTRA LUNAE. ET TUNC FUTURA PRAETERITAQUE NOSCEBAM; VITA POSTREMO VERBA EST TOTUM PER ORDEM UT DEMONSTRARIM ME OPTIMUM IN HOC CEPISSE STUDIUM MUSICAE... GOLDICUS MEUS... SATURNUS REVENIT.."

Coldie...

Affirmations

I. Entrapment

I see the white ghost as silence is cracked by dawn I fear the most when my body is torn it mourns fragile in the passage where I have been so many times before finding white noise in the rooms where I walk what I'm trying to find search for divine in a blind drawn in by a force night sets its course and I am still again a freeze frame a lifer's pain runs through these veins and I cannot stop the pulse the red is blue in search for true my wits may bring me back does my soul beckon the edge did my fate uphold a peace a deal already done but my body did the run I'm tired my veins run dry and hope of faith to get me through this sky's night once more as silence knocks on my mind's door it lets me know I've been here before.

2. Sonik Terrorism

Here come the drums the root of 'om' way back before the voice of song the sorrow tales of war and wails the barbarians from within are rising to free emancipation and tribe the rhythm of time may no pharaoh mute thine ears their eyes shall from black be given sight from rainbow eyes we thrive there night and sacrifice our sound the lambs we will be and pay the price the sonik sound shall give us light.

3.

Addiction is something that creeps like shadows at sundown it fades from colour to black and white and then casts you in the deepest black not even your eyes can find space within its vast abyss lost between genius and madness as the theory of paranoia or psyche do baron battle until your mind is that of pain and wound addiction is something that has fire in its own desire to take what you cannot comprehend and slay your doorways you have built in your conscious motive structure striking at the weakness of your hibernation of concept while static the very vulnerability at the fail gate of your condition through self manifestations of the sub demon the basic nature of your incapacitated log of every channelled energy the switchboard overload addiction is disturbing to the thespian at internal axiom of the written truth we all siphoned at this point of desire to be at peace with one's unsurable crosspoint being pushed in the shell addiction eats your fuel whether wise or fool we cannot escape it's my war that I must put those vivid conflicts of pain to the back of my mind addiction may trick.

4. Chameleon

Still the artists burns knowing no end beyond the frame of life's terrain whether madness or of sane I guess in the makers' spirit lies my blame I only bless for this I close my eyes, past night and paint my wish colours those have never seen and landscapes pure my own serene we do not sleep but only dream the ghosts that let us be I span my minds eye as far as it can see there is no boundary only infinity the shades I shape that make me the artist's life that breaks me my fear the grey will wake me the lines I draw mistake me so I stay my way on edge my focus point till death my canvas is to stretch and paint my whole life through whether red or blue the colour touched is true.

5.

The lifers that we know those that think and wait at life's debate concentrate to focus their point of trust in faith we cannot see it only feel for those that reveal their sixth sense at heaven's date a kind of braille we unveil in all we touch a must for those things in axiom or science concealed the fact is still based on mass man's trust so therefore if I conceive then yet it is to be for I at faith myself invest in pure energy construct my our us utopia that in all will one day be a lifer is my name to gain faith by this frame exist in my own picture.

6. The Book of Dikus – Prisms of Thought – A Chapter

No wonder as I look out of my window and see the full moon lights up all the sky and fills me with open energy big she glows the clouds pass over her at a pace I've never known the forever rapid change of time now she does not breathe still as if the blink in which I see hold me in her timeless awe her light is that of the universe bouncing through her as if the prism are made of her rainbows when I close my eyes from her blue still light and so the void in my head makes for night of its own design forward and backwards travelling in time not mine but the sight of dream in search to find and place those vivid rays of prism light at peace with life upon the crest of her full moon this her night no wonder I think yes wonder I must I feel at one and part join peace indeed my soul I trust.

7. Analogy

To face them you're identified the number known to the pharaohs way point of denial to pierce them incept the same deception they have decoyed your search for truth it exists yes we know where it lies entombed within the pharaohs columns its walls passages dusts sands particles of aristocracy traditions dust we cannot breath in the lie filtered because I closed my eyes fear of the blind the pure air of my life and those I breathe the rare breed the cougars who saw their young suffocate consumed by the pharaohs flood to the high ground damp paws left tracks in that we reverse circle bound tread rocks with cracks and move our packs in abstract they won't find us here this air is clear in that I feed a pharaoh's taste is that of need they bleed I saw it in the cracks as we pass I am conditioned to hunt to search purely because I see to strip the flesh of their own irony.

8. I Cry Therefore

A thought became the dream so it seemed thus love beamed to let me in to be exploded in me soul to let me free past shades confused the haze set tones confined my ways life's salts I taste as old as time seas sprayed the bitter slave of Abe in all save dignity for all to see the blind became serenity so therefore tears the seas that brought to me I cried therefore I am the shade blue in bliss was not the colours of my heart in love fired the spark the coals burned hot to be ignite to truly find the passion white at heart the pawns alone could not play the complex part a cupid simply stole the queen's part the arrows stricken pierced the kings down the armies marched against the clowns I cry therefore I am the joys of life my cupid's hands and somewhere lies the dream.

9. Those who Are Creative

A sleeping choice in all once awakened it will always seem like there is constant time to raise and love in surround and bound to be at destination we end up and are somewhat found and for those who wish for nothing are somehow caught in cloud a never ending misty exit a room without a crowd a life womb of anxiety faithful sometimes upon man's ego for that digital prophecy how can we measure life by these myths of code surely once shown purity in its cupid experience alone we look back at life in focus away from maddening crowd allow give time wipe lonely from your brow maybe not now but in future roads the signs will show you how curiosity may always lay rest but never be put down remember of how where at you are past of then but now back then the youth of clown played court and laugh to them to take away a frown fool teaches wish men of deaf bring song heard loud remember how?

10.

There's one voice that haunts as one the violent spirit of a demon strong in chaos though it may seem the chapter of a static dream a motion that in all frozen to anticipate before whence fall the truth in that may lay in the higher being a giant step away if not this presence can reveal a prophet through god did this seal a bond more close to god life points at us with many rods of true they be it not the road of destiny holds the plot the blueprint laid that points of compass a lie thus be not but esher and beyond X universal marks the spots pure treasure thought it's blind in all it seems is not beyond the decoy the pharaoh laid of roads they are all of babel end at point the map of man somewhat disjoint make

wide thy presence of signs for what brings of narrow lays
the blind.

11. Is This Nostradamus — The Eve of Wonder

My mind is unsure in this time right now it seems to be of
prophets and pagans a time they say of an end I guess I wouldn't
be anywhere else my fear is strong even though there is no
need because my soul has brought me this far I guess my human
instinct the primal scream is at its hottest demonz faith I pray
the act of mastering them is mine is this truly the nostrodamus
time it lays heavy on my mind right now days away but present
now it's as though being conscious has brought us here to most
and many unaware to me myself but only clear at least I can
truly say I bear witness to a revolution driven at technology's
end the overspill of man's will and power of the mind I watch
the sky again tonight and try to find peace in the uneasiness
I feel all will be revealed the genius of this intricate web of life
I just can't help but think that no matter how I try to conclude and decipher there is a beauty in the wonder of being
part of this the master's time the will be belong at one.

12.

Stabilise your thoughts for a second it is not an end to all of
this until it is purely yours alone and even then the ego
brought about by man's wish to take it all with us in his concept for a surround mass ending is a terrible fear of the flesh
it is primal and has always been so joyless we must be within
those seconds for we are joining moving up with other souls
together in something that cannot be explained until we reach
there beyond behind a never time.

13.

It is a revolution no doubt not like another for those I guess that have never been watching the ways of a changing wave before this came the youthful catalyst of want of change to leave ones name so it may seem redemption made extreme of faith made only by those that be a conscious wrong or right in a faithful hope that might bring us all to write our only dreams poets preachers artists readers science creatures all the cards laid for life's game in truth to learn there lies the axiom at bay from day or so they say were never meant to be the same why force the perfect utopia's hand surely spirit has no land so life is burdened with mortal man to roam thus look at what's at hand I think therefore I am I can I will in hope I sew this so-called land seeds of knowledge so we plant.

14. I Die Most Every Night

I die in me every night with what if or what might my body suspends the pain my mind transcends delight the fearless flight in dead of night I search for light between the purple blue dots when I close my eyes then pain I cannot describe my mind outwits the wise while word around demise my heart stretched wide it pumps but pays in life and cuts me like a knife I die once every night and yes there is light more powerful than white a shade more graced than life so pain sits opposite my room and shades me now and then my body is his only friend my spirit tells him you will end and once I leave my only room he cannot hurt again the pain you caused only set my course my spirit sails with wings they have eternal ends goodbye dear friend the life you died is where I begin the makers mind I learned to fly and in his sands of time he will tell me when I have patience on my stool and in my room I look at you through you beyond you my pained heart will only bless you until then you only count the grains dear friend named pain each one of them.

15.

At the edge of every tree in its age of lonely lies a base of nature that we cannot view in its darkest nature of its own organic nature that is and has outlived us all in its rings and growth of day and night in a time only made by our beliefs of time the self-made clock of man's design in an irrelevant decision of what might have been it's only written as we see before this in a frame that did not exist or so be it we persist to ridicule its past of myth far greater than our own our higher cycle crowned its own selfish throne dictate the roads of something that in essence we do not know and cannot bestow the tree of life that watched the embryo of life unfold for us to ponder a stolen seat of kings pharaoed for misconceptions they belong to us in only the frame we capture organic life and lie the wish in hope we have overthrown I wish to be that tree of life a branch I'm blessed and wish were my own to blossom flowers I'm dissatisfied in heart to be a part of flowers that began before my life could even start fragile as we are the tree a thousand leaves that fell in autumn breeze aged as wine and crushed to dust in evolution's time the silent organic me more fragile than the leaf we in our time watch fall to free caught by breeze a distant breath in that it reminds me it goes to dust just as we with open soul we are but the leaf I know god made that breeze in hope to carry me.

16.

And so the relativity of time distance space not so much in
its axiom as we know but for where we the individual soul
lies and ones own conscious thus conceptual abyssikl cord
of life I look through my prism to try to focus on pure
living wisdom and think how fragile we really are yet the
internal power and position man has often through faith
and war axed out I see the ant thirty feet away do I con-
sciously go toward its form and crush it or unconsciously
through cycle end its own life I ponder for those man made
seconds to the ant it was three-hundred years or thirty years
in relativity to my form it was only thirty seconds to its
fate so I ponder again and look at the stars the exploding
stars the fires that already have burnt burning burning out
beginning ending the slow photograph of the universe
through their distance like that of the ant three million light
years away three-thousand years away the relativity is somewhat the same they are already the past so I look through
the prism of my own consciousness and conclude we are
yet significant in our own internment but in relativity to
the ever conscious universe one spec of dust conclude yet
more to positively satisfy my own form whether I just begin
the slow burn whether I burn to my hottest point or fading
out like the stars or arriving at the complete white glow of
energy we are just burning and that is all to ensure we can
physically and positively combust life's source and decipher
from all form a forward positive shifting energy in what we
sometimes call soul the conscious soul that is the bare box
of the universe that may be one day I will be able to drive
and shift infinities realms one day in time hopefully I will
mastermind.

17.

The pharaoh exists a dark force manifests this purely the instrument for this force can dwell it cannot retract in its void its true evil can only be seen in its embodiment of the flesh to live in desire in form the pure form of energy that exists in our trait to survive our instinct for truth and consciousness grows within us the pharaoh however must to longevitate its cycle from beginning to deceive confuse to war the flesh condition our exists dissolve our belief our faith manifest betrayal our self denial its own pure evil cannot reach the beyond the pure spiritual energy of infinity after death in only the fractal of life this breed can live the necessity to survive contradict confuse conceive there is no need for this to be where it can't belong for in its own self denial the internal enemy is but itself its spirit is void vacuumed crushed in the exploding realm of an expanding universal of positive matter and spirit of energy the void in itself must live feel and justify through the eyes of pharaohs unbeknown to the flesh that kills to survive lies the man unconscious incepting thus is the doorway for this pure evil to dwell in this the greed will breed this time and sand is running out for both forces for pure consciousness to gain from this time in one man's mind the freedom of decline in sound for the void to gain in this time to force the hand of man in science it's fear to go beyond to create its superficial womb to confound faith and belief of the mind and manifest in the flesh that man began man and this is all I am there was energy before man there was a void before man I know where my soul stands.

18.

Ludus vitae saturnus revenit: cum memini me discere me scaccos spectare ludebam et laete movebam papilionem intra me metus timorque erat sensus ille sensus qui nunc ut scio libertas erat me movere intus non pro certo habui ubi viae per quadrata me duceant circumibam caudam meam persequens anguli margo quem circumire gestio numquam victor eram latrunculi cadebant devicto me nidus princeps laniatus est dum reges reginae corvi equites sicut familia solvuntur cursus primus est arcere secundus quidem ut lacessor ars movendi est novus mihi amor vestigia retro sequor et vias nunc veras specto apertus ego ad motus raptusque vitae discrimina appetitio me ad repugnandum pellit puerum inducite amor artis suus quem inveni providus haud est ars discendi visus ad oberservandum ut conspectum petat via longa patescit omnes propter quos sum ictus corvi vulnerati magna rependunt me docuerunt vitam firmare in vita versari et caverel semper exsistebat mihi est morsus regem necare eius rationem noscere signum eius pallidam faciem amo voluntatis ludum illum persaepe me dedebam ut peritus essem et fidus in omni qua caligine vita est comis in me quam oportet illo die si poteram delere res nunc de nihilo hic vivo hoc in loco saturni transitus finis postremo ruinae illa nocte candens saturnus erat a sinistra lunae et tunc futura praeteritaque noscebam vita postremo versa est totum per orbem ut demonstrem me optimum in hoc cepisse studium musicae goldikus meus saturnus revenit.

– Latin by Rosemary Andrew

Acknowledgements

Paul Gorman would like to thank the following for the time, assistance, advice and inspiration:

Simon Trewin, Sarah Ballard and Lucy Brazier at PFD; Katy Follain at Hodder; Margaret Pusey, Stuart Meade, Storm, Jessica Beard, Ben Green, David Bowie, Alan Edwards, Julian Stockton, Josh Evans, Noel Gallagher, Terri Hall, Kat at Ignition, Gus Coral, Sarah Gregory, Nellee Hooper, Trish and Lucy at Meanwhile, Pete Tong and Fiona Carlisle-Smith at ffrr/London Records, Michael Koppelman, Kate Pickworth and John Yorke at BBC *EastEnders,* Wendy Mandy, Neil Spencer, Ian 'Whitey' Whitehouse, Tyrone Lewis, Mark Sayfritz, Nick Ciraldo, David Lawson at Smoking Dogs Films . . . and of course, the Goldstar.
Most of all: the lovely Caroline Moss.

The authors and publishers wish to thank Gus Coral for permission to reproduce his photographs, and to Metalheadz for permission to reproduce the twelve-inch covers. The photographs of Chance and of Goldie in front of his *Survivors* graffiti are from Goldie's private collection.

Metalheadz Label Discography

'f the label was to end tomorrow I wouldn't be here. No deal, whatever deal, Metalheadz remains, because I don't learn anything if I don't go out and listen to the boyz.

'The label's my utopia.

'The label is a family.

'We take risks.

'This label is based on fate.'

By 1994 Goldie had established the Metalheadz logo as a brand by printing the distinctive logo of a metal skull wearing headphones on acetates for his and other artists' releases on the Reinforced label. As the drum'n'bass scene started to explode, Goldie found himself the centre of attention for an increasing number of new and emerging DJs and producers keen to release their material. So, as his deal to release his solo work with London Records/ffr got under way, Goldie launched the Metalheadz label as an independent record company, issuing as its first release a new twelve-inch version of his track 'Ghosts' as Rufige Kru and teaming it with Doc Scott's 'Drumz'.

'Grooverider had both tracks for a really long time, dropping them in the clubs and creating a stir. We decided to leave them for a whole year and then put them out. 'Ghosts' was about sampling my enemies and my friends. It's about ghosts that pass you and take you over.

'We got our Metalheadz sound from Rider and Fabio's sets. We sampled their sound. We took from their tapes. Never just cut and dried samples – we always processed samples to the max.'

Almost immediately Metalheadz was established not only as the movement's key label but also as the most exciting new British record company for years, representing every single one of the drum'n'bass pioneers and prime movers and spreading its wings with subsidiary imprints such as Razor's Edge. The label's rise coincided with Goldie's as 'Inner City Life' became a club anthem and the *Timeless* album made a huge commercial and critical impact. Simultaneously, Goldie launched the Metalheadz club night, which showcased many of the DJs and producers involved with the label. Starting with the infamous Sunday Sessions at the Blue Note in 1995, Metalheadz club nights moved to other outlets such as the Leisure Lounge and resulted in Metalheadz tours in the UK and overseas.

The Metalheadz label also successfully pioneered the drum'n'bass compilation business with its *Platinum Breakz* and *Metalbox* series, and branched into video and merchandising. Metalheadz continues to this day, a rare example of an independent record company with longevity.

1994

DOC SCOTT/RUFIGE KRU – Drumz VIP/Riders Ghost VIP [met h001]
PESHAY – Psychosis/Represent [met h002]
ALEX REECE – Basic Principles/Fresh Jive/I Need Your Love [met h003]

1995

DOC SCOTT – Far Away/It's Yours [met h004]
WAX DOCTOR – Kid Caprice/The Rise [met h005]
DILLINJA – The Angels Fell/Ja Know Ya Big/Brutal Bass [met h006]
J. MAJIK – Your Sound/Tranquil [met h007]
ALEX REECE – Basic Principles remixes: Reprieve (Alex Reece)/Rollout (Wax Doctor)/Step 1 (Dillinja) [met h003r]
PHOTEK – Consciousness/The Rain/Into The 90s [met h008]
ASYLUM – Da Bass II Dark/Steppin' Hard/Desire [oodark]
HIDDEN AGENDA – Is It Love/On The Roof/The Flute Tune [met h009]
WAX DOCTOR – The Spectrum/The Step [met h010]

ALEX REECE – Pulp Fiction/Chill Pill [met ho11]
ALEX REECE – I Want You/B-Boy Flava [met ho12]
J. MAJIK – Jim Cutter/Needlepoint Majik [met ho13]
LEMON D – Urban Style Music/This Is L.A. [met ho14]
DOC SCOTT – Drumz 95/Blue Skies [met ho15]
SOURCE DIRECT – Made Up Sound/The Cult [met ho16]
HIDDEN AGENDA – Pressin' On/Get Carter [met ho17]

1996

J. MAJIK – Arabian Nights/The Spell [met ho18]
RUFIGE KRU – T3/Dark Metal [met ho19]
HIDDEN AGENDA – Swingtime/The Wedge [met ho20]
DIGITAL – Niagra/Down Under [met ho21]
SOURCE DIRECT – Stonekiller/Web Of Sin [met ho22]
ADAM-F – Metropolis/Mother Earth [met ho23]
ED RUSH – Skylab/Density/The Raven [met ho24]
HIDDEN AGENDA – Dispatch#1/Dispatch#2 [met ho25]
PESHAY – Predator/On The Nile [met ho26]
OPTICAL – To Shape The Future/Raging Calm/Undersea Flight (By Matrix) [met ho27]

1997

J. MAJIK – Repertoire/Shiatsu [met ho28]
SCI-CLONE – Melt/B.O.D. [met ho29]
CODENAME JOHN – The Warning/Structures Of Red [met ho30]
HIDDEN AGENDA – Channel/Channel Beyond/No Man's Land [met ho31]

1998

J. MAJIK – Freefall/Transmission [met ho32]
RUFIGE KRU – Ark Angel [met ho33]
SCI-CLONE – Everywhere I Go Rmx/Red Fever [met ho36]

1999

TOTAL SCIENCE – Silent Reign/Colony/Shift [met ho35]
SCI-CLONE – Lucid/Hold On [met ho34]

2001

RUFIGE KRU – Beachdrifta/Stormtroopa [met ho37]

MARCUS INTALEX – Universe/Loose Control [met ho38]
TOTAL SCIENCE – Borderline 2000/Jungle Jungle [met ho39]
FUTURE CUT – Obsession/Tear Out My Heart [met ho40]
JOHN B – Up All Night/Take Control [met ho41]

2002

THE INVADERZ – Winter Sun/Controls My Mind [met ho42]
KLUTE – Curly Whirly/Splendour – [met ho43]
LOXY & INK – Skitzaphonic/Shine/Twisted Third Mind/Delta Ras [met ho44]
JOHN B – Up All Night Rmx/Diversify Rmx [met ho41r]

Razor's Edge

PHOTEK – Still Life Remix/The Rain Remix [razorsoo1]
PESHAY/DILLINJA – Jah Remix/Deadly Deep Subs Remix [razorsoo2]
SOURCE DIRECT – This Is A Baad Remix/The Cult Remix [razorsoo3]
GROOVERIDER/J. MAJIK – Your Sound Remix/Kemistry VIP [razorsoo4]
SOURCE DIRECT – Dark Metal Remix/Stonekiller Remix [razorsoo5]

Goldie

1995

GOLDIE – State Of Mind/State Of Mind (VIP mix) [fx273]
GOLDIE – Angel/Saint Angel/Angel [fx266]

Compilations

1996

PLATINUM BREAKZ (compilation)

cd.o1

01. RUFIGE KRU – v.i.p. riders ghost
02. PESHAY – psychosis
03. DOC SCOTT – far away
04. DILLINJA – the angels fell
05. J. MAJIK – your sound
06. PHOTEK – consciousness
07. HIDDEN AGENDA – the flute tune
08. WAX DOCTOR – the spectrum
09. ALEX REECE – pulp fiction

cd.02
01. DOC SCOTT – the unofficial ghost
02. LEMON D – in my life
03. SOURCE DIRECT – a made up sound
04. DIGITAL – down under
05. ASYLUM – da base ii dark
06. J. MAJIK – final approach
07. DILLINJA – armoured d
08. PESHAY – the nocturnal (back on the firm)

1997

PLATINUM BREAKZ II
cd.01
01. DIGITAL – metro
02. HIDDEN AGENDA – pressin' on
03. J. MAJIK – arabian nights
04. SOURCE DIRECT – stonekiller
05. ADAM-F – metropolis
06. ED RUSH – the raven
07. HIDDEN AGENDA – dispatch 2
08. PESHAY – on the nile
09. DILLINJA – promise*
cd.02
01. OPTICAL – to shape the future
02. J. MAJIK – repertoire
03. SCI-CLONE – melt
04. CODENAME JOHN – the warning
05. J. MAJIK – your sound remix
06. SOURCE DIRECT – dark metal remix
07. OPTICAL – swift glide*
08. LEMON D – chainsaw*
* exclusive tracks

METALBOX SERIES (CD 1)
1. DIGITAL – far out
2. DIGITAL – special mission
3. DOC SCOTT – swarm
4. DOC SCOTT – honey
5. ED RUSH – sabotage
6. ED RUSH – westway
7. HIDDEN AGENDA NO GUARD – (dispatch #3)
8. HIDDEN AGENDA – big lamp

9. J. MAJIK – futurestate

METALBOX SERIES (CD2)
1. J. MAJIK – elysian fields
2. LEMON D – whats up
3. LEMON D – urban style music 90bpm reprise
4. OPTICAL – to shape the future remix
5. OPTICAL – reckless mission dub mix
6. DOLLIS HILL – 'desist' da black
7. DOLLIS HILL – desist reprise
8. PHOTEK – neptune
9. DILLINJA – warrior jazz

2002

MDZ.02 THE ALBUM
1. USUAL SUSPECTS – Tribute
2. LOXY & INK – Shine V.I.P.
3. JONNY L – Part Of U
4. MARCUS INTALEX & ST FILES – My Soul
5. SONIC & SILVER – Innacorna
6. KLUTE – Unwind Yourself
7. THE SPIRIT – Solitaire
8. HIDDEN AGENDA – Relentless
9. TEEBEE – White Venom
10. TOTAL SCIENCE – Screw Ball
11. THE INVADERZ – Revealed

MDZ.02 (6 x vinyl)

A. USUAL SUSPECTS – Tribute
B. FUTURE CUT – Popcorn
C. LOXY & INK – Shine V.I.P.
D. JONNY L – Part Of U
E. MARCUS INTALEX & ST FILES – My Soul
F. SONIC & SILVER – Innacorna
G. KLUTE – Unwind Yourself
H. THE SPIRIT – Solitaire
I. HIDDEN AGENDA – Relentless
J. TEEBEE – White Venom
K. TOTAL SCIENCE – Screw Ball
L. THE INVADERZ – Revealed